THE GOD OF ECSTASY

STONEWALL INN EDITIONS

Michael Denneny, General Editor

THE GOD OF ECSTASY

SEX-ROLES
AND THE
MADNESS OF DIONYSOS

ARTHUR EVANS

ST. MARTIN'S PRESS
NEW YORK

Design by Jaya Dayal

Library of Congress Cataloging-in-Publication Data

Evans, Arthur.
The God of ecstasy.

1. Dionysus (Greek deity)—Cult. 2. Sex role—
Religious aspects. I. Euripides. Bacchae. English.
II. Title.
BL820.B2E9   1988   292'.211   87–16322
ISBN 0-312-01033-8
ISBN 0-312-02214-X (pbk.)

In Memory of Arthur Bell

CONTENTS

ACKNOWLEDGMENTS

Many thanks to those who helped make possible both the writing of this book and the 1984 Valencia Rose production of Euripides' play *Bakkhai*, on which the book is based:

Ron Lanza and Hank Wilson, for creating and long sustaining the Valencia Rose Cabaret in San Francisco at great personal expense to themselves; Brian Smith for crucial initial support for the play's production; Buzz Benze and Jeanne Thomas for valuable theatrical criticism; Ambisextrous for dazzling props; the cast and crew of the play for their hard work and devotion during its production (their names appear with the text of the play in the appendix to this book); Jim Gordon for documentation concerning the early San Francisco Faery Circle; Charley Shively for scholarly leads; Arlynn Friesen for understanding and support while I was typing the manuscript; Edwin Kennebeck for editorial criticism; Aaron Shurin and Judy Grahn for advice on marketing; and, most cherished of all, Billy Amberg, my lover, and José-Luis Moscovich, my dear friend, for their unfailing nurture.

INVITATION
TO A
LABYRINTH

❂

IN 406 B.C. the Athenian playwright Euripides died at the age of seventy-five in the Kingdom of Macedon, estranged from his homeland of Athens, which he had left two years before. Among the papers found in his Macedonian home at the time of his death was a heretofore unknown play: *Bakkhai* (or *Bacchae*, with the Latin spelling). This play, whose title literally means *Women Possessed by Bakkhos*, has long since struck readers as one of the most bizarre ever written, and many have thrown up their hands in dismay at this tale of a god who drives a whole city insane, entices its king to dress up like a woman, and goads its real women into tearing him apart with their bare hands.

The following pages are a journey into a labyrinth, the strange and seemingly twisted path that unfolds before us as we descend into the mythic world created by the genius of Euripides in his *Bakkhai*. It is a world I have spent much time exploring, first by translating the play anew into English (the translation appears as an appendix to the present book), then in producing and directing it at the Valencia Rose Cabaret in San Francisco, and finally by researching its historical and cultural milieu. As a result of this tortuous journey, I have made some rather startling discoveries, not only about this particular play, but also about ancient Greece, the emergence of Christianity, the historical development of sex-roles, and the nature of the present-day culture we live in.

I have also discovered that within the heart of Euripides' labyrinth a god is waiting, a not-so-distant relative of the fabulous Minotaur in the original labyrinth of yore. I have found my way to this god and back again by following a few simple threads of ancient and not-so-ancient history. And each time I emerge from his labyrinth I feel that I am a slightly different person, for my encounters with him have helped me to look at the world—not just Greek myths, mind you, but the actual world I labor and live in—to look at this world with different eyes, to see connections in things that previously seemed disjointed, and even to experience anticipations of—dare I say it?—a new definition of what it means to be human.

I invite you to come with me now as I descend to visit again this god who is both so strange and yet so familiar. In this journey, I will be examining the text of the play itself as well as a number of selected commentaries and studies on it (all translations of both primary and secondary sources are my own unless otherwise indicated). Moreover, I will be exposing a bit of my own values, feelings, and life experiences in the face of this evidence, and some of my conclusions will be quite controversial. Naturally I cannot guarantee that you will have the same kind of reaction to the play that I have had, but at least you will be able to judge for yourself why human beings for nearly 2,400 years have been so challenged both by this play and by its ecstatic god.

I

WHAT CHILD
IS THIS?

❂

EURIPIDES sets the scene of his play in the distant past, distant even from *his* point of view of 2,400 years ago. The time is that of the legendary era of Greek heroes, a time as conveniently nebulous for ancient Greeks as the European Middle Ages are for modern fantasy writers. The place is Thebes, a city in Greece, in fact one of the holiest cities in ancient Greek religion.

Onto this scene comes an effeminate young stranger with long hair who confides to the audience that he is really a divinity in disguise—Dionysos (also known as Bakkhos and Iakkhos). The stranger insists that he is the Son of God, that his father is Zeus, the father of gods and men, who once slept with his mother Semele, a mortal from Thebes.

As a result of this tryst with Zeus, Semele became pregnant, and when Zeus's jealous wife Hera found out, she was furious. So Hera plotted a vengeance worthy of a goddess. Appearing in human disguise, Hera urged Semele to ask Zeus a favor: to expose himself to Semele in all his glory as a god. After all, she insinuated to Semele, Zeus does so all the time for Hera, his wife. Is Semele to be less favored than Hera?

Semele swallowed the bait, and on her next rendezvous with Zeus begged him to please grant just one little favor. Beguiled, satisfied by his new playmate, and spent, Zeus nodded in assent. When Semele made her request, the god was aghast and tried to dissuade her, but without success.

Semele obtained her wish: ominous roarings of thunder filled the air, jagged bolts of lightning sizzled across the firmament, the earth heaved, and the great lord of Olympos was transfigured into the likeness of the

3

sun. Semele herself was instantly burned to a crisp, expelling from her womb the fetus named Dionysos.

Zeus, in pity, took up the fetus and pressed it into the massive, fleshy folds of his thigh, clamping the skin shut with pins of gold. In time, Zeus went into labor, and from his body there was born a god with horns on his head and snakes writhing in his hair.

This same astounding god now stands before the audience, but disguised as the Effeminate One. In an opening monologue he reveals that no one in Thebes believes this story of Zeus and his mother, least of all his dead mother's very own sisters. So he has driven these sisters—and all the women of Thebes—insane. They have left the constraints of home to loom and run about the mountains at night, frenziedly worshiping Dionysos. Ironically, another group of women *do* accept him, but they are foreigners who have followed him to Thebes.

In their revels the native women driven from Thebes are led by Agaue, an aristocratic matron of the city and the sister of dead Semele. When sane, Agaue could never believe that someone like Dionysos could be the Son of God, much less that the low-life foreign women that followed him to Thebes could be inspired by religion. But now driven mad, Agaue believes indeed.

How do the men of Thebes feel about this insane revel by their wives and daughters in the hills? A few recognize that a god is present and go to join the revels, wearing the fawnskin drape that is viewed as a kind of women's clothing. Most, however, are furious—not only at the seeming madness of it all, but also at the *nerve* of these women to leave the city and flout men's authority and rule! Their resentment finds a focus in Pentheus, the young and brash King of Thebes, and, ironically, the son of Agaue.

Enter young King Pentheus, his sharply chiseled face flushed, his bearing cock-sure. What is this outrage? he asks. Have the women of Thebes really all gone mad? And who is this effeminate foreigner who goads them on? I'll soon put a stop to all this craziness! Send out the troops to find the stranger and bring him here in chains!

Sure enough, Pentheus' thugs find their prey and bring him chained before the king. On seeing his catch, Pentheus is profoundly and unexpectedly torn: on the one hand angered and repelled by the spectacle of effeminacy before him, but on another, deeper level, sexually aroused. And so the ancient ritual begins, with Pentheus first threatening—but then touching, indeed almost caressing—the disguised god, and with Dionysos at first coyly and then ever so determinedly leading him on. In

4

the end, Pentheus' masculine image of himself and of Thebes wins out. He snaps back to himself, orders Dionysos' long hair cut off, and throws him in jail.

"Hell hath no fury like a god scorned," as one reviewer has aptly characterized Dionysos' reaction to this rejection (Spundberg, p. 27). To unfold his sacrament of vengeance, the god first causes an earthquake. The prison that contains him and the palace that contains the king are both shaken to the ground. Next, as lord of the emotions, he drives the king insane, but with a campy twist: he entices Pentheus, distraught and mad, to dress up like a woman in order to spy on the Raving Women in their nightly mountain rites. Pentheus, at this point completely mad, throws himself into the project, as Dionysos leads him through the middle of Thebes, beyond the protection of city walls and into the untamed, tangled forest. There the god sets Pentheus up in a tree like an animal about to be sacrificed and summons the pack of Mad Women to surround and kill him.

Agaue, the king's mother, leads the attack. With her mouth drooling and her body wracked by spastic jolts of superhuman energy, she leads the charge of driven women, all howling like a phalanx of Greek men when they charge the field in war. The women succeed in shaking Pentheus from the tree, then kill and dismember him. Agaue, finding herself with his head, hastens back to Thebes, deliriously believing she carries the head of a captured mountain lion.

On returning to Thebes, Agaue suffers the catastrophe of regaining her sanity. She realizes not only that her son has been murdered and dismembered, not only that she has led the attack, but also that she holds his head in her bloody hands. In the deepest moment of her agony, the god Dionysos suddenly appears in glory with his body golden and shiny, his hair twined with ivy, grape clusters, and snakes, his temples sporting horns, and his face contorted with a look of demented fury and ominous portent. He delivers the doom of banishment on Agaue, exults in his victory, and, like the breath of a bull on a cold winter morning, vanishes. Defeated, Agaue retreats from the scene while a member of the chorus recites the standard lines with which Euripides ends five of his plays:

> How varied are the gods' displays of power:
> What we often don't expect,
> *That* they bring to pass.
> And what we look for most,

5

That goes unfulfilled.
And for the least expected things,
A god will find a way.
And thus did these events transpire.

(lines 1388–1392)

Although the play ends on the most somber of notes, the first half is in fact a comedy, a mix of two different genres, something highly unusual for Greek theater at the time and yet another sign of Euripides' innovative style. The most cutting scene is when Dionysos leads downstage the once-threatening Pentheus, now fully dressed as a woman, speaking in falsetto, actually enjoying this newly found dimension of self-expression, and totally oblivious to the ironic double meanings in the responses of Dionysos. So, for example, when Pentheus has a psychedelic-like vision of the disguised Dionysos as a bull (which he actually was in early Greek mythology), he says:

And you look like a bull to me,
Leading me on in front,
And your head has grown two horns.
Say, have you ever been a beast?
Why, you really are a bull!

(lines 920–922)

To which Dionysos dryly replies:

The god, though hostile once,
Is with us now in peace.
You see as you should.

(lines 923–924)

And when Dionysos asks to adjust Pentheus' loosened headband, the king unwittingly prophesies his own fate:

All right, then, you can fix it.
See—I offer you my head.

(line 934)

As with all Greek plays, the audience knew the general outline of the story ahead of time, so dramatic tension came not from unexpected turns of plot, but from the irony of the characters' unknowing actions and

6

speech in the context of the certain fate to come. Nowhere is this irony better illustrated than in the following exchange between the king and the god:

Pen. Lead me on,
And right through the middle of Thebes!
I alone am *man* enough to dare these things!

Dion. Yes, what you alone will do will save this city,
You alone.
And the struggle awaits you there that had to be.
Now follow me.
I will be your guide and keep you safe till there.
But someone else will bring you back.

Pen. Yes, she who gave me birth!

Dion. And your fame will be known to all.

Pen. That's why I go—

Dion. And you'll be carried when you return—

Pen. In splendid luxury, yes—

Dion. And in your very mother's hands.

Pen. You'll have me spoiled!

Dion. Spoiled, indeed.

Pen. Just as I deserve!

(lines 961–970)

The shift from comedy to tragedy is not the only striking contrast between the two halves of the play. In the first half, Dionysos in his mortal disguise quickly captures the sympathies of the audience. In the face of Pentheus' violent threats, he is generally patient and good-humored, deflecting the king's crudely barbed verbal assaults with deft humor and elegant irony. When Dionysos does finally explode with anger, the audience is on his side, for they have seen this meek man repeatedly abused by one clearly more powerful. As a result, when Dionysos leads forth the once-menacing Lord of Thebes now dressed as a woman, speaking in falsetto, and dizzily checking the hem of his dress, the audience howls at his deserved retribution.

7

But in the second half of the play, the audience turns against Dionysos. They have heard a messenger tell how the women driven from Thebes tore the king apart with their bare hands. They have seen Kadmos, the king's aged grandfather, hobble back from the scene of the carnage, shattered by the bloody fate of his grandson and by the downfall of his dynasty. They have watched Agaue, the king's distraught mother, return from the hills carrying her son's head in her own hands. And after her return to sanity, they have heard her scream with horror at the knowledge of the slaughter and seen tears pour down her face as she sobs at the fate of her son to have been torn apart alive and of herself to have been his killer. After such an avalanche of human grief, the audience now suddenly beholds Dionysos appearing in glory as a god, gloating over and taunting his victims, prophesying more suffering to come, and departing with a cruel laugh. His behavior at this point is an utter offense to their sensibilities.

The divergent ways in which Euripides portrays Dionysos in the two halves of the play have led to differing interpretations of his intent. Some, emphasizing the likeable characterization of the god in the first half, believe the play celebrates the need for a total release from all culturally imposed restraints. Dionysos is the hero, they argue, and Euripides extols the psychological need of human beings for cathartic episodes of uncontrolled madness, sensual indulgence, and even bloody violence.

Another school of thought, keeping its eye on the Dionysos of the second half of the play, sees the god as a villain and emphasizes the great inhumanity and destructiveness of those possessed by him (Carrière, p. 93; Kalke, p. 426). The most forceful statement of this point of view is found in R. P. Winnington-Ingram, who argues that Euripides actually hates Dionysos:

> This, then, is the subject of the play: the Dionysiac group and its disastrous potentialities; the natural life and the way in which it may dehumanize the men and women who lead it; the drugged peace which alternates with furious violence; the exclusive and undiscriminating cult of emotion.
>
> (Winnington-Ingram, p. 178)

Both these divergent interpretations have something in common: each interprets the Mad Women who have been driven from Thebes and who wildly roam the hills and eventually kill the king as practitioners of the religion of Dionysos. To the first interpretation, these women are something positive, the bearers of spontaneous natural feeling throbbing for release against the arbitrary restraints of conventional behavior and values; to the second, they are mindless destroyers, ravaging everything that comes into their presence. But in the eyes of both interpretations, the Theban Mad Women remain the ones who define the practices of Dionysian religion.

The assumption that the two interpretations share is actually their common error, for Euripides makes it clear in the very beginning of the play that the Mad Women driven from Thebes are *not* the followers of Dionysos. Quite the contrary, they are the very ones who have rejected the god. Dionysos himself states that they have refused to accept him as a god and laugh at his mother's claim of having slept with Zeus. Hence he has driven them from the city as a punishment for this rejection:

> But the sisters of my mother,
> Those that I expected least,
> Denied that I was born from Zeus.
> They said some *man* had come and slept with Semele,
> And she blamed the affair on Zeus.
> They said her tale was a trick by her father, Kadmos,
> And because she lied, they sneered,
> Zeus had killed her.
> And so from their homes I drove these sisters frenzied
> To live beside themselves in hills,
> Wearing the dress of my rites.
> And I drove insane from their homes as well
> All the women who reside in Thebes,
> Each and every one.

> (lines 26–36)

Both the interpretations in question overlook the fact that there are *two* groups of women in Euripides' *Bakkhai*. The first are loyal followers who have come with Dionysos from Asia Minor in the East. These appear on the stage as the play's chorus of barbarian Mad Women. They display a wide range of feelings, from gentle eroticism to ferocious anger. They also describe two rites—ecstatic nighttime mountain dancing and raw-flesh sacrifice—that were actually practiced by women followers of Dionysos in historical times. But these women do *not* wander about aimlessly pillaging nor do they have any part in killing and dismembering the king.

The second group of Mad Women are native Thebans who have rejected Dionysos and been driven from the city. With the exception of Agaue, the king's mother, they never appear on the stage. Messengers report that the Theban women participate in all the rites of the first

9

group of Mad Women (the true, foreign followers of Dionysos); in addition, they indulge in wanton pillage and kill the king. They serve as examples of what happens to humans who *reject* the god's call (Vernant 1985, pp. 53–54).

Just as there are two different groups of Mad Women, so there are two faces of Dionysos. To those who accept the god and integrate his claim for reverence into the rituals of their lives, he shows the benign face. To those who reject him, however, he shows the face of destruction and death. In Euripides' *Bakkhai*, Dionysos first comes to King Pentheus with humor, sensual invitation, and rites of pleasure. That coming constitutes the first half of the play. When Pentheus rejects Dionysos, the god reveals that no human can afford to take him for granted. That revelation constitutes the second half of the play, as Dionysos himself clearly warns when he prepares to drive Pentheus mad:

> I go to put on Pentheus
> The dress he'll wear to Hades
> When his mother's hands destroy him.
> And this he'll come to know:
> The Son of God, Dionysos,
> Although to mortals he's most gentle,
> By nature is a god of dreadful power.

(lines 857–861)

The two masks worn by Dionysos are reflected in the very structure of the play: the first half a hilarious comedy, the second half a terrifying tragedy. They are also reflected in the historical development of Greek theater into comedy and tragedy, art forms that emerged from the actual cult of Dionysos in ancient Greece; hence the imagery of the twin masks of comedy and tragedy that have served as symbols of theater to this very day.

Euripides was a humanist and a skeptic, and of all the ancient Greek tragedians he most consistently challenged the conventional religious notions of his time. His sympathy for Dionysos in *Bakkhai* was partly due to the fact, as we shall explore later, that Dionysos was himself a stranger to those conventional notions, just as he appears as a stranger in disguise in the beginning of the play. Euripides' sympathy was also due to the fact that his play was not merely about Dionysos, or even Greek religion, but was a vehicle used to raise questions of far greater import, as will soon be seen. To view the play as nothing more than a commentary on Greek religion or Dionysos is to miss these wider implications.

In the end, Euripides finds fault with both Pentheus and Dionysos. The king, although succeeding legitimately to the throne, ruling according to law, and motivated by a sincere desire to protect Thebes against an apparently subversive threat, nonetheless was fatally out of touch with his own emotional needs and those of the people he ruled. The god, although a benefactor to human beings, a defender of the validity of emotion, and a victim of the city's fear of feeling, had nonetheless never learned how to forgive and grossly overreacted to the injustices against him. Euripides seems to say that the extremes of the one beget and encourage those of the other. His appeal here is to the traditional Greek ideal of *sophrosyne*, intelligent balance or moderation in leading one's life. But in contrast to the rising intellectualism of his time, Euripides sees as an essential part of that balance the validation of deep-seated emotional needs. By so validating emotion, Euripides presents a striking alternative to the later teachings of Plato and his school, who interpreted moderation as requiring the sublimation or repression of passion. A moderation based on emotional denial, Euripides argues, is an invitation to madness. Hence the playwright really delivers his own message when he has Dionysos proclaim these words in his very last speech:

> And I, Dionysos, declare to all,
> I who am no mortal father's son,
> The Son of God:
> Had you learned to balance your lives
> At the time you did not wish,
> You would have lived a happy life,
> Having Zeus's son as friend.

(lines 1340–1343)

In portraying the behavior of the chorus of barbarian Mad Women who were the real followers of Dionysos, Euripides did not just pull images out of thin air and string them together for theatrical effect. For as long as Greeks could remember, groups of women had regularly gathered together and held ecstatic, but structured, rites in honor of Dionysos. A woman who participated in such rites was called a *bakkha* ("woman possessed by Bakkhos") or a *mainas* ("mad woman"). The plural of the first term is *bakkhai* (in Latin, *bacchae*), and of the second, *mainades* (Latin *maenades*). In English, these women are usually called *maenads,* and their religious practices, *maenadism.* An understanding of the historical nature of maenadism will help clarify the meaning of Euripides' play, especially insofar as it relates to women and madness.

11

In 1960, E. R. Dodds published a memorable commentary on Euripides' *Bakkhai*, arguing that the historical women followers of Dionysos practiced two rituals in the god's honor: wild, nighttime dancing revels and the tearing apart and eating raw of a sacrificial animal. According to Dodds, these rituals, which were held every other year in winter, evoked a state of ecstasy in the women: "There must have been a time when the maenads or thyiades or bakkhai really became for a few hours or days what their name implies—wild women whose human personality has been temporarily replaced by another" (Dodds, p. xiv).

More recently, Dodds's assessment of the historical nature of maenadism has been challenged by Albert Henrichs. In contrast to Dodds's approach, Henrichs maintains that we must make a clear distinction between two kinds of evidence from Greek antiquity: epigraphical (inscriptions on stones, paintings on vases, and other records on durable materials) and literary (books, plays, and the like). Henrichs argues that evidence from the literary tradition is more likely to embellish and exaggerate the nature of maenadism (presumably because the writers were more likely to be creative artists than routine observers). After comparing the extant epigraphical and literary evidence, Henrichs concludes that "the cultic reality of maenadism was more subdued and less exotic" than suggested by the literary evidence, and especially so in the case of Euripides (Henrichs, 1978, p. 123).

Henrichs also makes an equally sharp distinction between myth and ritual. Just because the myths about a god and his followers describe the presence of a certain type of behavior, we need not automatically conclude that the actual rituals used in the god's worship incorporated that behavior. Although ancient myths about legendary maenads tell of women wandering the countryside at night, going into trances, and being possessed by Dionysos, all that really happened in the classical era of Greece, according to Henrichs, was some stylized dancing and vigorous physical exercise: "By all indications, the peculiar religious identity of the maenads had more to do with sweat and physical exhaustion than with an abnormal state of mind" (Henrichs, 1982, pp. 146–147).

Although Henrichs is right to note the twin distinctions of epigraphical/literary and myth/rite, the making of such distinctions does not really invalidate Dodds' original argument for the historical reality of ecstatic behavior among the women followers of Dionysos. For example, Henrichs points to a well-known stone copy, made in Roman times, of an earlier Greek inscription dealing with the rites of Dionysos. The inscription records a response from the oracle at Delphi that instructs the city of Magnesia to set up a sacred band of Mad Women in imitation of the cult at Thebes. Nothing mentioned in this inscription is inconsistent with Euripides' portrayal of his chorus of barbarian Mad Women. In fact, the same technical terms used to describe the cult in the inscription occur in Euripides. Likewise a Milesian inscription from 276 B.C., recording the sale of a state priesthood in the rites of Dionysos to a woman purchaser, provides nothing contradictory to Euripides, since private groups of woman worshipers continued to exist beside the relatively few state-run cults whose priesthoods were sold. Nor do vase paintings from ancient Athens provide any contradictory evidence; in fact, Dionysian women are often depicted on them in obviously ecstatic poses.

In addition, the Greek historians recount stories about Mad Women that were not fantasies derived from religious myth but observations of historical events. For example, the Greek traveler Pausanias reports that he never understood why Homer gave the city of Panopeus the epithet, "excellent for dancing," until he went there and found out for himself:

> . . . I could not understand why he called Panopeus "excellent for dancing" until I was shown by the women who are called Thyiades [another name for Bakkhai] by the Athenians. These are women of Attica who regularly travel to Parnassos every other year. They and the women of Delphi hold rites in honor of Dionysos. It is the regular custom for these Thyiades to hold dances at various spots as well as at Panopeus.

> (Pausanias, 10, 4, 3)

According to Pausanias' account, the women's rituals in honor of Dionysos were both of regular frequency and of great antiquity (since Homer apparently knew of them). Nothing in this anecdote contradicts Euripides.

The historian Plutarch has recorded another striking story about these same Thyiades. During a winter war between Thebes and the tyrants of Phokis, the Mad Women got lost wandering about and ended up in the town of Amphissa, which was then under the control of the Phokian tyrants:

> When the tyrants of Phokis seized control of Delphi and the Thebans were fighting them in the so-called Holy War, the women followers of Dionysos, known as Thyiades, while wandering about at night out of their senses happened to chance upon Amphissa. Exhausted and not yet in their right minds, they threw themselves down in the public square and fell asleep, lying about here and there. Now the married women of Amphissa feared that the Thyiades would be mistreated, since their city was an ally of Phokis and a great many of the tyrants' troops were there. So they all rushed out into the square and silently surrounded the sleeping women without coming close to them.

13

When the women awoke, they offered them help in turns and gave them some food. Finally with the consent of their husbands, they accompanied and safely escorted the women to the border.

(Plutarch, *Moralia*, 249E–F)

Plutarch explicitly states that the women were wandering about at night and that they were "out of their senses" (*ekmaneisai*). They stopped to rest at Amphissa, even though that was not their destination, because they were exhausted and "not yet in their right minds" (*medepo tou phronein parontos autais*). Here again there is nothing inconsistent with Euripides' account. In yet another incident, Plutarch records a case where wandering Mad Women were so carried away during the winter rites that they got lost and a search party had to be sent out to rescue them from the cold (Plutarch, *Moralia*, 953D).

Henrichs's treatment of maenadism also overlooks the psychological impact of certain physical elements of the women's worship of Dionysos. The women left the city at night in the winter, wandered about for days without much food, held frequent ritual dances at various stopping points, and continually played flutes, reed instruments, and tambourines. The net effect of sleep deprivation, lack of food, strenuous exercise, exposure to cold, and suggestive music is to induce an altered state of consciousness (Bremmer, 1984, p. 281).

Henrichs is also wrong to say that the experiential content of the Mad Women's rites must forever remain unknown to us (Henrichs, 1982, p. 144). That content was continuously and vividly reaffirmed in numerous myths about the Mad Women: they were women who temporarily threw off the rule of men, re-established close sensual and religious ties with each other and the animal world, gave vent to their most intense emotions, and were possessed by a god. It is one thing to distinguish between myth and rite, but quite another, once having made that distinction, to dismiss myth as of little value, as Henrichs does. Greek myth was precisely that cultural mirror into which practitioners in any cult looked in order to define the experiential significance of their ritual behavior. This function of myth as an experiential mirror was especially prominent in the religion of Dionysos, since participants deliberately modeled their dress and mannerisms on characters in the mythical entourage of Dionysos, as reported in the following passage from Diodoros of Sicily: "The women sacrifice to the god by groups, celebrating the revels of Dionysos and everywhere proclaiming his appearance. Thus they imitate the Mad Women who are reported to have accompanied the god in antiquity" (Diodoros, 4, 3, 3–4).

14

Henrichs is again on shaky ground when he claims that there is no evidence for believing that historical maenads engaged in *omophagia*—tearing apart and eating raw a sacrificial animal (Henrichs, 1978, p. 148). In reality, the Milesian regulations of 276 B.C. for the public cult of Dionysos, mentioned earlier, contain a provision specifying the order of precedence for performing this very rite: no one is to perform it until the priestess first does so on behalf of the city.

Henrichs is correct to point out that the Greek phrase in question (*omophagion embalein*) is vague and can mean anything from throwing the animal victim into the crowd (to be torn apart) to simply consecrating it to the god. Nonetheless, the use of the word *omophagion* is proof that some ritual involving raw animal flesh was practiced. Henrichs's speculation that the rite simply entailed cutting and handling raw animal flesh is unconvincing, since in both sacrifice and cooking the Greeks routinely handled and cut raw animal flesh. Why would they regard such a routine function as remarkable in the worship of Dionysos? In reality, no Greek source anywhere states that the rite of *omophagia* was merely the handling of raw flesh. On the contrary, Greek sources consistently stress that the worshippers in their rituals imitated the god in his mythology. In Euripides' *Bakkhai*, the chorus vividly and approvingly describes their male leader's imitation of the god in his hunt for raw animal flesh:

> What a delight he is in the hills,
> When he breaks from the speeding pack,
> Down on all fours,
> Clothed in a priestly fawnskin dress,
> Stalking the blood of goats just killed—
> Rawflesh delight!—
> Hurling himself from mountain to mountain
> In Phrygia and Lydia,
> Our priest and leader, possessed by Bakkhos—
> Hai-ee!

> (lines 135–141)

Henrichs is on firmer ground when he argues that there was no wanton pillaging, mayhem, or murder among historical maenads in the manner attributed to the escaped women of Thebes by Euripides in his *Bakkhai*. But as pointed out earlier, these latter women were the ones who *rejected* Dionysos; they were not the barbarian Mad Women who willingly embraced the god and practiced his alternate-year feasts. Likewise the many Greek myths that tell of the psychotic and violent be-

15

havior of others who rejected Dionysos do not describe the behavior of the god's followers. They rather serve as warnings that rejection of the rites of Dionysos will result in individual and societal catastrophe.

The Mad Women of Dionysos were real, not the mere invention of myth-makers. They did more than tire themselves out on long journeys and handle raw flesh, but less than indulge in random pillage and murder. By gathering in the winter mountains every other year, dancing hours on end to the pulsing sounds of reedy wind instruments and tambourines, devouring their animal sacrifices raw, and calling on their ecstatic god to come and join the dance—by doing these things they experienced a kind of madness, not an open-ended, relentless madness, but a madness articulated through a supportive ritual structure that had itself evolved over many generations of such practices.

The madness of Dionysos enabled these women to come together in large groups and to feel their solidarity and power independent of the control of men. The opportunity to do so was precious, for in classical Greece, outside of Sparta and Crete, the status of women was low. For example, in "democratic" Athens, women had no vote, were not allowed to speak on their own behalf in public assemblies and courts of law, and were kept in guarded seclusion within the innermost chambers of the house.

Athenian women also had no right to decide whom to marry and were prohibited from disposing of any significant amount of property in their own right. A husband had the power to determine in his will who his wife's next husband would be in case he should die. If the husband died without a will, the wife was "assigned" by a government official to be the wife of her nearest kinsman according to an order of precedence fixed by law (J. Gould, p. 43). In effect, the Athenian wife was considered as part of the patriarchal estate, or rather as a conduit for its safe transmission to a legitimate male heir. She was effectively reduced to the status of a perpetual minor incapable of mature decision making on her own.

If a married woman was raped, the act was viewed as an offense against the prerogatives of her husband and as a spoiling of his property. The rape victim herself was often held responsible for the act. Husbands were legally compelled to divorce wives who were raped, and the penalty for the rapist was only a monetary fine (Pomeroy, p. 87). In the eyes of the law, women had virtually become nonpersons (J. Gould, p. 44; Pomeroy, p. 74).

The anti-woman bias of Athenian law was mirrored in its social conventions. Although women had the responsibility for preparing the

16

household's food, they generally were not permitted to dine with their husbands, who maintained separate eating arrangements with their male friends in the men's half of the house. Athenian men also avoided making public mention of women by their own names, generally referring to them as so-and-so's wife or daughter. Even in lawsuits, the orators (who were the ancient equivalents of attorneys) were reluctant to mention by name any women involved in cases (J. Gould, p. 45). The essential social and legal reality was the husband or father; wives and daughters were mere appendages.

Athenian husbands were usually much older than their wives, whom they married when the women were in their early teens and they themselves in their thirties. Athenian men customarily spent little time with their wives, who most often had minimal opportunity for any kind of sexual affection, either with their husbands or with other women (Pomeroy, p. 87). Athenian women were not educated beyond the skills necessary to run the household, and scholars still debate whether they could read and write.

Ironically, it *was* possible for women living in Athens to enjoy a great deal of independence and mobility, but only if they were not "respectable" citizens. The *hetairai*—concubines, who included resident aliens, ex-slaves, and independently working prostitutes—moved freely in Athenian male society, were sexually and economically autonomous, and often had a high degree of education. They, and not Athenian wives, provided the men of Athens with most of their heterosexual companionship and sexual contact.

Some of the *hetairai* became quite renowned and formed their own cultural associations, as in the case of Aspasia, whom Sokrates and his pupils visited. They were also permitted to live with Athenian men in a kind of loose, common-law marriage but with the provision that children born to the *hetairai* were not considered citizens and had problems inheriting property (Pomeroy, p. 91).

In effect, Athenian society made a sharp cleavage between two types of woman: the legal wife who was kept restrained within the inner part of the house for the purpose of breeding legitimate male heirs and serving as a conduit for the patriarchal estate; and informal sexual playmates and companions who were autonomous agents but who could not bear legal heirs or transmit property and the rights of citizenship.

The only real outlet for the "legitimate" wives and daughters of Athens was to be found in those ancient religious rites that were primarily or exclusively run by women. Of these, the two most important were the cult of the goddess Demeter and the cult of the god Dionysos.

17

In the worship of the latter, women found a religiously approved vehicle for venting their feelings in an ecstatic manner that contradicted and transcended the male-defined mentality of the Greek city-state. When possessed by the madness of Dionysos, women suddenly found themselves free of the patriarchally imposed definitions of self, womanhood, and sanity. Hence, from a nonpatriarchal perspective, the madness of Dionysos had a certain logic after all.

The maenadic revels of Dionysos did not occur every day, however, or even every year, and they only lasted a short time when they did occur. Hence they could never really be a consistent force for changing patterns of male domination in Greek society. Nonetheless it would be a mistake to dismiss them as a mere mechanical release valve for pent-up wifely frustrations as, for example, Jan Bremmer does by comparing them to a modern disco:

> . . . the cult was an integrative factor in Greek social life . . . just as visits to the disco, where we find [that] the same phenomena of auditory and photic driving, headshaking, and strenuous activity, help modern youths to get through the boredom of everyday life: maenadism as Saturday Night Fever *avant le lettre*—a sobering thought.
>
> (Bremmer, 1984, p. 286)

Such a comparison misrepresents the rites, for it ignores the fact that they were grounded in a very ancient religious tradition with an emphatic mythological message. To disparage or impede women in these rites was a grave offense against a god and an invitation to catastrophe. They were not viewed as a mere human diversion.

Bremmer's comparison also slides over an important historical question: How did it happen that a ritual complex that so values women and emotion had obtained a recognized place in a society that was so dominated by men and intellectualism? In the next chapter, we shall see that to answer this question more is required than a comparison of the madness of Dionysos to disco fever.

Euripides' audience was well aware of the ritual practices of historical Mad Women; hence when the playwright introduced the chorus of barbarian Mad Women into his *Bakkhai*, they were not a novel item. There *was* novelty, however, in the way Euripides developed the theme of feminine power in the chorus, in the driven Theban women, and in Dionysos himself and contrasted it with the masculinity of King Pentheus. In effect, Euripides uses the character of Pentheus as a foil to expose the entrenched misogyny of Athenian civilization. The ultimate cause of the king's bloody death is not so much the seeming madness of women but his hatred for their power when they act in groups independent of men. Claire Nancy correctly observes that Pentheus' misogyny is the underlying destructive madness at work in the play: "The lesson is unequivocal: it is Dionysos in person who descends on the scene to unmask the character of and expose the celebrated *moria* [folly] in the camp where one hardly expected it, that of order and power" (Nancy, pp. 81–82).

Euripides' approach here is consistent with his other plays, where he often puts extremely misogynist statements in the mouth of a character who is about to be undone. His use of such misogynist lines has sometimes misled commentators into thinking they represent the playwright's own views. But a closer reading shows that the context is always one of exposing the misogyny of an entire social system (Nancy, p. 81).

Euripides' critical attitude toward Greek misogyny is not the only key to understanding his treatment of historical maenadism. Another lies in exploring the context of Dionysos' effeminacy and Pentheus' putting on of women's clothes.

Transvestite practices by both sexes were long associated with the actual rituals of Dionysian religion in antiquity. In fact, such ritual transvestism was so well established in Greek society from an early date that a number of sixth-century lyrical poems assume its existence as a matter of routine and can only be adequately understood by reference to its context (Slater, p. 190ff). In addition, a number of vases depicting the Dionysian festival of *Lenaia* in ancient Athens show men dressed as women and women dressed as men (Gallini, p. 215, n. 7). In some vase depictions, women wear a long phallus (Keuls, plate 314, p. 372). In the Athenian festival of *Oskhophoria*, a public procession marched from the sanctuary of Dionysos in Athens to the shrine of Athena Skiras in Phaleron. The procession was led by two young men of outstanding birth and wealth who carried branches laden with grapes and who were dressed as women (Parke, p. 77). And, of course, in Greek drama—performed in the theater of Dionysos—all women's roles were performed by men.

This same Dionysian transvestite tradition lasted until quite late in antiquity. In the second century A.D., the writer Lucian notes this odd behavior of a certain Demetrios: "He alone of all the rest did not put on women's clothing in the rites of Dionysos" (quoted in Greek by Dodds, p. 181). Again in the second century, Aristides says: "The rites of Dionysos customarily put women in the clothes of men [*eis andron taxin kathistanai*] as much as they dress men as women" (Gallini, p. 257, n. 7).

19

In the third century A.D., Philostratos says: "In the revel it is permitted women to dress like men and men to put on a woman's dress and walk like a woman" (Philostratos, 1.2).

So persistent was transvestism in the rites of Dionysos that it continued well after Christianity had become the state religion. In 691 A.D., the Council of Constantinople condemned the practice with these words:

> Moreover, we forbid dances and initiation rites of the "gods," as they are falsely called among the Greeks, since, whether by men or women, they are done according to an ancient custom contrary to the Christian way of life, and we decree that no man shall put on a woman's dress nor a woman, clothes that belong to men, nor shall any disguise themselves with comic, satyr, or tragic masks, nor call out the name of disgusting Dionysos while pressing grapes in the press or pouring wine in vats, thus ignorantly and vainly committing insane errors.
>
> (Quoted in Greek by Henrichs, 1978, p. 158, n. 117)

The Council here acknowledges that these practices are ancient (*kata ti ethos palaion*), that they occur in the context of religious rites, that both men and women are involved, and that they are still common enough to warrant condemnation. Since the evidence cited shows the continuity of this practice for a span of over a thousand years, Albert Henrichs is mistaken to argue that transvestism is rare in Dionysian rites and comparable to idiosyncratic behavior at "stag parties" (Henrichs, 1978, p. 133, n. 40).

In addition, Greek writers and painters often depict the god Dionysos himself as effeminate or else as actually wearing clothing associated with women. In Euripides' *Bakkhai*, for example, Pentheus several times scorns the god for his effeminacy, as when he shows his reaction to the rumors he has heard about Dionysos:

> They say some stranger—a sorcerer, an enchanter—
> Has come to the city from the land of Lydia.
> He wears, they say, sweet-scented locks of auburn hair,
> That his face is flushed,
> That his eyes have the grace of a goddess, Aphrodite . . .
>
> (lines 233–236)

When he sends out his thugs to hunt down the god, Pentheus says:

> Let those who patrol the land of Thebes
> Hunt till they find the effeminate foreigner . . .

(lines 352–353)

Here the word for effeminate is *thelymorphos*, literally "having the appearance of a woman."

Fifty years before Euripides wrote his play, the Athenian playwright Aiskhylos (Aeschylus, with the Latin spelling) wrote a similar work about Dionysos called *Edonoi*, only fragments of which have survived. Here as well Dionysos is arrested and humiliated, and the first question put to him by his captors is, "Where's this sissy from?" (Dodds, p. 133). In Greek comedy as well, Dionysos is often mocked for being effeminate.

The historian Diodoros of Sicily, summarizing in the first century A.D. the known myths of his time, describes Dionysos thus: "And they say that the Dionysos born of Semele in more recent times was quite soft and delicate of body, by far excelling others in his beauty and devoted to sexual pleasure . . ." (Diodoros, 4,4,2).

Some commentators believe that the depiction of Dionysos as effeminate was a rather late development and did not exist before the fifth century B.C. (Dodds, p. 133). But a number of vase paintings before this period show him as a bearded adult wearing clothing associated with women (Kerényi, p. 281). On some of these, he is represented in ritual scenes by a mere vertical pole on which are hung a bearded mask and a woman's dress, apparently a very ancient way of depicting the god. Moreover, the traditional costume of Dionysos on the stage—a fixed style of garment of great antiquity—was a long, saffron-colored dress. The Greek writer Pollux describes this garment as follows: "The saffron gown: Dionysos wore this and a flowery sash and a wand" (Sandys, p. xlvii). The word translated here as "flowery" is *anthinos* in Greek, a word usually used in connection with women's clothing, as indicated by its various associated meanings: "*Anthinos:* flowered, bright coloured, of women's dress . . . gay-coloured dresses worn by the *hetairai* [female consorts] at Athens . . . also dresses worn at the Anthesteria [a feast of Dionysos] by the Satyrs" (*Anthinos* in Liddell-Scott-Jones). This traditional dress of Dionysos is the same as that depicted for women long before in Bronze Age art (Gimbutas, p. 56).

Christians were later scandalized that the Greeks would worship a male god who wore a dress. In the third century A.D., Clement of Alexandria wrote a book titled *Exhortation*, in which he appealed to pagan Greeks to stop believing in gods he and other Christians found offensive.

Calling attention to the way these gods were typically portrayed, he said: "At any rate, if one goes around examining pictures and statues, he will at once identify your gods from their disgraceful depictions, Dionysos from his dress . . ." (Clement, 4, 50).

The most typical article of clothing long associated with Dionysos was a drape of fawnskin, which in antiquity was also linked with women, since men usually wore the skin of a panther (Sandys, p. 93). This fawnskin was not just a strip of skin but an embellished garment having tufts of wool or strips of goat hair fastened to it and sometimes embedded with pearls (Sandys, p. 112). Euripides calls this garment "a priestly fawnskin dress" (*hieron enduton*, line 137). Because of the traditional association of this garment with women and with the cult of Dionysos, Pentheus is horrified in Euripides' play when he sees his own grandfather Kadmos and the aged and blind prophet Teiresias both wearing fawnskins:

> What?! What a sight is this!
> There's Teiresias, the blind seer,
> Wearing a spotted fawnskin dress!
> And there's my mother's father, Kadmos—a joke!—
> Shaking a giant fennel stalk.
> Father, you make me ashamed when I see
> In old age how you've lost your mind.

> (lines 248–252)

Pentheus is also revolted by Dionysos' pale skin, since the Greeks viewed the latter as a female characteristic (Dodds, p. 135). Indeed, paintings from the earliest period of Greek history generally show women with light skin and men with very dark skin.

Both Dionysos and his followers wore the *mitra*, a head scarf borrowed from Lydia and worn by Athenian women (Bourlet, pp. 25–26). Without the *mitra*, the god is often shown with long, untied hair, which at the time was regarded as a woman's characteristic (Bourlet, p. 26).

The overall dress and appearance of Dionysos were thus distinctly feminine. By wearing these same artifacts, his followers—both men and women—imitated the god, and hence their Dionysian clothes were like a religious habit, as Michael Bourlet correctly argues:

In sum, the ritual costume that we have just described clearly appears as a collection of signs revealing the consecration of the believer to his god (hence putting it on is like taking the habit), but even more it expresses the attempt at making an identification with the god, especially insofar as he is man-woman. In itself such a costume *invites* possession and ecstasy.

(Bourlet, p. 27)

Such an association between transvestism and religious practice is also found in ancient myths involving other Greek gods and heroes. It seems to be a relic of an earlier tribal form of social organization, since ritual transvestism is often found in such societies (Gallini, *passim;* Segal 1982, pp. 169–170).

Thus the representation of Dionysos as effeminate was not a new trait in the fifth century B.C. What was new, however, was the greater emphasis placed on the concept of the god as a youthful beauty. This shift can be seen by comparing two descriptions of the god at sea, one by Homer in the eighth century B.C. and the other by a poet imitating Homer three hundred years later. In the first description, a scene where the ax-wielding Lykourgos attacks Dionysos and his followers, no attention at all is given to the god's physical description:

> Indeed, not even Dryas' son, Lykourgos, not even he lived long
> When he fought against the gods who dwell above.
> He charged, one time, raving Dionysos' nurses,
> Down and through the land of holy Nysa.
> All at once threw down their ritual things,
> Assaulted by the two-edged axe
> That killer Lykourgos waived.
> Dionysos, frightened, dived right in the sea . . .

(Homer, *Iliad,* 6, 130–136)

Compare now the second, later poem describing a scene where pirates are about to kidnap Dionysos:

> And as for Dionysos, Semele's famous son,
> I will tell how he came by the shore
> Of the ever rolling sea,
> Disguised like a young adolescent
> In the flower of his years.
> His dark, lovely hair danced in the breeze,
> And over broad shoulders
> Wore a cape that was mauve.

(Pseudo-Homer, *Hymn to Dionysos,* I, 1–6)

23

The same poet ends his account with these evocative lines:

> Farewell, then, son of Semele, you with lovely eyes.
> None will ere compose a song of charm
> Who has not remembered you.

(Ibid., 58–59)

What was the cultic relationship between the feminine-identified male followers of Dionysos and the Mad Women? Today most scholars are of the opinion that men and women held separate rites and did not practice maenadism together until later, in the post-classical period in Greek history. Nevertheless, there are reasons to conclude that mixed groups existed for such purposes from early classical times.

One reason for an early date is the chronology of Greek vase paintings. The first visual depictions of Mad Women in classical Greek art appear in the sixth century B.C. From the very start, scenes occur in which they are seen dancing in the presence of satyrs—male creatures who have a human body, a huge erect penis, a horse's tail, and sometimes women's clothing (McNally, pp. 103–104). In these depictions, the Mad Women display the characteristic body poses and costumes of classical maenadism.

Many believe that these satyrs are purely mythical beings, creations from folklore that imaginative artists decided to portray on their vases along with the Mad Women because of their wild appearance (Jeanmaire, p. 278ff). However, several of the earliest vase paintings of satyrs clearly show them as male human beings wearing furry costumes (McNally, p. 108, fig. 1, and p. 112, fig. 4). Moreover, when the worship of Dionysos gave birth to theater in the sixth century B.C., three theatrical genres appeared: tragedy, comedy, and satyr plays. The last were burlesque sexual displays performed by men wearing satyr masks, phalluses, and horse tails. The implication is that the satyr play emerged from previous Dionysian rituals in which men wore such costumes. In his *Poetics*, Aristotle argues that satyr spectacles also gave birth to comedy and that they continued to be celebrated in their original form in his own time (Aristotle, *Poetics*, 1449a).

The most explicit evidence on the satyr question comes from Plato in a typically prudish passage from his *Laws*. As often, he is vexed by the thought of people having too much pleasure (in this case dancing), and he gives this advice to rulers to help them distinguish between good and bad dance forms:

Now first we must distinguish objectionable dancing from unobjectionable dancing. What, then, is the former and how is it to be separated from the latter? Whatever belongs to Bakkhic revelry or to those who indulge in such—claiming to imitate drunken Pans or Silenoi or Satyrs—while carrying out purgations or other kinds of initiation— . . . this kind of dancing is not worthy of citizens . . .

(Plato, Laws, 815B–D)

Here Plato explicitly states that men imitate satyrs in their dancing, that these dances are part of the ecstatic worship of Dionysos (*hose men bakkheia t'esti*) and that they involve ritual initiations (*perikatharmous te kai teletas*). Hence the early depiction on vases showing Mad Women and satyrs dancing together (and sometimes having sexual relations) cannot be brushed off as the mere fantasies of imaginative artists.

Another important source of evidence on this point is Euripides' *Bakkhai* itself. At the very beginning of the play, after Dionysos announces that he has driven the women of Thebes out of the city to hold wild rites in his honor in the mountains, the aged and blind seer Teiresias hobbles onto the stage. Aware of the god's power, Teiresias tries to cajole the reluctant and equally aged Kadmos, the king's grandfather, into joining him in honoring the god.

In their exchange at this point, Teiresias and Kadmos seem to imply that they are going to the mountains where the women driven from Thebes have already fled. For example, Kadmos, who is embarrassed at wearing women's clothes, angers Teiresias by wanting to hurry out to the mountain in his chariot.

> Kadmos. Shouldn't we drive our chariot, then,
> Up to the mountain heights?
>
> Teir. No! For the god would not have fitting honor.
>
> Kadmos. Then I will take you by the hand,
> Age ahead of age.

(lines 191–193)

Ross Kraemer argues that this passage is still rather vague and does not explicitly state that Kadmos and Teiresias join the women's rites (Kraemer, p. 70). However, when Kadmos later returns at the end of the play, carrying the bloody pieces of Pentheus' body in a basket, he moans:

I heard about my daughters' violent acts
As I walked along the town within the walls,
Just back with old Teiresias
From the Raving Women's rites.
So back to the mountains I returned
To retrieve a son just slain by mad ones.

(lines 1223–1226)

Here Kadmos states explicitly that he and Teiresias have come from the Mad Women themselves (*Bakkhon apo*).

Although it is true that the rites of the Theban women are abnormal because they have rejected Dionysos, when Teiresias and Kadmos leave to join them at the beginning of the play they do so under the assumption that they are joining a regular band of Bakkhai. It is only later that the women's terrible destructiveness is unleashed, and when it is, Kadmos is not present, as the passage just cited indicates.

Commentators on Euripides' *Bakkhai* often overlook the fact that there is another male who joins the revelling Mad Women—Dionysos himself. His presence there cannot be discounted as a mere metaphor (on the ground that, of course, the god is in some sense present to his worshipers). On the contrary, until the very end of the play, Dionysos is disguised as a human being, as he states in his opening monologue:

I've changed my form from a god's to a man's,
And here I stand by Thebes' two streams . . .

(lines 4–5)

At the end of this same monologue, Dionysos announces that he will join the rites of the escaped women of Thebes, still disguised as a man:

I myself will go to the glens of Mt. Kithairon
And join the dance
With the women possessed by Bakkhos there.

(lines 62–63)

In a later scene, after Dionysos frees himself from Pentheus' prison by causing an earthquake, he is reunited with the chorus of barbarian Mad Women who have followed him to Thebes from Asia Minor. They still do not know that he is the god, and they address him as the mortal man who is the leader of their rites:

26

> It's you,
> The leading light in our ecstatic rites.
> How glad I am to see you.

(lines 608–609)

This is the same male leader whom the chorus earlier celebrates in a song describing the nature of their rites:

> The priest of Bakkhos,
> With pine-cone torch aflame
> And placed atop a fennel stalk,
> Its smoke like Syrian frankincense,
> Runs out,
> Inciting wanderers with dances,
> Shaking and shouting,
> Throwing his delicate locks to the air.
> With shouts of joy,
> He bellows as follows:
> 'Oh come, women of Bakkhos, come!'

(lines 145–153)

The Greek text in the above passage is unclear in some parts, but there is no doubt that the subject of the episode is a *male* priest (*bakkheus*—the male form of *bakkha*).

In view of the previously discussed evidence from vase paintings and the literary tradition, it is incorrect to argue, as Albert Henrichs does, that the presence of male maenads in Euripides' *Bakkhai* is "a striking illustration of the perversion of genuine maenadism" (Henrichs, 1982, p. 139). Quite the contrary, Euripides' feminine-identified male participants in the rites are consistent with this other evidence. Although, as we shall see, Euripides does draw novel conclusions from the religion of Dionysos, he does not pervert or misrepresent the basic nature of those rites as they were practiced. To do so would have been foolish, since his audience consisted of Athenian citizens who knew the rites from their own experience. Although Euripides' *Bakkhai* became well-known and widely discussed after its production, no ancient source has come down to us that accuses the author of perverting the basic nature of the rites. In fact, many subsequent Greek authors viewed him as an authoritative source.

In the rites of Dionysos during classical times, there were indeed cases where men and women celebrated the god in sexually separated groups and with different kinds of rites. But there were also occasions where the sexes acted together, even in maenadism. In the latter case, male participants were few and apparently always feminine-identified. Originally, in the prehistoric past, maenadism may very well have been an all-woman affair, but by the time of the classical era instances of male participants were not unknown. With the passage of time, they became ever more common, even involving foreign males. In a suggestive passage, the historian Herodotos relates that Skyles, the king of the Scythians, was overthrown when his subjects discovered that he had been secretly participating in what was apparently a Greek maenadic band (*thiasos*) (Herodotos, 4, 79–80).

The striking feature about male participation in maenadism is that in order to be acceptable men had to lay aside all signs of male privilege and adopt a feminine persona. This is precisely the thing that King Pentheus finds most offensive in the rites, and his resistance to this demand leads to his utter downfall. His unyielding attitude on this point is brought out early in the play when his grandfather Kadmos pleads with him to put on the ritual garb of Dionysos and come with the two old men as they wander off to the mountains to join the women of Thebes in their rites:

> Kadmos. Come, crown your head with ivy,
> Join us.
> Show the god respect.
>
> Pen. Aawwgh! Don't beg me with your hands,
> But go and dance with Bakkhos.
> Your madness won't rub off on me!
>
> (lines 341–344)

In an important sense, the whole action of Euripides' *Bakkhai* turns on the king's refusal to join the maenadic rites; hence to deny the historical reality of male maenadism is to rob the play of much of its meaning. It would be pointless for Euripides to have Dionysos demand such participation from Pentheus if most Greeks thought it had nothing to do with the rites of Dionysos in the first place.

The scene in Euripides' *Bakkhai* where the mad Pentheus finally puts on women's clothes surely reminded viewers not only of the transvestite rituals associated with Dionysos but also of the effeminacy of Dionysos himself. But it would be a mistake to see in Pentheus' behavior nothing more than an allusion to traditional rites and myths, as E. R. Dodds seems to do when he says, "The disguise was a traditional feature of the story that Euripides had to account for" (Dodds, p. 181). In fact, the transvestism scene is, above and beyond such allusions, an integral part of the inner dynamic and meaning of the play. The key to understanding this inner meaning lies in appreciating Pentheus' ambivalent attitude toward women.

On one hand, Pentheus is clearly sexually attracted to women, a fact indicated by his fantasies about the behavior of those women who have fled Thebes. His mind always turns to sex:

> I hear the bowls are full of wine amid their feasts
> And they sneak off to this or that deserted spot
> To service men in bed,
> Pretending to be some kind of raving priest,
> But serving, instead of Bakkhos,
> Love-goddess Aphrodite.

(lines 221–225)

Dionysos finally entices Pentheus to leave the city for the mountains by suggesting to him that he can thereby play the voyeur:

Dion. Well,
But wouldn't you like to spy on them there,
All gathered in the mountains?

Pen. Why, yes . . .
I'd give a pile of gold!

Dion. Why does that arouse you so?

Pen. I want to watch them when they're stinking drunk.

Dion. What!
You want to watch what galls you?

Pen. Yes, but hidden among the pines.

(lines, 810–816)

The Greek word translated as "arouse" in this exchange is *eros*, which means *sexual* arousal.

But like all men with entrenched patriarchal values, Pentheus also has great contempt for women: they are not to be trusted, they should stay in their place in the home, they must never challenge male authority or engage in male endeavors. He is, for example, horrified at the thought of women drinking wine in their Dionysian feasts:

With women, when grapes appear at the feast,
The rites, I say, can never be good.

(lines 260–262)

A number of recent commentators maintain that women never drank wine in the rites of Dionysos because many Greek cities in the classical era forbade them its use. But this line of reasoning ignores the fact that the religion of Dionysos allowed women to do many things usually forbidden them, such as gathering together in large groups outside their homes and holding dances in the middle of night on mountains. Moreover, ancient vase paintings show women in the grape harvest—work whose patron was Dionysos. It is a sign of sexist thinking to argue, as Albert Henrichs does, that despite these paintings women had no part in wine-making because "the laborious task of collecting and treading the grapes required strength and stamina, and was naturally left to men" (Henrichs, 1982, p. 140).

Euripides implies that women did in fact use wine in their rites (although without getting drunk), for when Pentheus proclaims that the mixture of wine and women is a bad thing, he is immediately rebuked by a member of the chorus for sacrilege against Dionysos:

What disrespect for religion!
Stranger, don't you respect the gods . . . ?

(line 263)

In addition to disapproving of their use of wine, Pentheus finds it hard to believe that women can regulate their own behavior when off by themselves, unsupervised by their husbands, as shown by this exchange:

Pen.   These rites, do you do them at night or in the day?

Dion.   Mostly at night. In darkness is holiness.

Pen.   This is a treacherous way for women
And one not sound.

Dion.   One can also find shame in the day.

(lines 485–488)

When Pentheus gets word that the driven women of Thebes have routed a group of herdsmen who tried to capture them, he practically has a fit:

> By now the Raving Women's outrage burns
>   nearby,
> A grave reproach to Greeks,
> And I must not hold back!
> Go to Elektra's Gate,
> Assemble all the troops . . .
> We march against the Bakkhic women!
> For this, indeed, is just too much—
> Am I to continue to suffer so at *women's* hands?

(lines 778–786)

In short, Pentheus regards women as an inferior class of human beings, suitable no doubt for satisfying men's sexual needs, bearing children, making clothes, and cleaning the house, but hardly the equal of men in the right to enjoy the pleasures of life on their own or in the power of running their own lives, to say nothing of running the collective life of the state as manifested in politics and war. In having these values, Pentheus typifies the general attitude toward women of the Greek establishment outside of Sparta.

It immediately follows from such a belief-system that any man who seems to look or act like a woman is degrading himself, and in lowering himself to the level of a supposedly inferior class of beings is the fit object both of the scorn of other males and of shame in his own mind, at least if he has any regard for himself as a real man.

That Pentheus is quick to draw this conclusion is shown by his response to Dionysos' goading suggestion that he dress up as a woman to spy on the Theban women:

> *Dion.* Want me to show you how to reach that place?
>   Do you really want to take this trip?
>
> *Pen.* Get on with it then.
>   I resent the time I have to spend with you.
>
> *Dion.* Okay, first put on a linen dress.
>
> *Pen.* What's that!?
>   Am I, a man, to be reduced to a woman?

(lines 819–822)

The Greek verb used in the phrase "to be reduced" is *telein*, a word borrowed from the language of taxation and literally meaning to be placed in a certain bracket or category for tax purposes (Dodds, p. 177, and *telo* in Liddell-Scott-Jones). Pentheus' question in which this word occurs literally means, "Am I to be removed from the category of a man and be placed into that of women?" The clear implication is that by putting on a woman's dress Pentheus feels he is degrading his status, and that feeling makes sense only if he believes women should have a significantly lower status than men. Had Pentheus believed in the equality of the sexes, it would have been impossible for him to express such a sentiment with these words.

Hence there is an essential link between Pentheus' fear of wearing women's clothes and his contempt for women. The same, of course, applies to his attitude toward the effeminacy of Dionysos, previously discussed. His contempt for signs of femininity, both in himself and in other men, is a natural consequence of his contempt for women.

Burdened by such a value system, Pentheus, not surprisingly, is also deeply conflicted in his sexual feelings toward Dionysos. As soon as the captured god is brought into his presence, Pentheus lurches back and forth between two modes of feeling: his natural sexual attraction to a man of Dionysos' beauty and his patriarchal values, which say such feelings are unworthy of a real man. First his eyes linger on the lines of the god's body, he probably even fondles Dionysos—but then he quickly pulls away and snarls an insult, reminding himself that such feelings belong to a woman, not a man like he. Next he caresses the god's hair, but quickly catches himself and snarls again. Finally, he strokes the god's smooth, pale skin, only to draw back abusively a third time. Here is the scene as Euripides paints it:

> Henchman. This man has come to us in Thebes with many wonders.
> What happens next is up to you.
>
> Pen. Release his hands. He's in my net.
> He can't move fast enough to fly from me.
>
> So, stranger, your body's not bad . . .
> At least as a *woman* would judge! . . .
> Which is why you came to Thebes.
>
> And your hair's so long . . . not athlete you!
> And falls below your cheeks . . . so full of lust!
>
> And your skin is fair and pale . . .
> Because of the life you lead!
>
> Not in the rays of the sun, but in the dark,
> You pursue with your beauty Aphrodite.
>
> (lines 451–459)

32

In the statement "Your body's not bad," the Greek for "not bad" is *ouk amorphos,* literally "not unappealing in form," derived from the root *morph,* meaning "shapely to the eye." The erotic connotation of this root is shown by the fact that at Sparta the name of the beautiful love goddess Aphrodite was *Morpho* (*Morpho* in Liddell-Scott-Jones).

The emphatic nature of Pentheus' pulling back after making this statement is underlined by the words *hos es gynaikas* (literally, "as at least from women's viewpoint") which immediately follow at the beginning of the next line and which abruptly limit and correct what he just conceded about Dionysos' physical beauty (Dodds, p. 134). The remaining Greek phrases in the scene are carefully balanced and juxtaposed, the latter half of each sequence immediately retracting and denying the meaning of the first half. The net effect both of Euripides' choice of words here and of his antithetical structuring of these words is to show Pentheus deeply divided against himself in the face of Dionysos' physical beauty.

Pentheus' behavior in this short scene was quite significant in the eyes of an ancient Greek audience in view of the reputation of Dionysos and his retinue (the satyrs) for homosexual activities. Scenes depicting or implying the homosexual ambience of Dionysos are among the most well-attested and enduring of Greek art, appearing from the earliest to the latest periods. I was vividly reminded of the prevalence of this theme while recently re-inspecting the Greek collection at the Metropolitan Museum of Art in New York. A jar from Athens from about 500 B.C., for example, shows, on one side, a bearded Dionysos closely facing a bearded satyr with an erection (cat. no. 41.162.32). On the other side, a naked adult man with an erection is courting a naked male youth, while another man stands nearby. Another jar from the same place and period shows Dionysos on one side with a nude male youth, while on the other, two bearded men caress each other's hands (cat. no. 18.145.15). Scenes similar in content, if different in style, can also be found much later, well into Roman times (Kerényi, plates 140, 141, 142).

Many vases have been preserved that show actual homosexual sex acts, in great profusion and variety, among the satyrs. The Dionysian homoerotic motif, both implicit and explicit, appears on jars and other objects used in temples, homes, storehouses, and markets. Through such artifacts, this theme permeated the consciousness of the ancient Greeks. Phallic motifs were also common in a number of Dionysian festivals. Albert Henrichs argues that their presence, though "rampant," had nothing to do with sexuality, since they were "confined to the male sex" (Henrichs, 1982, p. 148). But his underlying assumption that to Dionysos sexuality meant only heterosexuality is false, as is his argument that the cult's sexual imagery in general was but a celebration of "reproduction" (Henrichs, *loc. cit.*).

Literary records also bear witness to Dionysos' homosexual activity. The Christian writer Clement of Alexandria reports a rather colorful incident involving a certain Prosymnos:

> Dionysos wanted to descend to Hades but did not know the way. A certain Prosymnos promised to show him but for a price. The price was indecent but not for Dionysos. The price he asked of Dionysos was a sexual favor. Dionysos was receptive to the request and promised to yield to him if he would set him on his way, confirming his promise with an oath. After finding out, he departed. On his return he could not find Prosymnos, since he had died. To discharge his obligations to his lover, Dionysos went to his tomb and committed a perversion. He cut off the branch of a fig tree he chanced upon and fashioned it into the shape of a male member and then sat on the piece, thus carrying out his promise to the dead man. As a ritual reminder of this event, phalluses are set up to Dionysos throughout cities.

> (Clement, 2, 29–30)

The implication of Clement's passage is that Dionysos used the wooden phallus as a dildo in anal masturbation. In fact, a number of ancient vases depict satyrs masturbating in this way. The passage also suggests that some kind of widespread ritual was practiced in memory of this story.

The Greek traveler Pausanias refers to the same myth in his mention of a certain *Polymnos* in the context of rites practiced at the Alkyonian Lake near Korinth:

> And I saw the so-called Spring of Amphiaros and the Alkyonian Lake, through which the Argives say Dionysos travelled to Hades to bring back Semele and that the descent by this means was shown to him by Polymnos.

> (Pausanias, 2, 37, 5)

Pausanias adds that rites are practiced by the lake whose content he dare not reveal. Considered together, these two passages suggest that homosexual rites may have been part of the worship of Dionysos in his capacity as the lord who returns from the dead.

A more lyrical account of Dionysos' sexuality can be found in the work of Nonnos, a poet of the fifth century A.D. who, writing in Greek, undertook to synthesize most of the pagan myths of his time into one coherent story having the exploits of the god Dionysos as its central core. This poem, *The Epic of Dionysos [Dionysiaka]*, is the last great literary work of Greek paganism. It includes the description of Dionysos'

34

feelings on first seeing the young man Ampelos (his name literally means "vine"):

> Now once while hunting in shady recesses of woods
> He was charmed by the rosy-cheeked beauty
> Of a boy companion.
> Ampelos, the youth at play, had just come of age
> At the foot of the Phrygian mountains,
> A bud newly raised for the Passions.
> The delicate down on his ruddy jaws
> Still traced no shade on smooth and snow-white cheeks,
> This golden flower in the prime of youth.
> Spiraling locks of back-flowing hair
> Fell untied past silvery shoulders,
> Swirling together from the clear, brisk breeze,
> Tossed by its puffs.
> Then, as the strands of his hair blew aside,
> The nape of his neck, uncovered, was exposed to view,
> And flashed with a light, unobstructed,
> As the moon, when it breaks through a cloud,
> Shines out in its midst.

(Nonnos, 10, 175–187)

In imitation of Dionysos, Ampelos dresses himself in the womanish type of clothing worn by the god:

> Often he saw the Raving One's tunic with spotted back,
> So he dressed himself in mock dappled clothes
> And slipped nimble feet into purple buskins
> And wore a motley gown

(Nonnos, 11, 60–63)

Dionysos for his part falls deeply in love with the youth and dotes on him:

> And still it pleased Bakkhos to watch him,
> For the eyes can never be sated
> Of one who watches his love.
> Often, with the Raving One seated beside him at meals,
> The youngster would play wrong notes on is pipes,
> Altering the tune.
> Mixing the pitches of the reeds.
> But even when he made a note squeak,
> Bakkhos—as if the boy made lovely sounds—
> Would jump with a rush of air from the floor

And loudly clap his hands.
While the boy was even still singing,
He planted his lips on his mouth
And gave him a big, loving hug
In praise for his song.
He would swear by the son of Kronos
That neither Pan with his musical grace
Nor sweet-voiced Apollo
Had yet made such beautiful sounds.

(Nonnos, 11, 101–112)

When Ampelos is killed in a bull-riding episode, Dionysos transforms him into a grape vine that will eventually produce wine, and eulogizes him:

Ampelos, even in death
You bring joy to the heart of Bakkhos.
I will mix your drink with all my body parts.

(Nonnos, 12, 270–271)

In view of Dionysos' association with homosexual practices, Pentheus' emphatic rejection of him should be seen not only as religious but also as sexual. Although at first sexually aroused by Dionysos, Pentheus finally suppresses his feelings and snaps back into his patriarchal pose, repudiating the god's invitation to both sexual and religious initiation. Hence the great fury of Dionysos and his intense desire for vengeance resulted from having been spurned both as a god and as a lover.

Despite the homosexual ambience of his cult, Dionysos was not viewed by the Greeks as exclusively homosexual, but rather as pansexual, since there are also accounts of his love affairs with women. Moreover, even in the case of his lover Ampelos, Dionysos regretted that the boy never had a chance to marry—not because the boy had somehow been sidetracked into homosexuality but because he would never know the joys of sleeping with a woman in marriage as well. With regret, Dionysos compares himself to the god Poseidon, who gave his male lover a carriage with which to pursue a wife:

Only I have had a boy who died unwed.
Enticing Ampelos had no life-sustaining marriage,
Nor did this youngster yoke my marriage cart
To take his ride to the wedding bed.
No, he died and left but grief to joyous Dionysos.

(Nonnos, 11, 276–279)

36

In consolation, Eros, the god of love who appears in the form of a beautiful young man with wings, gives Dionysos this matter-of-fact advice:

> Relieve the smart of your love by another love.
> Exchange the sting you feel for a boy in bloom.
> Stop grief.
> For an older love
> A newer love is always the best of cures.

(Nonnos, 11, 356–359)

In effect, Dionysos is an expression of the sensual joys of life unrestrained by the state and unchanneled by the patriarchal family. In the apt words of one commentator, his religion is "an expression of the aimless joy of life" (Kerényi, p. 170). For him, the primary purpose of sex is not to beget but to enjoy, an attitude well described by another commentator's characterization of his Indian counterpart, Shiva: "All the beauty and all the joy in the world is manifested by means of an erotic explosion. Flowers cast their pollen to the wind. Fecundation is but an accident in the manifestation of erotic joy. Eros recognizes no difference of sex or object" (Daniélou, p. 157).

To Pentheus, with his straitjacket mentality about masculinity, sex, and the family, Dionysos naturally looks like a raving lunatic hell-bent on overthrowing civilization. In the face of this apparent threat, the king's first inclination is to resort to violence—to call out the troops and put the offenders down. He reveals this penchant for violence at his very first appearance on stage, where he says with self-satisfaction:

> So my men are guarding in the jail,
> Chained by their arms,
> All the women I've had arrested.
> And as for those who fled to the hills,
> I'll hunt them down:
> Agaue—my very mother!—
> As well as Autonoe and Ino,
> My mother's sisters.
> I'll tie them together with a net of steel
> And soon put an end to this evil frenzy.

(lines 226–232)

Later, when he confronts Dionysos in person, the king makes similar threats, but Dionysos rebukes him by pointing to his fatal flaw—he is so out of touch with his real feelings and needs, so repressed, that he is setting himself up for disaster. In short, he has violated the first rule of

Euripides' friend and mentor, Sokrates: Know yourself. This is how the scene goes:

> Pen. Seize him! This man's in contempt of Thebes and me.
>
> Dion. As sanity calling the insane,
> So I bid you not to bind me.
>
> Pen. When it comes to the power to bind,
> My reach is greater than yours.
>
> Dion. You don't know what you're saying,
> Or what you're doing,
> Or who you are.
>
> Pen. I am Pentheus, the son of Agaue,
> And son of my father Ekhion.
>
> Dion. Your name resembles *penthos*, Greek for "grief,"
> And fits you well for your misfortune.
>
> (lines 503–506; reading *pheis* for *zeis*)

Such is the conflict, then, that Euripides establishes early in this play: in one corner an up-and-coming butch young man with power who is contemptuous of women and of femininity in men, out of touch with his own homosexual capacities, and eager to smash with a fist every challenge to his narrow definition of the world. In the other corner, a feminine male who dresses like a woman, delights in every form of sexuality, and says he represents the power of the gods. Thus the whole thrust of the play would seem to be nothing more than a study of the interplay between these two distinctly defined character types. On one level, indeed, that is exactly what the play is about. But there is also a deeper level—a level of half-forgotten historical memories, vague collective yearnings and fears, strange mutterings in broken and distant voices almost recognizable yet strangely inaccessible, the grinding sound of great, transpersonal historical forces in slow but momentous movement. This deeper dimension of Euripides' *Bakkhai* is what takes it out of the realm of soap opera and raises it to that of great tragedy. To explore and understand this dimension we must now turn our attention to yet another kind of labyrinth: early Greek history.

II

BULLS, GODS, AND WOMEN

○

FOR many centuries after the revival of classical learning in the Renaissance, a general notion of early Greek life prevailed that was based on episodes in the poems of Homer (written in the eighth or seventh century B.C.). The *Odyssey* and the *Iliad* depict the early Greeks as a warlike collection of tribes in which men exercise all significant political, military, and religious power and women are mere accessories, desired only for their physical beauty or their access to good connections. Strength in battle and strategic ability are the hallmarks of male greatness, and obedience and fidelity are the marks of worthy women. The gods live in the sky above, where Father Zeus maintains his patriarchal sway among the clouds. At times these gods intervene in human affairs, even taking sides on the battlefield, but they never involve themselves in the inner emotional life of human beings. They are prayed to or avoided because they are powerful and can influence the outcome of a battle or the course of the weather. They are never loved. In effect the Homeric world-view is that of a band of recently settled nomadic invaders whose economic growth is based on pillage, whose ideal men are "heroes" (a word that literally means "warriors" in ancient Greek), whose women are property, and whose gods embody brute force and are imagined to live in a patriarchal social organization like that of their followers.

There is no doubt that the Homeric world-view is a fairly accurate representation of the dominant values of the upper classes in a certain period of early Greek history (from about 1200 B.C. to 700 B.C.). Only recently, however, has it been discovered that things were once quite different.

In the early years of this century, the traditional understanding of early Greek history was completely upset by the astounding archeological discoveries in Crete by Arthur Evans (no relation to me, as far as I know). Evans uncovered the ruins of a previously unknown civilization which he named Minoan after the legendary King Minos who was said to have once ruled in the island.

In the town of Knossos, Evans unearthed a palace complex that is remarkable for several reasons. The paintings on its walls show a high degree of refinement and delicacy, with a great deal of attention given to scenes from nature and to playful pastimes, and very little to subjects of a warlike nature. Women, often nude from the waist up, routinely appear in roles of leadership. The chief deities appear to have been female, not male, and the labyris (the double-bladed ax that was a principal symbol of authority) is never shown in the hands of a male god (Nilsson, 1950, p. 226). Except for a small flying male figure, no clearly identifiable evidence of the worship of sky gods can be found, and the oft-recurring image of the labyrinth (or maze) suggests a religion based on earth deities.

Since Evans's discoveries, other sites have been excavated, and it is now known that Minoan civilization was highly developed throughout Crete, had branches on the Greek mainland and on other islands, and maintained extensive trade relations with many distant countries. Among those who have studied this culture, both on Crete and on the mainland, the following is a typical assessment: "It was peaceful, agricultural, seafaring, and artistic" (Hammond, p. 37).

Excavators have found examples of the writing of this civilization (so-called Linear A), but have not succeeded in deciphering the script. Linear A is probably not part of the Indo-European family of languages and is suspected of being Semitic.

Minoan civilization reached its peak in the period from 2000 B.C. to 1600 B.C. Around the latter date, waves of nomadic invaders speaking Greek appeared from the north. Organized socially into a patriarchy and worshipping sky gods, they eventually conquered the Minoans and formed a two-tiered society. On the top, the conquerors took over the elaborately built structures of the conquered, spoke an early form of ancient Greek (recorded in the so-called Linear B script), and imported a religion that was eventually reflected in the poems of Homer; on the bottom, the original inhabitants continued to work the land and maintain their own traditions.

The Minoans and the invading Greeks formed a hybrid civilization called Mycenaean from the important city of Mykenai (or Mycenae) in mainland Greece, ruled by the legendary Agamemnon, Lord of Men, as he is called in Homer. Tablets inscribed with Linear B and surviving from this period in Mykenai, Thebes, Pylos, and Knossos have been deciphered. They show that women of the period played an important role as both skilled and nonskilled workers in nondomestic occupations and in religion. They also suggest that among the upper classes (the invading Greeks) family descent was reckoned through the father, but through the mother among the conquered lower classes (Billigmeier, pp. 2–3).

A number of passages in the later poems of Homer apparently refer back to Mycenaean customs concerning women. As Sarah Pomeroy has shown, certain Homeric myths imply that succession to kingship in some areas was obtained only by marriage to an existing queen or princess (Pomeroy, p. 19). Such appears to have been the case with Menelaus, who became King of Sparta through his marriage to the beautiful Spartan Helen. After Helen ran off with Paris to Troy, Menelaus had to regain her in order to keep his kingship. Hence the Trojan War. And hence also his inability to take vengeance on Helen after he regained her (Pomeroy, p. 21). Homer also implies that certain queens in the Mycenaean era had significant power in their own right (Pomeroy, p. 22).

In time, new waves of even fiercer Greek invaders appeared, and in the middle of the thirteenth century B.C. all the sites of Minoan and Mycenaean civilization were burned and sacked. A dark age ensued until about 800 B.C., when classical Greek civilization as we know it first began to emerge. Though speaking Greek, this new civilization was in fact a hybrid of both Greek and earlier Minoan elements, which did not always form an easy mix. As will be shown, a memorable expression of the clash between these two cultural elements is found in Euripides' *Bakkhai*.

Among the Linear B tablets surviving from Mycenaean times are a number referring to the god Dionysos. For example, at Pylos two tablets are inscribed with the phrase "Of Dionysos" and probably refer to a storage record for wine (Kerényi, pp. 68–69). Another refers to "Eleuther, Son of Zeus," another title later associated with Dionysos (Kerényi, p. 165). The names "Pentheus," "Iakkhos," and "Silenos" (a satyr) are found at Knossos (Kerényi, pp. 69, 71, 77). These records prove that Dionysos was known from the time of the very first introduction of the Greek language into the area now known as Greece.

The discovery of these early inscriptions caused quite a sensation because many myths treat Dionysos as a *new* god only recently come to Greece. Found in many different parts of Greece, these stories recount the sufferings of Dionysos as the rejected Son of God and tell of his subsequent vengeance when triumphant (Kerényi, p. 175). The most celebrated example is Euripides' *Bakkhai*, where Dionysos says in his opening monologue:

> I am Dionysos—the Son of God!—
> And I have just arrived here in the land of Thebes . . .
> But the sisters of my mother,
> Those that I expected least,
> Denied that I was born from Zeus . . .
> And so from their homes I drove these sisters
>   frenzied . . .

(lines 1–2; 26–27; 32–33)

The Linear B tablets show that Dionysos is as old as any of the Greek gods, including Zeus. Why, then, are there myths about his late arrival and of Greek resistance to his worship?

The answer lies in the two-tiered nature of Greek history just mentioned, which was reflected in a two-tiered religion. On the top were Zeus and the conquerors' other gods: "We have a warlike upper class which created a State of the Gods on the model of their own feudal organization" (Nilsson, 1950, p. 32). On the bottom was the great mass of agricultural workers and slaves who retained the agrarian and nature deities of the old Minoan religion and their special rites. In the course of time, both fusion and conflict occurred between these two religious traditions.

Dionysos was the Greek god who most resembled certain male deities from the Minoan era. Accordingly, he rapidly assimilated many of the beliefs and practices of the agrarian lower classes. This assimilation of the Minoan world-view brought about a tremendous change both in his importance and in his nature. In Homer, for example, he is only peripherally mentioned. But by the time of the classical era a few hundred years later, he had become the center of a massive cult that was everywhere well entrenched and the source of practices and beliefs that disturbed the upper classes.

Dionysos also had a second source of strength. A similar resurgence of suppressed old beliefs and practices occurred in the Eastern Aegean in Asia Minor (now Western Turkey) after a patriarchal conquest there. In the classical period, with the resumption of a seafaring trade, Greeks from the West discovered that the deities Sabazios and Bakkhos were performing the same functions in the Eastern Aegean as Dionysos in the West. Furthermore, many immigrants came to Greece in this period from

42

Asia Minor, bringing the cult of Sabazios or Bakkhos with them. As a result, there were convulsive religious upheavals from the eighth to the fifth centuries B.C., as the various countercultural gods blended together into Dionysos-Bakkhos. The long-repressed lower classes at last had a new focus and momentum for their ancient beliefs and clamored for their piece of turf in the religious and cultural hierarchy. The upshot was that the old aristocracy suddenly found itself confronted by a powerful and alien god who simply would not go away and with whom it was forced to come to terms.

The coming of Dionysos represents, therefore, the return of the repressed. But this "repressed" was not just a collection of long-subdued underclasses at last making their social clout felt. It was also the resurgence of a world-view, a way of regarding nature, sexuality, and religion that directly threatened the established concepts of the time. To understand this concept of Dionysos, we must examine those traits he brought with him from the labyrinth of Minoan religion.

To begin with, one of the most striking but nonetheless well established features of Dionysos was his practice of wearing horns or appearing in the form of a bull, a depiction repeatedly mentioned in Euripides' *Bakkhai*. When the chorus first enter, they relate the marvelous birth of Dionysos from the thigh of Zeus, saying:

> And when the Fates matured him,
> Zeus gave birth to a bull-horned god,
> And crowned his son with a wreath of snakes.

(lines 99–102)

Later, after Pentheus is stricken with madness, Dionysos relates how the king had tried to bind him with rope in the stable where he had been imprisoned. But in his madness, the king actually attacked a bull, thinking it was Dionysos:

> This is how I made a *fool* of him:
> I made him think he jailed me,
> When in fact he neither touched nor bound me
> But fed on expectations.
>
> By the stable there where he had led and held me
> He found a bull
> And tied a rope around its knees and hooves.
> And all the while he dripped with sweat,

Seethed with hate,
And bit his lips
Nearby I sat at peace and watched.

(lines 616–622)

When totally insane and dressed as a woman, Pentheus looks at Dionysos and swears he sees a bull, to which the latter replies:

> The god, though hostile once,
> Is with us now in peace.
> You see as you should.

(lines 923–925)

After the death of Pentheus, the chorus gloats in a sing-song voice:

> He took for himself a woman's dress
> And a sharpened fennel stalk
> (What a worthy thyrsos for Hades!)
> And followed a bull to guide his doom.

(lines 1156–1159; reading *nartheka te pikron Haida* in place of Dodds's *nartheka te, piston Haidan*)

In a number of ancient hymns mentioned by Plutarch, women invoke Dionysos as a bull (Plutarch, *Moralia*, 299B). In addition, all-male Dionysian cult societies existed whose members were called *boukoloi*, which literally means *herdsmen*, "though the true meaning of the title was doubtless 'worshipper of the bull god'" (Dodds, p. 159). In Euripides' *Bakkhai*, a herdsman is the first to give the king a detailed eyewitness account of the god's power, and when Pentheus arrests Dionysos, he locks him up in the stable with bulls and horses. In Nonnos' epic about Dionysos, the god's youthful lover Ampelos is killed while riding a wild bull (Nonnos, 11, 218–220).

As it happens, one of the most common motifs in Minoan art is that of the bull. Minoan murals show dancers performing elaborate acrobatics on the backs of bulls, drinking cups for wine are made in the shape of bull heads, altars are decorated with bull heads or bull horns, and several paintings show the head of a bull with the labyris—the double-bladed ax—between its horns.

Since the original language of the Minoans—Linear A—has never been deciphered, none of these depictions in itself is foolproof evidence that a bull god existed among them. Hence some scholars dismiss the idea of such a god, arguing that the bull depictions are just decorative or that the pictures of acrobats with bulls simply show nonreligious pastimes. This is the position taken by Martin Nilsson, who argues that, on the basis of the available evidence, we can safely conclude only that the *head* of the bull played a part in Minoan religion (Nilsson, 1950, p. 232).

But Nilsson's argument fails to explain *why* an admittedly animistic people would revere only a part of a certain animal and not the whole. Where would the head get its power, if not from the whole? The Phoenicians, who were culturally related to the Minoans, worshipped a bull god named *Baal Moloch*, which they usually represented by its head alone (Nettleship and Sandys, p. 394). The head is a convenient symbol for the power of the whole because the rest of the animal is usually used up—eaten, in fact, as is the practice in animistic societies that believe they commune with a god by eating its flesh.

Further, to argue that the bull-leaping games were devoid of religious content flies in the face of everything known about public spectacles in early antiquity. Holding games in a god's honor was a common and well documented practice. Games were even held on the occasion of funerals. Purely secular games did not occur until very late in antiquity. Moreover, one of the most conspicuous features of Minoan culture in general was this fusion of the secular and the sacred (Hawkes, 1968, p. 121).

Finally, Nilsson dismisses Minoan depictions of men having the upper torso of a bull because "the crouching position and grotesque appearance (resembling a fetus) of these man-bulls are absolutely inappropriate for a divine being, even in the Minoan age" (Nilsson, 1950, p. 375). This argument simply begs the question, since the whole issue here is what is to be considered divine and what is not. To Nilsson it may be inappropriate for a god to be a fetus with a bull's head, but not to Euripides, who wrote thus:

> And when the Fates matured him,
> Zeus gave birth to a bull-horned god.

> (lines 99–100)

But the telling blow against Nilsson's position is a Minoan myth that survived well into the classical era: the story of the Minotaur (literally, "Bull of Minos"). This was a creature, half man and half bull, who lived in the labyrinth at Crete, to whom both criminals and young Athenians sent as tribute were sacrificed. According to this myth, the Athenian culture hero Theseus, helped by Ariadne, a Cretan woman who had fallen in love with him, eventually killed the Minotaur and freed the Athenian captives. Every year, in a festival already mentioned—the Oskhophoria—the Athenians celebrated this event with a public procession associated with the god Dionysos and led by two young men dressed as women. The purpose of this festival was to thank Dionysos for *not* returning with Theseus *from* Crete *to* Athens (Kerényi, p. 145). Further, in the earliest Greek reference to this myth (in the *Odyssey*), Dionysos has the turncoat Ariadne killed for helping Theseus, as indicated in the passage where Odysseus is observing the ghosts of the dead:

> And Phaidra I saw and Prokris and lovely Ariadne,
> Daughter of sharp-witted Minos.
> Theseus was taking her off as a bride from Crete
> To mighty Athens' heights,
> But never took his joy of her.
> Golden Artemis killed her first
> At the request of Dionysos.
>
> (Homer, *Odyssey*, 11, 321–325)

The implication of these tales is that a god in the form of a bull-man existed on Crete and that Greek myth later identified him with Dionysos. The myth of the Minotaur probably had a historical reference to the time when Athens was a tributary subject of Crete and when human sacrifices were performed, that is, when criminals and war captives were executed in a ritual context, since the ancients did nearly everything in a ritual context.

A number of Greek myths suggest that human sacrifices may once have been offered to Dionysos. An echo of these myths occurred in historical times, in the fifth century B.C., in the war between Athens and Persia. The Persians had sent a huge fleet to invade Athens, and the population of that city was panic-stricken and desperate. Plutarch reports this incident involving the Athenian naval commander Themistokles:

> While Themistokles was slaughtering animal victims in the sacrifice near the Admiral's warship, three prisoners of war were brought in, gorgeous-looking men dressed in sumptuous clothes and gold jewelry. They were said to be the sons of Sandauke, the Persian King's sister, and Artauktos. When Euphrantides the seer caught sight of them, a bright flame flared up from the animals on the altar and someone on the right sneezed, a good omen. Euphrantides addressed Themistokles and urged him to begin with the young men and to offer them up with an invocation for help to Dionysos Flesh-Eater. In this way the Greeks would win both deliverance and victory.
>
> (Plutarch, *Lives*, 13, 3)

Themistokles was horrified at this suggestion, but the war-frenzied crowd rioted, dragged the prisoners to the altar, and sacrificed them to Dionysos.

Debate continues over whether human sacrifice in connection with cannibalism ever existed in ancient Minoan religion. Although nearly all paintings from Crete show a fairly peaceful civilization, archeologists in 1981 discovered anciently buried human bones that showed knife-nicks, suggesting that the flesh had been sliced off. At the time, some interpreted this find as a sure sign of cannibalism. More recently, however, it has been shown that an odd burial custom persists in the modern Greek village of Leonidi: the body of the deceased is allowed to decompose in a temporary grave, after which the remains are exhumed, the bones stripped clean with a knife and bleached, and the cleaned bones reburied (Tumasonis, p. 307). Hence the bones from ancient Crete may have been treated in this fashion. Although stories of cannibalism in so-called "primitive" societies often capture the popular imagination, documented cases of the practice are rare.

Dionysos' affiliation with Crete is implicit in myths about his family relationships, since he was the son of Semele, who was related to King Minos of Crete. The poet Nonnos recalls this relationship in the story of Asterios of Crete, who once came to Dionysos' aid with a troop of Cretan warriors ("the people of the hundred cities"):

> He came at that time to wine-sparkling Bakkhos
> With the people of the hundred cities
> To honor the kindred blood of his father's family,
> Since Minos was cousin to Semele
> And common kin of Kadmos.
>
> (Nonnos, 13, 227–230)

Another link between Dionysos and the Minoan bull is the double-ax, which frequently appears as a symbol of religious power in Cretan paintings, often between the horns of the bull's head. Its placement in this position is appropriate, since the instrument was probably used in Minoan bull sacrifices, either to slit the throat of the sacrificial animal or to cut off its head (it takes a very strong implement to cut through a bull's neck). In classical times, even when an animal was slaughtered just for food, the act was done in a ritual context laden with religious significance. The taking of life to support the community was a bloody spectacle provoking participants' feelings about the balance of life and the prerogatives of the gods. (The institution of the impersonal, mechanized

47

slaughterhouse, so typical of modern industrial culture, did not exist in antiquity.)

Although also known by the Minoan-derived word *labyris*, the double-ax was called *bouplex* in classical Greek, which literally means "bull slammer" or "cattle slammer." Nonnos has given us a memorable depiction of the sacramental feeling of animal slaughter among the ancients and of the use of the *bouplex* in his account of the slaughter of a cow by Kadmos, the grandfather of King Pentheus, after his victory over the Giants:

> Now when Kadmos had reaped his snake-like crop of foes
> And cut the stalks of Giants that grew from teeth,
> And gave the war's first fruits as gifts to Ares,
> He washed his hands in River Dirke,
> The stream that nourished dragons,
> And slew on an altar made by the gods
> A cow from the land of Delphi
> As Athena's worthy offering.
> When he led the cow at first to the altar,
> He sprinkled her horns about with barley.
> Then he reached for the top of the unsheathed sword
> That he wore by his thigh, held by a belt from Assyria,
> And cut some hair with hilted blade
> From the shaggy heifer's head.
> Then Theoklymenos, pulling the young cow back by her horns,
> Stretched her neck out tight.
> Thyestes slashed her sinewy throat
> With the axe that has two sides,
> And Ongkaian Athena's stone-made altar
> Turned red from the young cow's blood.
> They slammed the cow on her forehead,
> And down the heifer fell . . .

(Nonnos, 5, 1–17)

Not surprisingly, Dionysos was often associated with the double-ax. On the island of Tenedos a Dionysian ritual existed in which a man put hunting boots on a newborn calf and slaughtered it with the double-ax. Bystanders then threw stones at the man, and he ran away until he reached the sea (Nilsson, 1950, p. 228, and Kerényi, p. 190). This rite recalls the scene in Homer when young Dionysos and his nurses are attacked by ax-wielding Lykourgos and to escape, the god runs and jumps in the sea:

> All at once they dropped their ritual things,
> Assaulted by the two-edged axe
> That murderous Lykourgos waved.

> (Homer, *Iliad*, 6, 133–135)

The poet Simonides, writing in the sixth century B.C., called the double-ax "the bull-killing servant of Lord Dionysos" (Nilsson, 1950, p. 228). In other accounts, Dionysos is himself called by the name "Double-Ax" (Kerényi, p. 192, n. 11).

Once the bull was slaughtered, its head was removed and nailed to a tree in a holy grove or to a temple wall (Nilsson, 1950, p. 232). In fact, it became a common Greek practice to attach the head wherever the power of the bull was needed as a protector. So, for example, an ancient commentator remarks: "Farmers are accustomed to nail legs and skulls to trees to avert their being dried up from evil spells" (Nilsson, 1950, p. 232, n. 76). From this practice came the artistic device in classical Athens of decorating altars and temples with paintings or sculptures of bulls' heads (Nilsson, 1950, p. 232). Euripides' *Bakkhai* contains a clear and strikingly ironic reference to this practice in the scene where the mad Agaue rushes home with the head of her son Pentheus in her hands, deliriously thinking it is a mountain lion's head. On entering Thebes, she calls to her father Kadmos, saying:

> I bear in my arms, as you can see,
> The trophy of victory that I have won,
> So you can nail it on your house's wall.

> (lines 1238–1240)

The absorption by Dionysos of many of the traits of the Cretan bull-god was of enormous significance, for it affirmed and reinforced in classical Greek culture the continuity of animal-human-divine. Human to the chest, bull above, worshipped as a god—such was the Cretan god who was echoed in the myth of the Minotaur. Disguised as a man, sporting horns, worshipped as a god—such was Dionysos as he appeared in his rites and in his myths.

In affirming this continuity, Dionysos flew in the face of the major religious trend of his time. Most of the Greek gods had long since ceased to be worshipped in any animal form, and in addition, were felt to be removed from real human experiences and feelings. Like Athena at Athens, they had become symbols of the corporate identity of the city

49

where they were worshipped in cults whose priests were public officials. Or like Zeus, they were images of the power of the patriarchal family or the warrior aristocracy. Dionysos was God made flesh, animal made human, the visible incarnation of nature's continuities.

The cleavages between human, animal, and divine that came to dominate classical Greece were no accident but the natural results of profound social and political changes that had been occurring for hundreds of years. For one thing, the populace was divided into two radically distinct classes: free citizens and slaves. The former, descendants of the original conquerors, enjoyed a greater mobility and tended to move within the walls of the cities, while slaves performed the actual labor on their farms. Urban slaves, though many, always maintained a subordinate status and influenced the climate of opinion only indirectly. It was the urban free citizens, especially those who were relatively well-off, who participated in the deliberations of government, enjoyed the pastimes of sports and theater, and discussed questions of philosophy. When they needed food or supplies, these were simply shipped in from their farms. As a result, the dominant classes were losing touch with the earth, with animals, and with the great cycles of nature. Their concept of what it meant to be a human being was changing, as were their concepts about gods and animals. "The general tendency in the arts, literature, and philosophy of the fifth century is to assert man's independence from nature, a tendency since then stamped on all of Western thought" (Segal, 1982, p. 31).

Not only was there a sharp distinction between animal, human, and god, but the human experience itself was becoming fragmented. The "nobler" or "better" or "higher" part of human beings was increasingly identified with reason, or rather with abstract, discursive reason. Feelings and passions, especially sexual passions, tended to be associated with animal behavior, that is, with a type of being now considered distinct from and inferior to humans.

This general tendency found a rather extreme expression in the writings of the Athenian philosopher Plato, who flourished in the fourth century B.C. Although initially influenced by the wit, sensuality, and playfulness of his mentor Sokrates, Plato eventually hardened into a stern-faced ideologist who basically regarded the body as an impediment to the best of human potentials. Puritanical in morals, authoritarian in government, distrustful of any knowledge based on the senses or feelings, hostile to artists, he was the new spirit of alienation from nature taken to its logical conclusion.

Although his extreme views made Plato atypical of the Athenians of his time, he became nonetheless the voice of the future in classical civilization. A harshly elaborated version of his basic mentality finally triumphed with a vengeance when the successors of the Emperor Constantine made Christianity the state religion of the Roman Empire in the fourth century A.D.

In addition to the distinction between slavery and freedom, another cleavage that fostered alienating tendencies was the great gulf between women and men, especially in Athens. As shown in chapter 1, Athenian wives and daughters were expected to stay at home in the women's quarters, tending children and overseeing domestic affairs. They were not allowed to vote, participate in government, or directly plead their own causes before law courts, even in cases where their rights within the family were at stake (Keuls, p. 101). Themes of rape—popular among the original Greek invaders—were approvingly represented in myth and in the visual arts. The only women to enjoy a significant degree of release from this domination were the *hetairai*. These informal common-law wives or companions were often former prostitutes or foreigners and had a dubious legal status (Keuls, pp. 272–273).

In stunning contrast to the accustomed practices in Athens, Euripides' *Bakkhai* depicts women as completely independent of men. Scenes may shift from their tender feelings for each other when left alone to their ferocious aggressiveness against outsiders when provoked, but in either case they act on their own with no other motive force for their action than their direct experience of the divine.

Just as significant is the play's defense of their sexual autonomy. When Pentheus complains (falsely) that the women are debauching themselves with men at the rites of Dionysos, the prophet Teiresias rebukes him, saying that is a matter for the women to judge for themselves:

> And Dionysos will *not* compel, in sex or love,
> A woman to act with self-restraint.
> No, for whether she is modest or not
> Is up to her own nature.
> You must consider this:
> Even in ecstatic rites,
> She who is really moderate will not become corrupt.

> (lines 314–318)

To hear these lines put into the symbolic voice of the Athenian religious establishment must have caused quite a stir in the audience. But, as previously indicated, both myth and artifact indicate that women had once held a much higher status in the religion of the old Minoan culture.

As a result of their exclusion from power and public life in Athens, women had little chance to develop a sense of solidarity with each other or to influence the dominant value system of the city. Hence the worst patriarchal attitudes of the early Greek invaders continued to be largely unchallenged. Qualities popularly associated with women—softness, tenderness, physical receptivity in the sex act—were looked down upon, whereas qualities associated with men, especially men in war, were praised—aggressiveness, competitiveness, insensitivity to suffering, the active role in the sex act. The language itself reflected this bias. The word for courage in ancient Greek is *andreia*, literally "manliness;" the word for virtue is *arete*, originally meaning "valor in war."

The religion of Dionysos, with its historical connection to the old, conquered populations and their world-view, with its emphasis on natural feeling, became enormously popular among slaves and women, who in fact also happened to constitute the majority of the Athenian population. And so Dionysos' rites were remarkable in two respects: they were one of the few religious events in which slaves were allowed to participate, and they were one of the few occasions when women could assemble in groups and act in unity. As E. R. Dodds has aptly put it:

Dionysos is a democratic god: he is accessible to all, not like the Pythian Apollo through priestly intermediaries, but directly in his gift of wine and through membership of his *thiasos* [sacred band]. His worship probably made its original appeal mainly to people who had no citizenship rights in the aristocratic "gentile state" and were excluded from the older cults associated with the great families.

(Dodds, pp. 127–128)

Because of its association with the lower classes and women, the Dionysian religion inspired the contempt of those in power in Athens. A good example of such an attitude can be seen in the Athenian orator Demosthenes, who lived in Athens in the fourth century B.C. and was a staunch defender of Greek democracy (such as it was) against the imperialism of Philip and Alexander of Macedon. Although truly committed to the Athenian democratic ideal, Demosthenes nonetheless sneered at those who had to make a living by labor and at the Dionysian religion they tended to support. He betrays these feelings in a speech against his arch political foe Aiskhines, a leader of the pro-Macedonian party, who had previously criticized Demosthenes for inflicting his personal bad luck on the affairs of the state. As it turned out, Aiskhines had once worked as an attendant in a school and his mother was a member of a cult that had been influenced by the rites of Sabazios, a god from Asia Minor similar to Dionysos. Demosthenes uses these associations to discredit Aiskhines personally:

> You, the proud one who would sneer at others, just take a look at the kind of life *you* have had—as a child to be raised in poverty and to help your father at the school house, making ink by hand, scrubbing down the benches, and sweeping out the lobby. You have had a life like a slave and not like a free-born son. And as an adult, when your mother conducted rites, you would read from their scriptures and help her out with the other things—at night dressing initiates in fawnskins, washing them with wine, and scraping off the clay and the bran. Helping them up from this cleansing rite, you would have them shout, "I have escaped the bad and found what's better."

(Demosthenes, 258–259)

With his voice heavy with sarcasm, Demosthenes ridicules the use of animals and plants in their rituals and the participation of older women:

> And in the day you led those fine revellers of yours through the streets, crowned with fennel and poplar leaves. You would grab puffy snakes and hold them above your head, shouting, "Euhoi! Saboi!" And you danced to the cry of "Hyes, Attes, Hyes, Attes!" And old hags hailed you as leader and chief of the dance . . .

(Ibid., 260)

Arriving in Athens in the fifth century B.C., the cult of Sabazios fused with and reinvigorated the cult of Dionysos (Picard, p. 132ff). In effect, Sabazios was a reaffirmation of the wilder aspects long since lost by Athen's tamed version of Dionysian practices (Dodds, p. xxiii). The new cult's emphasis on emotionalism and sexuality in its rites and its popularity among women and slaves caused consternation in the Greek establishment and a renewed attitude of suspicion and hostility toward Dionysos himself. The cult's fusion with that of Dionysos and the Athenian establishment's negative reaction provided the immediate social backdrop against which Euripides wrote his *Bakkhai*.

The cult of Sabazios subsequently spread throughout the Mediterranean, even to North Africa. It eventually influenced the formation of an important new development in Dionysian religion, Orphism, which will be discussed later (Picard, p. 150).

The subversiveness of the Dionysian religion to the established

53

culture of the Greek city-state was particularly apparent in its rite of *omophagia*—the eating of raw animal flesh. As Marcel Detienne has brilliantly shown, to eat raw flesh in a Greek religious ceremony was a shocking affront to established values because the whole politico-religious system was sanctified by ritual sacrifice—that is, by the act of slaying an animal, burning part of it as an offering to the gods, and cooking and eating the rest (Detienne, p. 56). Whenever a fleet was launched, a treaty was signed, or a building dedicated, the civil authorities sanctified both the deed and the social system of which it was a part by this ritual sacrifice. Indeed, in an important religious sense, the community could be defined as those who shared and participated in such sacrifice.

As discussed in chapter 1, participants in the rite of *omophagia* ate some of the flesh of a sacrificial animal in raw form. Not only did this act completely bypass the ritual sacrifice of the established religion, it required humans to act like beasts of prey in the wild. In effect, it abolished "the frontiers between men and beasts" (Detienne, p. 62).

In breaking through this division, the followers of Dionysos call to mind the Cynics, an ancient school of philosophers who repudiated, somewhat in the style of American hippies of the 1960s, most of the conventions of Greek urban life and called for a return to more natural conditions. Their motto was *Ton bion apotheriosai*—"Live like an animal" (Detienne, p. 64, n. 42). The Cynics were also one of the few philosophical traditions that called for the emancipation of women, and there were a number of famous Cynic women philosophers, such as Hipparkhia (Pomeroy, p. 136). Because of their blatant disregard for established values, the Cynics shocked the respectable citizens of their time, who compared them to dogs (*kynes*). Hence they were called *Kynikoi* ("doglike"), which became *Cynici* in Latin, the source of our word "Cynic."

Commentator Charles Segal has correctly pointed out that the scene in which Dionysos destroys Pentheus' palace is an image of the assault on the institution of the city-state (Segal, 1982, p. 97). To see the beautifully balanced and proportional columns so typical of Athenian architecture brought crashing down by an unexpected irrational force no doubt deeply unsettled the Athenian audience:

> *Dion.* Let Goddess Earthquake shake the land!
>
> *Chorus.* Ahhhhhhhhh!
> Soon the palace of Pentheus will be shaken down!

54

Dionysos—look, he moves upon the palace!
May he be praised.

Yes, praise the god!

Look, the stone caps there on the columns,
They're starting to move!

Within the walls, within the walls,
A Raving God is screaming.

Dion.   Strike, fiery flashes of lightning, strike!
Burn the royal palace of Pentheus down!

Chorus.   . . . Oh Raving Women of Bakkhos,
Throw yourselves to the ground and shake,
For he is upon the palace,
Now to tumble it down,
Our Lord, the Son of God!

(lines 585–603)

The independence of women in Dionysian rites and the subversiveness of the cult to the Greek establishment are also reflected in another rite also discussed in chapter 1—*oreibasia*, the wild nighttime dancing revels held in the mountains by women in honor of Dionysos.

The phenomenon of the Mad Woman was not a new development in Greece, but had existed since the earliest times, as is shown by a metaphor used by Homer to describe the grief of Andromakhe for her slain husband:

Thus she spoke, and shot through the house
Like a Mad Woman, her heart pounding.

(Homer, *Iliad*, 22, 460–461)

Although these dances had been considerably tamed in classical Greece, they continued with their original intensity in Macedon to the north, the place to which Euripides had retired after leaving Athens and which many native Athenians regarded as only half-civilized. Euripides has his chorus of barbarian Mad Women sing this song about Pieria, a southwestern region of Macedon:

Oh Happy Pieria,
The God of Ecstasy reveres you
And will come with revelry and dance.

55

He will cross the swift-flowing stream of Axios
And will lead his Mad Women whirling.

(lines 565–570)

So closely associated was Dionysos with these wild dances that he was known in antiquity as the Lord of the Dance and the Giver of Ecstasy. Another choral passage of *Bakkhai*, again referring to Pieria, attributes both these functions to the god in the same context:

> I wish I were in Cyprus . . .
> Or where Pieria is, fairest spot of all,
> Olympos' holy slope,
> The Muses' temple.
> Oh Raving One, Ecstatic God,
> Master of the Sacred Dance,
> Take me, take me there!

(lines 402–413)

The actual Greek epithets used in these passages show the god's character in this respect more concretely than can any English translation. The word I have translated as "Ecstatic" or "of Ecstasy" is *euhios*. This adjective is derived from the loud shouts of *"Euhoi! Euhoi!"* that the celebrants made when possessed by the god. To convey into English the sharp sound of this shout in Greek, it should probably be rendered as "Hai-ee! Hai-ee!" Dionysos is the bringer of ecstasy in the sense that he makes his followers go into an altered state of consciousness while they are wildly dancing and shouting, "Hai-ee! Hai-ee!" His women devotees also make the shrill, trilled sound of *olololo* that can still be heard to this day among Middle-eastern women. In fact, Euripides has Dionysos claim that he was the first to introduce this cry into Greece:

> Yes, in Thebes I first raised the
> women's cry
> Of *olololo* in the land of Greece . . .

(lines 23–24)

In the passages referring to Pieria, Euripides uses the word *daimon* for "god" instead of *theos* in reference to Dionysos. Although these two words for "god" are sometimes used interchangeably, the Greeks generally preferred *daimon* when speaking of divinity as the presence of a supernatural force. For anthropomorphic personifications (especially with Zeus and his family), they preferred the word *theos*. Moreover, *daimon* has a slightly eerie connotation and is the source of our word "demon." Hence the phrase *euhios daimon*, "the God of Ecstasy," connotes the sudden presence of a supernatural force that leads people into altered states of consciousness through group ritual. In his role as the bringer of ecstasy, Dionysos retrieves those human psychological aptitudes locked out by urban Greek civilization, just as he retrieves animal-associated qualities in his role as successor to the Minoan bull-god.

Greek artists depict women and satyrs who dance in the Dionysian rites with a definite style of body pose: the head is turned to one side, one arm is bent up and back, one arm down, and the legs are slightly flexed and sticking out (for examples, see Kerényi, plates 10 and 17). In looking at a scene with more than one dancer, if the viewer rapidly moves his or her eyes back and forth from one dancer to the next (which is probably the way such group scenes were intended to be viewed), the effect is a bit like movie animation, with one dancer appearing to be bounding about. Viewed in this way, the dance scene conveys a feeling of stylized, throbbing intensity.

The Greeks' stylized depiction of dancing Mad Women is strikingly similar to scenes of women or goddesses dancing in Minoan art. For example, the seal of a Minoan gold ring from Isopata (now in the Heraklion Archeological Museum) shows the same positioning of head, arms, and legs (Kerényi, p. 107). This continuity of style in women's dancing is one more indication of the impact of Minoan civilization on Dionysian religion. Its full significance will be discussed later in a look at the role of Minoan goddess figures.

Dionysos had another means besides the raptured choral dance to lead his followers to altered states of consciousness: he was the inventor and dispenser of wine. Euripides on several occasions refers to this aspect of the god, mentioning wine not only as an accessory to dance but also as a gift of compassion that adds to the joy of human life and helps soften its pains. So the chorus, after hearing the threats of stone-faced Pentheus against their god, offers up this prayer:

> Oh Heavenly Justice,
> Queen of the Gods,
> You who lower your golden wings to earth,
> You see what Pentheus did.
> You see it's against what's right,
> This abuse against the Raving One,
> Semele's son,
> The god with his festivals and lovely crowns,
> He who's happiest of all.

57

> This is his role:
> To revel in dance with his sacred band,
> To laugh with the flute,
> To scatter cares
> Whenever the fruit of the vine
> Is served at the feasts of the gods
> Or when, at holidays decked with ivy,
> A bowl of wine can clothe our cares in sleep.

(lines 370–385)

To turn one's back on this joy, to have a hostile attitude toward the natural pleasures of life, is an offense against Dionysos, as the chorus indicates in a later passage of the same choral sequence:

> The god that is the Son of God
> Delights in celebrations.
> And he loves the goddess Peace,
> The bearer of prosperity,
> The nurturer of children.
> To rich and poor alike
> He gave the gift of wine that kills our pain.
> He hates those men who aren't concerned
> To live their days and treasured nights
> In happiness and in joy

(lines 417–426)

To his believers, Dionysos was in a sense identical to the marvelous power of wine to transport its drinkers from the monotony or pain of sobriety to the pleasure and euphoria of intoxication. For them, to drink wine was to consume Dionysos, to become *entheos*, filled with his divinity (Dodds, p. xiii).

Recently Albert Henrichs has challenged the idea that wine drinking in the rites of Dionysos had a sacramental character, arguing instead that such practices were merely "social" (Henrichs, 1982, p. 141). But this argument overlooks the fact that even mere "social" wine drinking among the Greeks had almost a sacramental character. Bernard Sergent rightly points out that Greek wine drinking was usually done in a specific ritualized context with symbolic implications about manhood, sociability, and patriotism (Sergent, p. 27).

In the rites of Dionysos, this symbolic function of wine drinking was intensified, since metaphorically Dionysos himself was the wine that was being drunk. In Euripides' *Bakkhai*, the prophet Teiresias reminds Pentheus that at all Greek sacrifices wine is spattered on the altar and thus so is Dionysos:

> Being himself a god,
> He is poured on our altars as an offering to gods,
> And so through him do mortals have good things.

(lines 284–285)

This concept of the Son of God who is physically present on the altar in the form of wine was later to have a significant impact on Christian mythology.

Many of the festivals celebrated by the Greeks in honor of Dionysos concerned the growing of grapes or the making of wine, or else they were revels in which much wine was drunk. For example, in the Athenian festival called *Anthesteria*, which occurred in early spring, people brought newly fermented jars of wine from their houses to the temple of Dionysos in the swamps, where they first opened the jars and tasted the new wine (Kerényi, pp. 302–303; Parke, pp. 107–108). This swamp site was regarded as the oldest temple of the god in Athens and the doorway to the underworld. Since the ghosts of the dead were believed to emerge from the swamp and drink from the jars, the festival "was marked by an erotic atmosphere and the presence of ghosts" (Kerényi, p. 303). On the principal day of the feast, the chief religious official at Athens, the *archon basileus*, dressed up as Dionysos, led his wife into the civic center, and had sexual intercourse with her in his official residence, the *Boukoleion*, literally the "Bull House" or the "Cattle House." In a typically Dionysian manner, the *Anthesteria* emphasized the continuities of nature. It celebrated the nourishment and sustenance of the community, which was conceived not merely as the city-state of Athens, but as the great community of nature: mortals, gods, animals, plants, and the dead.

The ancient Minoans also drank wine. One of the implements they drank from was called a *rhyton*, a horn-shaped vessel with a small hole at the bottom. These vessels may originally have been bull horns, not only because of their shape, but because they are often decorated with representations of bull heads (Kerényi, pp. 53–54). Interestingly, some of the tablets found in Knossos describe bulls by an adjective in Linear B Greek that later became the word *oinops* in classical Greek (ibid., p. 54). This word occurs several times in Homer, usually in relation to the sea, and is often rendered as "wine-dark." Literally, however, it means "with a surface like wine" and may actually mean "sparkling" or "shimmering." In any case, the same word is also an older name for Dionysos (ibid., p. 54, n. 9).

Several myths mention Dionysos as the inventor of honey, from which the intoxicating drink mead is made. Euripides recalls this aspect of the god:

> He makes the land to flow with milk, with wine,
> With the nectar of bees . . .

(lines 141–142)

In a similar vein, the herdsman who has witnessed the miracles of Dionysos among the Theban Mad Women reports how the god fed his followers in the wilderness:

> And from an ivied thyros top
> There dropped sweet honey drops.

(lines 710–711)

C. Kerényi has shown that the ancient Minoans placed a high value on honey collection and on mead making, that a male deity (the so-called "Cretan Zeus") was connected with these endeavors, and that Dionysos later absorbed the attributes of this god (Kerényi, p. 30ff). That the ancients at some point in their history associated honey with intoxication is shown by the Greek word for getting drunk, *methyskein*, whose Indo-European root *methy* means "honey" (ibid., p. 36).

In fact, the ancients generally seemed to associate all intoxicants with Dionysos. So, for example, Diodoros of Sicily says about a kind of beer: "He also discovered the drink made from barley, called *zuthos* by name, with nearly the same fragrance as wine. This he taught to those whose land was not suited for growing grapes" (Diodoros, 4, 2, 5).

Interestingly, Indian myths report that a parallel god, Soma, who was once sewn in the thigh of the sky god Indra, invented the intoxicating drink named after him (Dodds, p. 78; Davis, p. 134).

After the decline of classical civilization, Dionysos was probably remembered more for his association with wine than for any other attribute. Especially under the name of "Bakkhos" (derived from Asia Minor and latinized into "Bacchus"), he was later depicted as a kind of congenial cherub who was always tipsy. In Renaissance art, this Bacchus was sometimes associated, as in the works of Caravaggio, with homosexual themes (Henrichs, 1984, p. 215). Possibly he was also turned into the figure of St. Bacchus, a supposed Christian martyr and soldier of the fourth century A.D., who was said to have been deeply attached to his fellow soldier, St. Sergius. Church tradition claims that both saints were forced by pagans to wear women's clothing before their martyrdoms (De Smedt, p. 380). Their feast day on the church calendar is October seventh.

Bull-god, drunk god, god of women and transvestites, giver of ecstasy, master of dance, lord of the emotions—such were the various masks worn by the *daimon* whose lineage went back to ancient Minoan civilization. In his myths and rituals, Dionysos embodied both a feeling for the living continuities of nature and a concept of the human personality as an organism deeply rooted in the nonrational forces of the cosmos. Serving as the focus for the spiritual needs of Greece's underclasses, he became the god that the patriarchal establishment could neither accept nor eliminate. And so Dionysos represented the return of the repressed in several senses: return of the religious needs of the lower classes, return of the demands of the nonrational part of the self, and return of the Minoan feeling for the living unity of nature. And so in turn he threatened several repressors: the aristocracy of well-to-do male citizens, the domination of intellect over emotion, the alienated ethos of the city-state. In each of these confrontations, he is personified by the character of Dionysos in Euripides' *Bakkhai,* just as the opposing tendencies are likewise personified by Pentheus.

III

THE
TWO
ESSENTIALS

❂

DIONYSOS did not act alone in his role as a divine focus for the return of the repressed. He had an associate deity in this role, and their relationship went back a long way—to the earliest ages in Greece, Crete, and Asia Minor. This associate, whose importance in the beginning was much greater than his, was his mother.

As soon as he steps onto the stage in Euripides' *Bakkhai*, Dionysos proclaims the significance of his mother both for his own identity and for the actions that follow:

> I am Dionysos—the Son of God!—
> And I have just arrived here in the land of Thebes.
> My mother was Semele, a mortal, Kadmos's daughter.
> While pregnant by Zeus
> She was hit by the fire of his lightning bolt
> And then gave birth—to me.
> . . . But the sisters of my mother,
> Those that I expected least,
> Denied that I was born from Zeus.
> They said some *man* had come and slept with Semele
> And she blamed the affair on Zeus . . .
> And so from their homes I drove these sisters frenzied . . .
>
> (lines 1–3; 26–34; 32–33)

Although she appears in Greek myth and in Euripides' play as Dionysos' mortal mother, this same Semele was once neither restricted to Greece nor merely human. She was in fact an import from the religion of Asia Minor (Western Turkey), whose inhabitants had long worshipped her as a great goddess, Mother Earth. As E. R. Dodds observes of Semele: "When the legends of Dionysos were grafted upon Theban tradition, she became a mortal princess; but traces of her original exalted status survived both in saga and in cult, and the learned guessed that she was Mother Earth" (Dodds, p. 63). In the language of the Phrygian inhabitants of Asia Minor, the word "semele" means "earth," a word related to the modern Russian *zemlya*, also meaning "earth" (Humbert, p. 165; Nilsson, 1950, p. 567 and n. 19).

The Phrygians, however, did not invent this goddess. When they arrived in Asia Minor in the twelfth century B.C. (at a time corresponding to the final overthrow of Minoan civilization in Crete and Greece), they found the worship of Mother Earth already entrenched among the native inhabitants and they simply added their own name for her (Nilsson, 1950, pp. 567–568). In fact, the worship of a great-goddess figure in Asia Minor can be traced back to the Stone Age (Turcan, p. 49; Rawson, p. 15; Gimbutas, p. 135). For thousands of years, she was the central figure in the religion of the inhabitants of the area, and when people from other nations first encountered her, they simply called her by the name of a goddess in their own pantheon. Hence she was variously invoked as Semele, the Great Mother of the Gods, Artemis, Diana, Dindymene, Kybele, and Rhea.

Although Euripides settles on the name of Semele for the mother of Dionysos, he also points to a close relationship between the latter and the goddesses Kybele and Rhea. For example, he implies that Bakkhos and Kybele are linked together and that those who participate in their common rites are blessed with a special wisdom:

> Happy is she whose luck is to know
> The rites of the gods,
> Who makes her life into something holy,
> Who joins her soul to the sacred band,
> Who worships Bakkhos on mountains
> With sacred rites of cleansing.
> She observes the mysteries of Great Mother Kybele,
> And shaking high her thyrsos,
> Crowned with ivy,
> Worships Dionysos.
> Come, women of Bakkhos, women, come!
> Raving Dionysos, a god's son, a god—
> Bring Dionysos down from Phrygia's high peaks,

Yes, down, down to the very highways of Greece,
The Raving One!

(lines 72–87)

In regard to the goddess Rhea, Euripides claims that she and Dionysos
were the co-inventors of the tambourine, as Dionysos indicates when he
first summons forth his chorus to enter Thebes:

> Now you who left Mt. Tmolos,
> Lydia's famous fortress,
> My sacred band,
> Women I've gathered from out of barbarian lands,
> My comrades on the move, my aides—
> Lift up, lift up your tambourines!—
> The ones you brought from the land of Phrygia,
> Devised by me and Mother Rhea.

(lines 55–59)

In an extraordinary passage that has sometimes puzzled commentators,
Euripides again invokes the names of Rhea and Kybele, but shifts the
scene of their worship far from their accustomed habitat of Asia Minor to
the island of Crete. To further complicate matters, he also mentions a
festival of Dionysos in the context of an old Cretan myth about the birth
of Zeus, the King of the Gods. On the surface, this passage seems to be
nothing but a hodgepodge of different gods, goddesses, and locations, but
in fact it makes an important statement about the identities of Dionysos
and his mother and also about the development of their worship. Here is
the passage in question, ostensibly a short history of the tambourine:

> Oh den of dancing warriors
> And holy haunt in Crete where Zeus was born,
> Where Kybele's thick-plumed priests
> Devised in a cave this tight-skinned tambourine—
> In the rites of Bakkhos they mingled its sound
> With the clear, sweet air of Phrygian flutes,
> And into the hands of a goddess, Mother Rhea,
> They put the beat with shouts from Raving Women.
> Frenzied satyrs then took the skin
> From the Mother Goddess' hands
> And mixed its sound
> With the dance that's done on alternate years
> In feasts that delight Dionysos.

(lines 120–135)

The first part of this passage refers to a well-known Cretan myth that Zeus was born on that island in a mountain cave and that a band of warriors (*Kouretes*) danced around the infant, clanging their swords against their shields to hide the sounds of his crying from his murderous father, Kronos. In reality, this infant god was an ancient Minoan deity associated with animals, vegetation, and the cultivation of honey and worshipped with orgiastic rites (Kerényi, p. 30ff; Nilsson, 1950, p. 534ff; Dodds, p. 84). The Greeks called him "Zeus" because he seemed to be the chief male deity of the island, but his nature was really much closer to that of Dionysos.

After mentioning this Cretan scene, Euripides abruptly introduces, from Asia Minor in the North, the priests of Kybele (*Korybantes*) who also worshipped their goddess with orgiastic rites. In making this juxtaposition, Euripides implies that Crete and Asia Minor share the same religious tradition. In fact, there are striking similarities: both have a holy mountain named Mt. Ida; the *Kouretes* and the *Korybantes* have similar ecstatic rites; and the names of both these groups appear to be derived from a common root meaning "young man." By Euripides' time, many Greeks had come to a similar conclusion about a shared religious tradition, a conclusion supported by modern research.

Next Euripides narrows the scene in Asia Minor, to Phrygia with its wild religious dancing in the cults of Bakkhos and the goddess whom Greeks called Rhea. From there, he directs the reader back to mainland Greece, to the satyrs and Dionysos. That the Greek satyrs performed the same role as the orgiastic dancers in Crete was recognized by the geographer Strabo, writing in the first century A.D.: "In Crete the rites of Zeus were celebrated in a unique way with orgiastic features and attendants like Dionysos' satyrs. These were called *Kouretes*" (Strabo, 10, 468).

In view of these considerations, the "tight-skinned tambourine" mentioned in the quoted passage should be seen as a symbol for the Dionysian religion of which it was an essential part. Euripides uses the story about its history to convey a veiled meaning about the history of the worship of Dionysos: it originated in Crete in the orgiastic worship of a young vegetation god, spread to Asia Minor in the form of the cult of Bakkhos and Rhea, and finally entered Greece in the entourage of Dionysos and his satyrs. In all its habitats, the religion involved the same basic orgiastic rites and was centered on a divine pair: the ecstatic son and his holy mother.

Euripides was close to the truth in making this claim, for we now know that such a divine pair was both ancient and ubiquitous in the areas under consideration: "From very early times a Divine Mother and a Divine Son were worshipped with dances and *oreibasia* [ecstatic mountain revels] under different names" (Dodds, p. 76). Just as the mother appeared with various names (Kybele, Rhea, Semele) so the son took on different forms (Dionysos, Bakkhos, Sabazios, Cretan Zeus). Sometimes the cults appeared separately; at other times, mixed. Sometimes, they were quiescent; other times, aggressive. But they all shared a highly emotive approach to religious ritual, a concept of humanity as deeply rooted in nature, and an influence, direct or otherwise, from Crete.

Although Dionysos occupied a more central position than his mother in the myths of classical Greece, in earlier times a goddess figure was clearly more prominent, a situation well documented for Crete. Nearly everyone who has examined the archeological evidence for that island has remarked on the large number of depictions of goddesses and the relative scarcity of figures of male gods. This predominance of goddesses dates from the earliest periods of the Stone Age up until the time of the Greek conquest, when male gods appear in larger numbers along with more scenes of war.

Archeologists are right to caution that not every Cretan female depiction should be seen as a goddess, but even so, many clearly are. We can be sure of this because the Minoans often used certain definite symbols in their art to indicate the presence of a divinity. One such symbol is that of a stylized eye, seemingly suspended in the air, which they borrowed from the Egyptians, with whom they shared certain artistic conventions. Gems and seals survive with this eye placed next to a large female figure, indicating that she is a goddess. Another sign is a human gesture—the arm bent forward and up, with the hand touching the forehead and the elbow jutting out—used by the Minoans as a sign of religious reverence. Once again, a number of artifacts depict Minoans, sometimes exclusively women, facing a large female figure and displaying this gesture. Both these symbols for divinity appear less frequently with male figures.

Sometimes the reluctance to see female figures as goddesses stems from simple male chauvinism—the assumption that artists and cultural leaders in that period must all have been male and that all art reflects a male perspective. This bias is clearly evident in Martin Nilsson, who dismisses the argument that many Cretan Stone-Age figures were goddesses on these grounds: "This supposition does not reckon with the artistic and other impulses of man which may have caused him to model an image of a woman as he modelled images of—let us say—animals and cattle, at least in the neolithic age" (Nilsson, 1950, p. 291). It seems never to have occurred to Nilsson that the leading priests and artists of this early period could have been women.

Another stumbling block to interpreting these "idols," as Nilsson calls them, is the fragmented nature of modern research. Archeologists have spent much time digging through layers of soil and cataloging artifacts, but sometimes have not bothered to keep abreast of recent research in mythology. Despite this neglectful attitude, discoveries about a culture's mythology can illuminate its use of artifacts, since these artifacts sometimes express the collective consciousness embodied in mythology. To gain insight into a culture, we should be open to *all* the evidence—archeology, comparative mythology, and recorded history.

As I have shown in a previous work, a comparison of evidence from different sources on this subject reveals a striking result: throughout various societies situated in and around the Mediterranean, the oldest layer of religion focused on a great-mother goddess and an accessory male deity, often horned, who was the son or lover or brother of the goddess (Evans, p. 22ff and p. 30ff). Recent scholarship has confirmed this conclusion (Gimbutas, Lerner).

This old religion was an expression of human life when it was still centered on agriculture, foraging, and hunting, and before warfare (and hence male domination) became the mainstay of economic development and political expansion. The leading priests of this religion in its earliest period were women, and the rituals were often sexual in nature, including homosexual activity. With the subsequent rise of male power, the influence of the *potnia meter,* the great-mother goddess, was eclipsed: "The matrilineal world was brought to an end by a number of murderous assaults upon the heart of that world, the *potnia meter* herself. The opposition to the *potnia meter* seems to have been closely connected with the cult of Ares [the god of war]" (Butterworth, p. 51).

In ancient Crete, there appear to have been a number of different goddesses but they all seem to be expressions of one basic type: the power of nature (whether animal, plant, or human) articulated in female form. Whatever the individual names of these goddesses, many of their traits were subsequently identified with the Greek goddess Demeter, whose name is derived from the words *deai,* meaning "barley," and *meter,* "mother." As Mother Barley or Mother Grain, Demeter was in fact the giver and mistress of all cultivated vegetation, in other words, Mother Earth in her capacity as the giver of food to humans and hence a most important deity for any society living primarily by agriculture.

In this connection, C. Kerényi has shown that the Cretan version of

Mother Grain was sometimes depicted with poppies in her crown, and a close inspection of these poppies shows that they have the characteristic slits used for the extraction of opium (Kerényi, p. 24). The goddess Demeter was also often depicted with poppies in both her hands. It seems possible, therefore, that there was a continuous tradition from late Cretan to early Greek culture of the use of this hallucinogen in religious rites associated with a great-goddess figure.

The connection of Dionysos with such a goddess figure was natural enough because he was the male version of the image of nature as the supplier of human food, especially of foods that were drunk. He was also associated with other vegetation and in particular trees, from which he was called *Dendrites*, "The Arboreal One" (Sandys, p. x). As in the case of Demeter, he was worshipped in seasonal rites of an ecstatic and sexual nature.

In view of these considerations, we can appreciate the full significance of a remarkable statement made by the blind prophet Teiresias to King Pentheus in Euripides' *Bakkhai*. After the king denounces Dionysos and threatens his women followers with arrest, Teiresias makes this proclamation:

> The essential things for men are two, young man:
> First the goddess Demeter
> (She is also Earth, call her what you will).
> With dry-grain foods she rears the human race.
> He who came in next, the son of Semele, Bakkhos,
> Found the other half, the liquid food of grapes . . .

> (lines 274–279)

These lines represent far more than a superficial statement about food-stuffs, as they might at first appear. For one thing, they clearly demonstrate that Euripides was aware of the tradition of the old agricultural religion with its focus on two deities, a great-mother figure and a horned god associated with ecstatic rites. Moreover, the passage occurs as a *rebuke* to Pentheus, who has just derided the story of Dionysos' birth as something unworthy of the great patriarchal god Zeus (lines 242ff). Finally, in speaking here of what is essential in religion, Teiresias markedly makes no mention of that same Zeus or any other Olympian god. As grains and liquids are essential for human physical survival, so the two essentials for spiritual nourishment are Demeter and Dionysos, i.e. the old religion of the agricultural underclasses. These two deities were, in fact, the most popular in the entire Greek pantheon, because their rites responded to the spontaneous emotional needs of their followers—the goddess most notably in her mysteries at Eleusis, and the god in numerous private societies. In this respect, their worship was in clear contrast to the state religion of Zeus and company, with its priesthood composed of public officials and its deities as symbols of state or family power.

The supreme irony of this passage is that Euripides puts these words into the mouth of Teiresias, the traditional representative on the Greek stage of patriarchal religious values. Euripides was able to get away with this coup because he uses the character of Teiresias basically for comic effect in *Bakkhai*: he is a blustering, self-important windbag, acting as a foil in the early interlude with Kadmos, the king's grandfather. Nevertheless, while diverting the audience's attention with his comic mannerisms, Teiresias delivers lines that are corrosive to the established state religion, and he does so in the guise of its chief representative.

Despite this and other pleas from Teiresias and his own grandfather, Pentheus reacts as no doubt many others of his class did when confronted by the new aggressive form of this old religion:

> Aawgh! Don't beg me with your hands,
> But go and dance with Bakkhos.
> Your madness won't rub off on me!

(lines 343–344)

The tendency of the old agrarian religion to see its many divinities as expressions of two essential types, one male and one female, each with its own set of myths and ecstatic rites, was no accident but a reflection of ancient patterns of social organization, especially in regard to sexual behavior. These patterns functioned as a kind of power reservoir that kept the deities from ossifying into stiff and ashen statues like the Olympians of the state religion. To appreciate more fully the dynamics of the interaction between these social patterns and the corresponding religious forms, we must examine the sexual context of archaic Greek religion.

The Greek word most typically used as a name for the rites of both Demeter and Dionysos was *orgia*, a plural noun that is the origin of our word "orgy." Although the latter English word has a definite sexual meaning, some scholars argue that *orgia* as used in Euripides' time was a less charged word, simply meaning "religious rites," and that it did not have a sexual connotation until later. So, for example, E. R. Dodds says:

Orgia, from the same root as *ergon* ["deed"], are properly "things done" in a religious sense. . . . The modern sense of "orgies" derives from the Hellenistic and Roman conception of the nature of Dionysian religion; it must not be imported into the *Bacchae*.

(Dodds, p. 67)

Dodds is partially right, in the sense that one can translate *orgia* as "religious rites" throughout Euripides' *Bakkhai* and get results that make perfectly good sense. However, the context of the play in several places implies that something more is involved than this neutral sense of the word. For example, the first use of *orgia* occurs in a scene where Dionysos announces he has driven his mother's sisters mad because they have rejected him:

> And so from their homes I drove these sisters frenzied
> To live beside themselves in hills,
> Wearing the dress of my rites [*orgia*].

(lines 32–34)

The context of the word's use here is one of inflicted madness, of people having been *driven* from a routine domestic state into one of wildness and abandon. The passage also refers to a special dress, the fawnskin, an article of apparel made from a wild animal and traditionally associated in the Greek mind with the Mad Women who customarily wore it.

In view of the context of suggested wildness that often accompanies the use of the word *orgia*, Dodds may be mistaken in deriving it from the same root as the word *ergon* ("deed"). An equally likely derivation—and one much more in tune with its actual use in this play—is the verb *organ*, which means "to be aroused," "to run riot," and "to be in heat," just as this verb is generally agreed to be the source of *orge*, meaning "anger" or "intense passion." If this latter derivation is correct, then the word *orgia* suggests more than neutral deeds and is evocative of very intense states of feeling.

Even where Euripides uses other Greek words to describe these rites, the context is often highly suggestive. (In addition to *orgia*, he also uses *teletai*, "initiation rites," and *hiera*, "sacred rites.") An example is the scene where Pentheus first interrogates the captured Dionysos about the nature of his religion. Here the king clearly suspects that there is something more than meets the eye:

> *Pen.* What's the nature of these rites [*orgia*] of yours?
>
> *Dion.* It is forbidden to know the rites
> For those outside the sacred band.

70

Pen.   Do they bring the members some good?

Dion. You have no right to hear,
       But they're certainly worth the knowing.

Pen.   You've faked it so well, I want to hear.

Dion. The rites of this god
       Detest a man who does not respect the gods.

Pen.   These rites [hiera], do you do them at night or in the day?

Dion. Mostly at night. In darkness is holiness.

Pen.   This is a treacherous way for women
       And one not sound.

Dion. One can also find shame in the day.

(lines 471–486)

The scene right before Pentheus' death also clearly implies that he does not regard the rites of Dionysos as just neutral religious practices. In fact, the god calls to his followers to slay Pentheus precisely because of his hostile attitude toward these rites:

Oh maidens,
I bring and offer up to you
The one who laughs at you,
At me,
And at my secret rites [orgia].
Avenge yourselves on him!

(lines 1079–1081)

Historically, Dionysos was the Greek lord of the dance, and his *orgia* always included dancing. In the earliest period, Greek dance was wild and ritualistic, often including the wearing of animal masks, nudity, and transvestism (Lawler, pp. 34, 71, 92, 112). These associated features of cultic dancing were likely to come to mind when the ancients spoke or wrote of Dionysian *orgia*.

But granted that the *orgia* of Dionysos were more than just "religious rites," are we justified in assuming they were sexual? Pentheus, as just seen, seems to think so, but his suspicions might be another example of his madness when "sane." After all, the herdsman—the first one to give the king an eyewitness account of the Mad Women from Thebes—specifically rebutts the king's expectations on this score:

All were sober, despite what you say,
Not drunk from bowls of wine and the sound of flutes,
Not lost in the woods
In pursuit of the goddess of love.

(lines 686–688)

The word I have translated here as "the goddess of love" is *Kypris*, an epithet of the goddess Aphrodite. The herdsman's rebuttal in this instance is aimed at the king's earlier remark where he had said, in the fantasizing spirit of voyeurism:

I hear . . . they sneak off to this or that deserted spot
To service men in bed,
Pretending to be some kind of raving priest,
But serving instead of Bakkhos
Love-goddess Aphrodite.

(lines 216–225)

So the king was clearly wrong to charge the women with participating in drunken orgies with men.

But one of the great ironies of this play is that Pentheus—driven by his own sexual fantasies in regard to the Theban women—completely overlooks their real eroticism: with each other. Although nowhere made explicit in the play, this sexual ambience is hinted at by the slave who witnesses the king's eventual immolation and murder. Before the terrible scene when the women descend in fury on Pentheus, they are gathered together in a moment of quiet, appearing as they do when undisturbed by men: relaxing, attending to pastimes, disrobing in an atmosphere of lyrical eroticism:

Nearby was a grove, with cliffs all around,
Well watered with streams, shaded by pines.
And there the Mad Women sat,
Their hands devoted to pleasant pursuits.
Some decked out anew their tired wands
With curls of ivy,
While others slipped off their dappled robes,
Like fillies their yokes,
And answered each other in raptured song.

(lines 1051–1057)

Although this single passage is a slender thread on which to hang such weighty implications, its significance is made clear in the context of the historical background of women's religious circles and choruses. In particular, the role played by institutionalized lesbianism in these groups has been brilliantly revealed by Claude Calame in his book *Les choeurs des jeunes filles en Grèce archaïque,* published in 1977.

Calame maintains, correctly I believe, that in those parts of pre-classical Greece where the most ancient traditions survived (Crete, Sparta, the Aegean islands, and Asia Minor), women's circles existed that shared common religious rites, were devoted to artistic development and education, and incorporated lesbian relationships. In fact, in the geographical areas in question, these circles were the chief means of educating young women, and they combined the functions now separately exercised in modern patriarchal society by school, church, family, and lover.

Some of these groups attracted women of great ability and were headed by famous cultural leaders:

> Hence a number of women poets, especially in Eastern Greece, seem to have assembled around themselves a fixed number of young girls who were both their pupils and companions. Under their direction, these adolescents devoted themselves, often in the context of a religious cult, to a musical activity that bestowed on their association a form quite similar, if not identical, to that of the lyric chorus.

> (Calame, v. 1, p. 372)

On the island of Lesbos in the seventh century B.C. there were several such renowned circles, lead by Andromeda, Gorgo, and, the most famous of all, Sappho (Calame, v. 1, p. 370). Relationships within these circles was artistic, affectional, sexual, and religious. The special relationship between the leader and her pupils was described by the adjective *syzyx,* a term derived from agriculture, literally meaning "yoked together" and typically used in matrimony to describe the relationship between husband and wife (Calame, v. 1, p. 370).

The women in these circles were called *parthenoi,* usually translated into English as "virgins" or "maidens" (and into French as *jeunes filles*). Originally, however, the word "virgin" did not have its current meaning but simply indicated an unmarried woman. As a result, there was no incongruity in speaking of a virgin who had children, and several such are in fact mentioned (Calame, v. 1, p. 65).

The change in the meaning of "virgin" to denote a woman who has never had sexual relations probably happened as a result of the patriarchal triumph; thereafter, as women were not allowed to have sexual relations outside of monogamous heterosexual marriage, an unmarried woman was also a woman without sexual experience.

It should also be noted in this context that the English word "virgin" is derived from the Latin *virgo*, which happens to be related to a Greek verb discussed above—*organ*, the possible source of *orgia*, the ancient rites specially associated with Demeter and Dionysos. (For the etymology of *virgo* see the entry for this word in Lewis and Short.) This association is yet another bit of evidence showing the different meaning of "virgin" in antiquity and suggesting that the word *orgia* did in fact have interesting connotations.

Unfortunately, Calame's otherwise perceptive account of these women's circles is at times marred by an unthinking homophobia. For example, he correctly points out that many of the women would eventually leave the circles to marry and have children, but wrongly concludes that this situation shows their lesbianism was only an aberrant stage that they were passing though while young. The obvious fallacy of this argument is the persistent lesbianism of the leaders of the choruses. Calame basically describes these women as stuck at an arrested stage of development, as when he characterizes Sappho as a neurotic whose exclusive lesbianism "short-circuited all heterosexual sentiment" (Calame, v. 1, p. 430). But to say that the persistent lesbianism of the teacher is neurotic because the lesbianism of the time was only ephemeral begs the very point at issue, namely, whether this lesbianism was just a temporary stage. Furthermore, Calame verges on absurdity when he implies that the women, since they performed their lesbian sexual acts in the context of a higher educational goal, could not have done so with any real enthusiasm (Calame, v. 1, pp. 425–426). Can he really think that the initiating teacher had sexual relations with her pupils merely because this happened to be the educational format of the times? If so, how can he explain the intensity of feeling described in Sappho's poems? And if the students did not enjoy themselves, how can he explain the fame and popularity of their teachers? Finally, who is to say these women did not continue to enjoy lesbian relationships after they were married?

Despite these flaws, Calame's work has established the existence of a very ancient institution in archaic Greece: the circle of unmarried women who function independently of men, practice common religious rites, enjoy lesbian relationships, and serve as the vehicle for women's culture and education. Euripides' *Bakkhai* reverberates with historical echoes from this institution. As already shown, the slave's description of the Theban women depicts them in an atmosphere of lyric eroticism when not in the presence of men. In addition, the play's actual chorus—

the barbarian Mad Women from Asia Minor—recount that they are a sacred band (*thiasos*) who hold their own secret and ecstatic nighttime mountain rituals. On several occasions they express the wish that they could be free of Thebes and its men to practice these rituals without restraint. So, for example, right before the scene where Dionysos dresses Pentheus in women's clothes, the chorus says:

> When will I lift my naked feet
> In the night-long dance of Bakkhic frenzy
> And toss my head to the dewy sky?—
> Like a fawn
> Who frolicks in the pasture's verdant pleasure
> When she escapes, out of watchers' sight,
> The dreaded hunt
> And leaps beyond the fine-knit hunting nets.

> (lines 862–870)

In another passage the chorus uses explicitly erotic language to express its desire to escape and hold its rites:

> I wish I were in Cyprus,
> Aphrodite's land,
> Where the Passions dwell
> That enchant the hearts of men . . .
> Or where Pieria is . . .
> That is where the Graces are
> And young god Passion, too.
> And there the ones possessed by Bakkhos
> Are free to hold their rites.

> (lines 402–415)

This passage begins by referring to Aphrodite, the goddess of love, and to the Passions (*Erotes*, meaning *sexual* passions); it concludes with an allusion to the Graces (*Kharites*, personifications of physical beauty) and the god of youthful passion (*Pothos*, derived from *pothein*, "to yearn for sexually"). The last phrase, "to hold their rites," is *orgiazein*, literally "to celebrate the *orgia*." This erotic language, expressed in the context of a desire to be in a remote place free from men, is a clear echo of the religio-lesbian chorus of archaic Greece.

Analagous forms of institutionalized homosexuality could also be found among men in those areas of Greece that maintained older traditions. At Sparta, for example, the basis of the educational system was *paiderastia* (hence the English word "pederasty"), the sexual love of an older, more experienced man for a younger man. The older man was called *eispnelas*, which means "inspirer," and the younger man *aitas*, "hearer" or "listener" (Mueller, pp. 300–301). When young, the men in such a homosexual relationship learned the basic values and skills of Spartan culture. When older, they in turn became the sexual teachers of the next generation. Male Spartan children between the ages of seven and nineteen were also congregated into chorus-like groups called *agelai*, literally "herds," and the leader of such a group was called *agelarkhes*, meaning "ox-herder" or "herd leader" (Calame, v. 1, pp. 374, 375, and n. 30). This terminology calls to mind the old tradition of the worship of a bull-god, already discussed earlier, as well as a notable passage in *Bakkhai*, when the chorus calls upon Dionysos to appear in animal form and take a furious vengeance on Pentheus:

> Come, and be revealed a bull, my Raging One!
> Be a many-headed dragon!
> Be a lion, spurting flames!
> Come, and with a smiling face
> Throw a deadly loop of rope
> On him who seeks to hunt and seize
> A herd [*agela*] of Raving Women!

(lines 1016–1023)

Likewise in Crete, male homosexuality was institutionalized in an educational-religious context, where the older man was called *philetor* ("lover"), and the younger, *kleinos* ("renowned one") (Mueller, p. 302). A regular custom existed on the island where the elder man would elope with his youthful companion and live with him for two months in the forest, initiating him into men's mysteries. On their return to the city, the older man presented the youth with a set of arms for war, and the latter was given public honors (hence the name *kleinos*, "renowned") (Calame, v. 1, p. 422).

The institutionalization of homosexual relations in parts of Greece was probably a survival of old Minoan customs, since it appeared in just those places that held on most tenaciously to older customs and since no similar practice is mentioned in Homer as characteristic of the invading Greeks. In addition, several ancient authors—including both Plato and Aristotle—explicitly state that Crete was the original source (Calame, v. 1, p. 422, n. 142). Finally, in the famous myth where Zeus seduces and carries off the beautiful boy Ganymede, the Cretan historian Ekhimenes reported that it was originally King Minos of Crete and not Zeus who acted thus (Dover, p. 186). Plato also believed that the Cretans invented this myth because of the nature of their homosexual practices (Plato, *Laws*, 636C–D).

In precisely those areas where the older customs survived, women had a higher status than elsewhere—enjoying wide freedom of movement, participating in public athletics, giving counsel in war and politics (Bethe, p. 44). For example, the women of Sparta were educated in both gymnastics and in intellectual skills and moved freely in public areas among men, on occasion even in the nude (Cartledge, pp. 91–92). They had a reputation among other Greeks of being outspoken and held large amounts of property in their own right. Among married Spartan couples, if the husband was under thirty, the wife continued to reside at her parents' home, and the husband would visit but not live with her. Hence it was difficult for such men to dominate their wives. Spartan women could also have more than one husband at a time (Cartledge, pp. 102–103). They likewise experienced a high degree of sexual freedom in regard to their own sex, as witnessed by Plutarch's remark that "the unmarried women love beautiful and good women" (Plutarch, 1, 18, 4).

By contrast, at Athens (where, as we shall see, there had been a *decline* in the status of institutionalized homosexuality) women had a markedly lower status, as discussed in chapter 1. The Athenian philosopher Aristotle was appalled at the freedom of Spartan women when compared to the situation in his own city. He called their behavior a form of "license" (*anesis*) and claimed that it was undermining the Spartan constitution (Aristotle, *Politics*, 1269b).

Hence the old argument, repeated as recently as 1984 by Peter Mason (p. 33), that the prevalence of male homosexuality in ancient Greece was due to the suppressed status of women is quite false (Bethe, p. 440). In fact, the exact opposite is true: the status of homosexuality and the status of women tended to rise and fall together. Moreover, the older the system of law and custom, the higher in general was the status of both.

The important role of homosexuality in religion and education was not a phenomenon unique to archaic Greece. Among many societies which are tribal in nature, people tend to spend much of their time with members of their own sex. Sometimes men and women live and sleep apart, with one common house for men and another for women and children; in some cases, the sexes even live in separate villages (Briffault, v. 1, pp. 509–513). In those tribal societies where the sexes do live together in individual families, as was the case among many of the North American Indians, men and women nevertheless spend much of their time, whether in leisure or in labor, with the members of their own sex (Briffault, v. 1, p. 510). Under the social conditions of early hunting and foraging communities, "the most thorough survey of the evidence yields the generalization that in such societies the relative status of men and women is 'separate but equal'" (Lerner, p. 29). Among early tribal societies of this type, homosexuality often comes to play a prominent part in their initiation rites and their enculturation process (Van Gennep, p. 171). Such conditions probably appeared in the earliest period of many of the societies around the Mediterranean, including the ancient Cretans and the indigenous inhabitants of Greece before the conquest from the North. When the invading Greeks finally settled in the peninsula, they no doubt absorbed some of these sexual customs, just as they took up many other features from the conquered. Hence Calame is right to compare the tribal conditions of other early societies with Greek developments and to conclude that:

> . . . particularly for the archaic period and in the domain of ritual, Greek institutions display striking analogies, both structural and functional, with the reality falsely called "primitive." This is particularly the case with tribal initiation rites: several historians of religion have shown that this social institution, common to practically all people living in a tribal mode, also existed in the archaic period in several Greek areas and in particular at Sparta, and this was not as some kind of "vestige" but with its plain political and religious function. In light of these studies, it seems that the reservation of a certain number of Lacedemonian cults for young men or young women indicated a religious consecration of the different constitutive parts of that institution.
>
> (Calame, v. 1, p. 33)

The ancient Greeks often projected their own mores and behavior onto the gods they worshipped, so that the myth of a god's exploits became a clue to the actions of that god's worshippers. A notable example is the goddess Artemis (Roman Diana). Although by late classical times, poets and artists often depicted Artemis as chaste, pale, and ethereal, in the archaic period she was "a ruder and more primitive type of deity which was wide-spread specially in the Peloponnesos and among the Dorian peoples; she is, in fact, the most popular goddess of Greece, at least in the cult of the simple rustic people" (Nilsson, 1950, p. 503).

Later observers were puzzled by the fact that this Artemis was both the goddess of sexual power and a virgin, but they had forgotten the older meaning of "virgin" as simply a woman who was not married (Calame, v. 1, p. 65). In reality Artemis was quite famous for her sexual exploits—with other women (Kerényi, p. 433; Nilsson, 1950, p. 510). She also bore a remarkable resemblance to a similar goddess figure long worshipped with ecstatic rites in the city of Ephesos in Asia Minor, and for that reason the Greeks likewise called the latter "Artemis." Both these deities were but two versions of an older goddess, the Great Mother in her capacity as the patron of wild animal life, a goddess sometimes referred to as *potnia theron*, "Our Lady of the Beasts," and commonly depicted in ancient Minoan art (Nilsson, 1950, p. 507). In the same way, as we have already seen, Demeter was a form of the Great Mother in her capacity as the patron of cultivated foods.

The members of the archaic cult of Artemis were virgins (unmarried women) who held wild orgiastic dances in her honor, sometimes wearing masks (Nilsson, 1950, p. 503; Gimbutas, p. 199). So widespread was this dancing cult that it gave birth to a famous Greek proverb, "Where has not Artemis danced?" (Nilsson, *loc. cit.*). As should by now be evident, the behavior of the goddess in the archaic period was a reflection of that of her devotees: women involved in agrarian religio-lesbian circles.

The worship of Artemis (Diana) had a very long history. With the decline of classical civilization and the rise to power of Christianity, she tended to absorb other pagan goddesses (of whatever nature) and become *the* deity of rural women. As I have shown in my previous book, her worship eventually spread throughout Europe and persisted as an underground religious movement until quite late in the Christian era, becoming in fact the principal historical source for the phenomenon later called "witchcraft" (Evans, p. 63ff). She also influenced certain traditional Christian beliefs, especially those concerning the Virgin Mary and various women saints (Berger, p. 49ff; Moss and Cappannari, *passim*).

The exploits told of Dionysos and his mythical entourage likewise reflect the practices of his worshipers. As we have seen, both ancient art and myth tell of fantastic male beings called satyrs, humanlike creatures who have long, horselike tails and large sexual organs. They accompany Dionysos in a crowd, dancing and having sex with each other (and sometimes with the Mad Women). In reality, the satyrs were modeled on men who dressed up in masks and cavorted with each other in rituals dedicated to Dionysos (Kerényi, p. 325). In classical Athens they still appeared in public processions in honor of the god (Kerényi, p. 171). A number of vases have also survived showing men putting on satyr masks in preparation for public festivals (Walton, pp. 150–151). With the rise of urban values in classical Athens, the satyrs were often depicted in anomalous situations and in a humorous fashion but originally they were an integral part of the ecstatic agrarian rites of the god.

By a process well-known in its outlines but still poorly understood in detail, one of the male cult circles associated with Dionysos underwent an astounding transformation. In the small agricultural town of Eleutherai, not far from Athens, Dionysos was anciently worshipped in the form of a black goat and with the name Eleuthereus, a word connected both with the name of the town and the adjective *eleutheros*, meaning "free" (just as the Italian deity most similar to Dionysos was named *Liber*, also meaning "free"). C. Kerényi has argued that the god was connected with the goat here because this animal, since it eats grape vines, is the enemy of Dionysos as the god of wine (Kerényi, pp. 319–320). But a more natural explanation is that the association arose from the practice of keeping wine in goat skins, as when Homer has Odysseus say:

> And I had a goat-skin bottle of sweet, dark wine . . .
>
> (Homer, *Odyssey*, 9, 196)

In any case, all-male choral groups held the usual ecstatic dances and songs in honor of this Eleuthereus of the Black Goat Skin (*Eleuthereus Melanaigis*).

At some point in the sixth century B.C., Athens annexed the town of Eleutherai, and the cult of the black goat god enjoyed a revival in Athens itself, where it had probably been known for some time, although not well favored. By this time the rites had become rather tame, and the city set aside a public dancing platform (*orkhestra*) for participants that was inside a precinct called the viewing-space (*theatron*) of Dionysos Eleuthereus.

In this sacred spot in the latter part of the sixth century B.C. there occurred "the greatest miracle in all cultural history" (Kerényi, p. 331). At some point certain members of the Dionysian chorus stepped forth and began to recite individual lines in roles that were distinct from those of the chorus. Written records of these lines came to be maintained in addition to the usual librettos for the choral songs. In time, these episodes of interaction among the individuals and the chorus were formalized into two performance genres: tragedy and comedy, the former named from *tragoidia*, meaning "goat song," and the latter from *komoidia*, meaning "revel song." With these developments, theater was born.

In its heyday in classical Athens, the theater of Dionysos seated 17,000 people (Parke, p. 129). Dramatists of the caliber of Aiskhylos, Sophokles, and Euripides presented their plays there during the Great Dionysia—the city's major celebration that took place each year in March in honor of Dionysos. The holiday began with citizens carrying the statue of Dionysos from a temple to the town of Eleutherai and then back to the theater (Walton, p. 61). The production of plays began at sunup and continued for four days, with one playwright presenting three tragedies and a burlesque satyr play each morning and then a comedy later each afternoon after a long noon break (Parke, p. 131). Women probably attended the tragedies but not the comedies (Parke, p. 130). At the conclusion of the four days there was a huge public revel.

Initially each play was performed only once, although later there were smaller theaters for repeat performances in rural areas. All roles in both comedies and tragedies were performed by men. The Athenian playwrights themselves were quite prolific; Euripides alone wrote more than ninety plays, only a few of which have survived. The playwrights also often directed and sometimes even performed in their own plays.

The dramatic presentations at Athens were thus a major social and artistic event, involving large numbers of the population as spectators, and dominating the life of the city during their production. Moreover, they summoned forth from their artistic participants some of the most memorable works of art ever to be created. The effect of the plays on the audience must have been quite spectacular, for the actors and chorus wore elaborate masks and costumes, and the chorus sang their lines (and danced as well). In its overall effect, the Athenian theater was much like a play, an opera, a ballet, and a public fair all rolled into one. Despite these many aspects, however, it never lost its sense of being a religious event. The altar of Dionysos was always evident, and the front row seats in the center were reserved for his priests, their bench bearing the inscription in large letters, "Sacred to Dionysos Eleuthereus."

The sacramental setting of the theater no doubt added a special dimension to the audience's reaction to Euripides' *Bakkhai* when it was eventually produced, for here was a play about the god Dionysos being performed in his very own precinct. But even more arresting must have been the devastating thrusts made by Euripides in the name of that god against the very Athenians who gave him lip service on those special days. Standing within sight of his own altar, Dionysos addresses the Athenian political and religious establishment in the person of Pentheus and says, in effect, "You have repressed the sexual and emotional essentials of the old agrarian religion and are ignorant of your own inner self. The price to be paid for this repression is a madness that will tear you and your civilization asunder."

IV

WAR

"War is the father of all, and of all the king. Some he turns into gods, while others, men. Some he makes slaves and others free."

—Herakleitos

WHEN Pentheus is confronted with a challenge to his way of thinking, his gut reaction as a man with patriarchal values is to strike back with violence. Since he also happens to be a nation's king, he has the added ability to arm this reaction with the power of the state, in short, to wage war. So, when frustrated by Dionysos' miracle of an earthquake that destroys his palace and enraged by the herdsman's tale of ferocious Mad Women, he sends for his troops:

> Go to Elektra's Gate,
> Assemble all the troops
> That fight on foot with heavy shields,
> And all the knights
> Astride their swiftly running steeds
> And all the archers who brandish smaller shields
> And twang the strings of bows.
> We march against the Bakkhic women!

> (lines 780–784)

Pentheus' reaction here smacks of madness, for the god has just caused an earthquake and a messenger has already reported that the Mad Women have defeated the herdsmen in battle, tearing cattle apart with their bare hands. Against such supernatural power, what good are troops? Dionysos says as much when he warns:

> Pentheus, you've heard my words,
> But not been moved at all.
> Though you abuse me, yet I advise:
> You must not bear arms against a god . . .

> (lines 787–789)

Despite such obvious good sense, Pentheus, as if unable to help himself, still wants to wage war. Dionysos is finally able to divert him from such grievous madness only by inflicting a little "giddy madness" of his own. Although still in human form, the god invokes his divine power and reveals his plan to the audience:

> Dionysos, here's your chance,
> For you are not far off. Let's punish him!
> First, drive him from his mind
> And then inflict a giddy madness.
> He'll never wear a woman's dress when sane,
> But driven from his mind he will.

(lines 849–853)

The irony and tragedy of Pentheus' situation is that "his sanity" is really insane. Only when he wears a woman's dress—an insane act by his previous standards—does he see Dionysos as the bull he really is, and only so does he feel free enough to shake the thyrsos, dance, and let out the ecstasy repressed within. But since Pentheus in his previous sanity ridiculed and oppressed the rites of the god, Dionysos now uses his transvestism as a punishment, to humiliate the king in public and lead him so arrayed to a sacrificial doom. And so the king's fateful road to his death and dismemberment is in a sense predetermined—his character when "sane" drives him against all good judgment to the violent acts that ultimately backfire.

The character of Pentheus in this situation was the character of classical Greece as a civilization, just as his fate was also Greece's. To see how this is so, and thereby to see as well the dreadful brilliance of Euripides' critique, we must enter once again the labyrinth of early human history.

As noted previously, the discovery of ancient Minoan civilization earlier in this century by Arthur Evans caused quite a sensation. Here was a highly developed society whose artifacts showed women in positions of leadership and goddesses as more prevalent than gods. Scenes depicting everyday Minoan pastimes were striking. Whereas the artwork of the time from other Eastern Mediterranean nations, such as Egypt, was glutted with scenes of organized armies in combat, of kings personally smashing in the skulls of their enemies, of conquerors rounding up masses of slaves, of powerful overlords directing the mass construction of monumental buildings, and of crowds of subjects hailing the omnipotent male ruler, none of these themes is found in Minoan art (Hawkes, 1968, pp. 74–76; Willetts, p. 24). Up until the time of the Greek conquerors (in the fifteenth to the thirteenth centuries B.C.), Minoan art continued to concern itself with graceful scenes of nature and festive pastimes, and towns remained unfortified.

After the first influx of Greeks, artwork in Crete abruptly changed to reflect a greater interest in men, male deities, weapons, and war scenes, and walls began to appear around towns. After the second influx of Greeks in the thirteenth century B.C., all the settlements of Crete were burned and destroyed, and a dark age descended on the region that lasted until the emergence of classical Greek civilization in the eighth century B.C. Except for Sparta, the emerging Greek civilization was characterized by a systematic subjugation of women. Moreover, the entire Aegean area came to worship a pantheon of sky gods dominated by males, the economy was grounded on slavery, and warfare became an institutionalized way of national life.

We now know that the style of society existing in Minoan Crete was not an isolated fluke of history. Quite the contrary, an overview of a great mass of archeological evidence, from Europe to Western Asia, from the Old Stone Age to the Bronze Age, now proves what many analysts of ancient myths have long suspected: the Minoans were but the latest and most highly developed example of an ancient, universal mode of living that was quite different from what today is called "civilization."

The full implications of this archeological evidence have recently been explored by Marija Gimbutas (in *Goddesses and Gods of Old Europe*, 2nd ed., 1982) and by Gerda Lerner (in *The Creation of Patriarchy*, 1986). As these authors show, prior to 4500 B.C. (the onset of the Bronze Age), widespread cultural uniformity throughout Europe and Western Asia centered on the worship of a great-goddess figure, first in the form of a Mistress of Wild Animals (often depicted as androgynous or hermaphroditic) and later, after the invention of agriculture, in the form of a Grain Goddess. Commonly associated with this Great Goddess, especially after 7000 B.C., was a subordinate male deity, often depicted in the form of a bull or a horned figure.

In these early settlements, evidence is lacking for the existence of large-scale organized warfare, slavery, or government hierarchy. The clan, rather than the nuclear family or the state, appears to have been the essential unit of social organization, and religious rites were infused with a notable sexual content. Women appear to have had a generally high status and probably functioned as artists and the inventors of agriculture and sometimes even as hunters. An overview of the evidence confirms the conclusion reached early in the 1960s by Jacquetta Hawkes:

There is every reason to suppose that under the conditions of the primary Neolithic way of life, mother-right and the clan system were still dominant, and land would generally have descended through the female line. Indeed, it is tempting to be convinced that the earliest Neolithic societies throughout their range in time and space gave woman the highest status she has ever known.

(Hawkes, 1963, p. 264)

A little reflection will show why these qualities of Stone-Age life were not as unlikely as they might at first appear. Since all people lived directly on the land, initially either by foraging or hunting, it would be easy for individuals and groups to remain economically independent: people had no incentive to subject themselves to others in order to survive (in the way, for example, that modern workers rent out their labor to earn money to pay rent and buy food). Since weapons were simple and accessible to all (stone axes, wooden clubs, and the like), no one developed a monopoly on the means of social coercion (as nation-states do with police forces and armies). Hence, although there would be fights, group skirmishes, and other forms of personal violence, it would not be technologically feasible to subdue an entire people by violence. Since the mother of a child could always be known for sure but the father much less readily so, property and rights would naturally descend through the mother (as opposed to patriarchal societies where paternity is guaranteed only by keeping the wife's sexual activity under constant supervision). In sum, everybody would have access to basically the same resources for food and shelter, nobody would have a decisive edge in weapons, and women would define kinship.

As comparative anthropology has shown, societies living under such conditions generally feel a close emotional bond with nature and often personally identify themselves, both individually and collectively, with various animals. In addition, as their art usually shows, they display a great diversity of openly practiced forms of sexual behavior, often in a ritual context, including lesbianism and male homosexuality.

In an environment that was warm and well watered—and hence abundant with plant and animal life—societies so organized could expect to satisfy their basic survival needs without disrupting these simple patterns of existence. But in a cold and harsh climate where the margin of surplus in the necessities of life is much smaller or even nonexistent, there would be a constant economic incentive to move on and look for better conditions. If, in the process of so roaming, a group of nomads could develop a team of fighters and equip them with weapons superior to those of their neighbors, a situation would soon develop where one or more groups would begin supporting themselves by plundering others. Those plundered would, in turn, either have to submit or else change their ways and imitate the aggressors' methods in order to fight back. In either case, the new social and economic system would perpetuate itself.

Some such scenario repeated itself several times in early European history. On more than one occasion invaders appeared from the cold North, hungry for the greater goods and comforts of the South, armed with better weapons, and more disposed to battle. First they would steal and pillage, then conquer, then form a new hybrid culture with the defeated, combining elements of both the old and new societies. Eventually this hybrid culture would attain a state of comfort and stability, only to wait its turn as the object of the hunger of the next wave of invaders. And so stone was replaced by bronze, and bronze was replaced by iron in the pulse-beat of attack, consolidate, and defend. In the midst of these episodes of conflict, a clear overall tendency emerged toward greater efficiency in weapons-making and a greater reliance on fighters to create, stabilize, defend, and feed the society. After a certain point was reached, the ability to conduct warfare became *the* essential basis of both political stability and economic development. Once this point was reached, a quantum leap occurred in human history. Henceforth attacks could come from anywhere, not just the North, and from any type of society, not just nomads.

These cumulative political and economic changes had enormous social and religious consequences. For one thing, they meant a steady decline in the status of women. In the earliest periods, the labor of women was just as or even more crucial than men's to the survival of the society: foraging, making clothing and pottery, preliminary cultivation of plants, enculturation of young children. Among extant hunting and gathering societies, for example, women provide an average of 60 percent of the food (Lerner, p. 22). Later, survival and growth depended much more on organized fighting, which was usually reserved for men. War brought in tribute from the conquered lands, increased the land holdings of the triumphant military aristocracy, and opened up fresh markets for the commerce and agriculture of the new city-states. In addition, men now frequently obtained their wives and mistresses by seizing and raping the wives of their defeated and enslaved enemies. In effect, wives became the property of their husbands, who held and used them by right of conquest.

These changes also affected the way people related to members of their own sex. The solidarity of women was broken. Their old religio-

86

sexual circles tended to die out as women were secluded in the individual households of their husbands, on whom they became increasingly dependent for their emotional, economic, and sexual needs. More than ever before, the major avenue for the personal well-being of a woman was to be associated with a powerful man.

The religious and sexual solidarity of men was also transformed. Since the way for a society to survive and flourish was to win on the battlefield, the ideal man was now one who was trained and ready to fight and kill other men. In general other men became the objects against which a man continually tested and proved his own manhood through bravado, competition in sports, and fighting. Since women were now viewed as distinctly inferior to men, any quality conventionally associated with women, such as emotional sensitivity and vulnerability, was looked down upon and ridiculed. Hence the enormous psychological pressure on men to suppress within themselves any feelings or behavior they regarded as feminine. As a result, the old institutionalized homosexual practices tended either to die out or else be given a stridently militaristic coloring as in classical Sparta or Thebes.

These changes did not happen all at once nor in a steady stream nor in the same way in all areas. There were, in fact, many reversals, and often with time the mores of the minority of conquerors were completely re-absorbed into those of the vast majority of the conquered. This re-absorption was aided by the nature of archaic warfare itself, which, until well into the classical era, remained the province of those relatively few wealthy males who could afford to equip horses, hire retainers, and purchase armor made of metals that were then rare and expensive. The great mass of the people, both men and women, continued in their age-old agricultural pursuits and value systems. Their world, moved by the momentum of the ages, persisted, while militarist oligarchies rose and fell at the helm. Nevertheless, over the long haul, from about 4500 B.C. to about 1200 B.C., it was apparent that a stunning change had occurred in European life: the patriarchal revolution.

In the last century and a half, a great debate has raged among historians, sociologists, and anthropologists over the question of the existence and nature of this revolution and on the evidence for the status of women in so-called "primitive" societies, including peoples antecedent to the rise of ancient Greek civilization. Recently Rosalind Coward has given an excellent overview and analysis of this debate in her book *Patriarchal Precedents* (1983).

Coward shows that early in the nineteenth century scholars tended to assume the universality and inevitability of the patriarchal family (that is, a family institution characterized by the domination of the husband over wife and children and by a male line of inheritance for property and family names). This family structure was then regarded as the legitimizing model for patriarchy (that is, the systematic domination of men over women in society at large). In other words, the argument held that men should dominate women in society because husbands naturally dominate wives in the family.

In the mid and late nineteenth century a number of studies conducted in Southern India and Southwest Asia, largely occasioned by the spread of European colonialism, showed that forms of family organization in these areas were inconsistent with the patriarchal model. These discoveries led to a reassessment of existing information concerning the American Indians, ancient Europeans, and others.

On the basis of these new findings, Johann Bachofen in 1861 published his famous book *Das Mutterrecht*, claiming that in the earliest societies around the globe women and not men were the principal leaders. As a result of his work, the word "matriarchy" came into common currency, although at first with a wide variety of meanings. Since Bachofen at times argued that women once dominated men as men now dominate women, matriarchy came to be viewed as the mirror image of patriarchy, although that was not necessarily the intended sense in its usage by others.

Bachofen's work stimulated other authors interested in the early status of women, and the following years saw the publication of Lewis Morgan's *Ancient Society*, Friedrich Engels's *The Origin of the Family, Private Property, and the State*, and Robert Briffault's *The Mothers* (1927), which was the last exhaustive and systematic work on the subject in this tradition of thought.

In the twentieth century, a great tide of anthropological sentiment, stimulated by Bronislaw Malinowski, turned against the various versions of the matriarchal theory. The new anthropologists showed that in any given society there is no necessary relation between male power and the institution of private property, that matrilineal descent can coincide with a *subordinate* status for women, and that different patterns of ownership and control often exist in the same society. Most telling of all, the new anthropologists demonstrated that there is no documented case on the planet of a culture where women regularly held a leading position in politics, diplomacy, and the conduct of war.

As a result of this anthropological critique, the various versions of the matriarchal theory fell into discredit. Recently, however, with the rise of modern feminism, prevailing attitudes of anthropologists and sociologists on this subject have again come into question. As Rosalind Coward points out, the universal exclusion of women from positions of military and governmental leadership does *not* mean the same thing in all societies. In modern industrial cultures, this exclusion is a significant deprivation of power. But for hunting and foraging communities, where formal government is nonexistent and warfare only sporadic, the occupations traditionally filled by women are the ones that have the greater influence (Coward, p. 55).

Coward also shows how male anthropologists have lacked perceptiveness in regard to the importance of women's functions even when they have personally lived in a society. A striking example of this phenomenon is the case of R. S. Rattray, who spent several years living with and sympathetically studying the Ashanti. Despite this long-term effort, he was one day shocked to discover that the Queen Mother had an importance among the Ashanti of which he had been completely ignorant:

> I have asked the old men and old women why I did not know all this—I have spent many years among the Ashanti. The answer is always the same: "The white man never asked this; you have dealings with and recognize only the men; we supposed the Europeans considered women of no account, and we know you do not recognize them as we have always done."

> (Quoted by Coward, p. 55)

Most important of all, modern anthropologists and sociologists have a strong antihistorical bias. They tend to assume that an investigation can capture the essence of a culture the way a cook handles an onion: cut out a slice and examine the pattern of the fibers. This approach will indeed show how the fibers of the examined slice are all interconnected, but it will tell very little about the growth of the whole bulb of which the slice is but a part. For that larger view, an examination of patterns of historical development is required.

An examination of such patterns for ancient Europe—from both archeology and mythology—shows that the bulb has a very definite growth: in the beginning, essential social functions (and hence essential power) were fairly evenly divided between men and women. Only after the patriarchal revolution from 4500 B.C. to 1200 B.C. did a gross imbalance occur. Although Bachofen was wrong to see matriarchy as the mirror image of patriarchy, he was on to something nonetheless. In my own opinion, a qualified use of the term "matriarchy" is still appropriate, since its Greek root *arkhe*, which means "power," stresses the importance of the power and influence of women, not just the patterns of kinship or inheritance implied by the adjective "matrilineal." For those who find it hard to shake the associations given to the word "matriarchal" by Bachofen, perhaps a more precise term for describing the conditions in early human society would be "matri-equal."

In classical Athens of the sixth and fifth centuries B.C. the effects of the patriarchal revolution were everywhere in evidence. As previously noted, "respectable" women were kept secluded in the innermost rooms of the house, closely supervised when they appeared in public, not generally allowed to dine with their husbands, and even required to call their husbands "lord" (Mueller, p. 297). The class of the free male citizens increasingly tended to live in walled cities, alienated from nature and fearful of attacks from other cities. Most of the labor necessary to maintain the society was done by slaves, many of whom were either captives taken in war or the descendants of such captives.

The prosperity and wealth of Athens stemmed largely from its military, particularly its navy, whose power had turned its previous allies against Persia into tributary subordinates and from whom it extorted huge sums of money. In 416 B.C. Athens showed the extent to which it was prepared to go to maintain this empire. In that year the people of the island of Melos decided to withdraw from Athenian hegemony and pursue an independent political and economic policy. The Athenians dispatched ships filled with soldiers who dutifully carried out their orders to slaughter every adult male on the island and sell all the women and children into slavery.

Like all its Greek neighbors, Athens was constantly at war against other city-states. The most memorable conflict was the catastrophic war with Sparta. After exhausting themselves in these seemingly endless wars, the Greek states proved too weak to resist the subsequent imperialist onslaught of Philip and Alexander from Macedon in the North, who conquered them all and whose successors succeeded in effacing democratic government, however imperfect, from the West. Rome was to follow and then Christianity. Not until the seventeenth and eighteenth centuries, nearly two thousand years later, were the ideals of democratic government again to be openly articulated and translated into actual working institutions.

Athens was a male-dominated society, and all significant decisions pertaining to war, peace, religion, and economic policy were made by men. The manner in which these men made their decisions was to a large extent influenced and sometimes even determined by the male conditioning they had received since childhood, and this conditioning was in turn an outcome of the preceding patriarchal revolution. The nature of this conditioning is nowhere better illustrated than in their attitudes toward male homosexuality.

The subject of homosexuality in classical Athens has long been the target of poor scholarship, partly the result of homophobic approaches that try to deny, trivialize, or explain away the phenomenon, and partly the result of some who, going to the other extreme, seek to glorify particular cultural expressions of Athenian same-sex relationships. Fortunately, an informed and fairly balanced study in the subject appeared in 1978 with K. J. Dover's book *Greek Homosexuality*, the best treatment of the subject in the English language, although, as we shall see, there is a need for a number of important corrections.

One of the chief virtues of Dover's book is to draw attention to the real significance of various ancient sources on the subject. In particular, he correctly places great weight on a speech that was written by the Athenian orator Aiskhines in 345 B.C. In Dover's assessment, this speech is "the only surviving text which gives us access to the sentiments which it was prudent to profess in public on the subject of homosexuality in Athens during the classical period" (Dover, p. 14).

Aiskhines' speech has come to serve this function both because of his own personal circumstances and because of Athenian political conditions at the time. Aiskhines himself was an actor turned politician who rapidly rose to a position of influence in Athens because of his speaking ability in the public assemblies and courts. The burning political issue of his time was how Athens should respond to the growing empire in the North of King Philip of Macedon, the father of Alexander the Conqueror. Originally Aiskhines urged resistance to Philip, but after a certain point abruptly changed sides and became the leader of the Macedonian party, the group that favored conciliation and compromise with Philip.

Aiskhines' opponent was the formidable orator Demosthenes, the leader of the anti-Macedonian party. Demosthenes believed that Philip of Macedon was a threat to the very existence of Greek democracy and argued that the king, through a policy of playing off the various Greek states against each other, was bit by bit robbing them of any future potential for resisting his encroachments. Demosthenes called for a united front among the Greek states to prepare for war against Philip, hoping thereby to save democracy. Demosthenes also believed that his opponent Aiskhines was taking bribes from Philip (which was probably true) and hence was a traitor to his own country's cause of freedom.

As with politics today, so in ancient Athens political opponents often used whatever personal attacks they could devise in order to undermine the political standing of the other side. The process was actually much easier in ancient Athens because of the nature of its judicial system. For one thing, there was no independent government prosecutor. Any citizen who believed a crime had been committed brought charges against another citizen as in a civil case. At trial the accuser acted as prosecutor, presenting evidence, summoning witnesses, and arguing for his interpretation of the law. The person accused likewise conducted his own defense (except for women, who had to be represented by a man). There was no judge as in a modern American or British court, but only a presiding officer. Depending on the nature of the case, the jury could be quite large, up to several hundred persons, and only a simple majority was needed to reach a verdict. The rules of evidence and germaneness were quite loose, with the result that both the introduction of irrelevant considerations and attacks of a personal nature were quite common. In effect, the court was like a debating society. Since any citizen might someday find himself before such a court, there was a great demand at the time for teachers of the skills of public speaking, and accomplished public speakers were both admired and dreaded. Both Demosthenes and Aiskhines were among the most accomplished of their age.

In 346 B.C. these two orators were part of a delegation that left Athens for Macedon to negotiate business with King Philip. On their return, Demosthenes was convinced that Aiskhines had plotted with Philip to betray Athens. At this point he persuaded a friend and supporter of his, a certain Timarkhos, to bring an indictment in court against Aiskhines for betraying the interests of the state.

In response to this charge by Timarkhos, Aiskhines cleverly twisted some loose threads in the Athenian judicial fabric to tangle up the entire process. He uncovered an old law that forbade any man who had ever been a prostitute from addressing public assemblies or the courts. Invoking this law, he claimed that since Timarkhos in his youth, over forty years before, had prostituted himself to other men, his appearance now in court to bring charges against anyone else was illegal. Aiskhines demanded a public inquest (*dokimasia*) to resolve this issue before any further action was taken on Timarkhos' indictment against himself.

The speech that Aiskhines wrote for this inquest, entitled *Against Timarkhos,* is the very one that is now our best source for classical Athenian attitudes toward homosexuality. Ironically, his speech is a good source on this point because of Aiskhines' own unscrupulous motivation. He really had no concern at all for whether Timarkhos had ever been a prostitute or not; his only interest was to discredit him personally and thereby quash his indictment. Since it was in Aiskhines' interest to bring up everything he could think of to discredit Timarkhos, his speech spares no effort in finding fault with the latter's behavior, especially his sexual behavior. In addition, since Aiskhines' audience was a jury in a court of law, his speech also reflects the values of the average Athenian citizen of the time—in fact his whole point is to show how Timarkhos' behavior was contrary to those values. To accomplish these ends, Aiskhines consequently delineates both Timarkhos' sexual behavior and the values of his audience, and therein lies the value of his speech as a historical source.

Aiskhines begins by describing the legal justification for his action against Timarkhos. The law requires, he says, that no citizen may address a public assembly or court who has struck his parents or failed to support them in old age; who has deserted from the battlefield; who has wasted an inheritance; or who "has been a prostitute" or "hired himself out for sex" (Aiskhines, 28–30). Significantly, the majority of these exclusions deal with money. The reason the law makes the last exclusion is the fear that somebody who has sold his own body would do anything for money, including accepting bribes to vote a certain way in the assembly: ". . . for he [the legislator, in other words, the law personified] believed that anyone who made a scandalous business from his own body would also easily sell out the public interests of the city" (Aiskhines, 529). In other words, citizens who had prostituted themselves to other men were excluded, not because they had engaged in homosexual activities, but because they had accepted money for so doing. Moreover, apart from this civil exclusion, prostitution did not incur any criminal penalties in Athens (Dover, p. 31). The Athenian law on this point is, therefore, quite different from later Christian-inspired legislation that outlawed homosexuality *per se* and equated it in severity, not with such things as squandering an inheritance, but with murder.

Aiskhines adds that in his own opinion prostitution is an inherently abusive affair and that a prostitute, by engaging in this line of business, is guilty of a kind of self-abuse. Hence he should also be excluded from public assemblies on the ground that abusive people have no business there: "In short, someone who violates another, regardless of his status, is judged unfit to participate in the public life of a democracy" (Aiskhines, 17).

Using a style of prosecution typical of Athenian courts at their worst, Aiskhines admits that he is unable to produce any eyewitnesses to Timarkhos' alleged prostitution but urges the jury to make the assumption anyway in view of his public reputation. The following is an example of the type of innuendo he uses to descredit Timarkhos:

> Or what should one say when a young adolescent leaves his family's house to spend the night in others' houses—a boy with outstanding good looks—and feasts at lavish banquets without any contribution of his own, or when he has the best paid flute girls and courtesans and gambles, yet pays for nothing himself, but another pays for him?

> (Aiskhines, 75)

Timarkhos as an adolescent left his parents and lived the high life. Hence, Aiskhines argues, he must have been selling his body, for how else could he have lived so well? As an interesting aside, this same passage also implies that Timarkhos was active heterosexually with "flute girls" and "courtesans." Such a pansexual attitude was not at all uncommon among the classical Greeks. For example, Aiskhines says of one of Timarkhos' married male lovers that "he showed more lechery toward the wives of free citizens than anyone else ever has" (Aiskhines, 107).

In order to prejudice the jury against Timarkhos, Aiskhines insinuates that he was prone to a certain type of homosexual activity that should, according to Aiskhines' beliefs, compromise him in the eyes of his peers: he liked to play the physically receptive role in anal sex, even after he became an adult. So, for example, Aiskhines mentions a certain Misgolas, whom he characterizes as "a fine gentleman in other respects, and not at all blameworthy, but extraordinarily devoted to this sexual interest [anal sex] and ever accustomed to having singers and harpists in his company" (Aiskhines, 41). Aiskhines claims that when this Misgolas found out that a doctor friend of his was keeping the young attractive Timarkhos for just this purpose, Misgolas "offered him [Timarkhos] some money to have him leave and move in with him, since he [Timarkhos] was well built, young, dissolute, and fit for the thing that Misgolas like to do and that Timarkhos like to have done to himself" (Aiskhines, 41).

In the eyes of Aiskhines and the Athenian jury, for an adult man to enjoy receptive anal sex was degrading (although not illegal) because it gave him a woman's role, since women play the physically receptive role in heterosexual sex. Aiskhines brings out this implication quite clearly when he relates an anecdote about a well-known prior incident in Timarkhos' life when the latter was accused of stealing public funds. Aiskhines tells how the accuser of Timarkhos stood up in public and said, "Citizens of Athens, a husband and wife are stealing a thousand *drakhmas* from you" (Aiskhines, 110–111). When people were confused as to what this accuser meant, Aiskhines said he replied, "You don't know what I mean? The husband is Hegesandros [Timarkhos' lover], who previously was likewise the wife of Leodamas, and the wife is our Timarkhos" (*loc. cit.*). In other words, Timarkhos was like a wife because of his reputation for enjoying, even as an adult, the receptive role in anal sex.

Apparently to claim that an adult male enjoyed passive anal sex was a common insult in Athens at the time, because Aiskhines in the same speech gratuitously makes such a charge against his opponent Demosthenes, the friend and supporter of Timarkhos. Aiskhines delivers this jab by means of a pun on the Greek word *battalos*, which means "stutterer," and which was an old nickname Demosthenes had received from his childhood nurse because he once stuttered. However, the same word, when spelled with one *t*, *batalos*, means "buttocks" (Martin and de Budé, in Aiskhines, p. 64, n. 1). Recalling this double meaning, Aiskhines says that Demosthenes' character is well known to all, since by nickname he is rightly called *Batalos* ("Buttocks"), not from his nurse, but from his reputation, "getting this name from his debased effeminancy" (Aiskhines, 131).

Aiskhines continues this type of insult against Demosthenes, who was present at the inquest, by claiming that even his style of dress is like a woman's:

For if someone stripped off that fine little mantle of yours and that soft tunic—the clothes you wear while writing speeches against your friends—and took them around and put them into the hands of the jury, I think—if someone did this without warning—the jury would be at a loss as to whether they held a man's or a woman's clothes.

(Aiskhines, 131)

Aiskhines even insinuates to the jury that Demosthenes' preference for anal receptivity should discredit him when he attacks the policies of Philip of Macedon:

His speech's blundering with regard to Philip is crude and untimely. . . . At least he makes such slanders against a man, though he himself is not one. But when he concocts digressions against Philip's son [Alexander] and extraneously introduces base suspicions about *him*, he makes the city look ridiculous.

(Aiskhines, 167)

95

Whether Demosthenes actually enjoyed the practices attributed to him by Aiskhines is not known. The important thing here is the nature of the insult itself—to be receptive in anal sex is to be like a woman, and to be like a woman is to be unfit to participate in politics.

Aiskhines sums up his case by appealing to the jury not to slough off Timarkhos' behavior as so many peccadillos, but, being mindful of the ancient severity of the law in other matters, to render stern judgment here as well: "Have your fathers, then, made such a sharp distinction between good and bad, while you will acquit Timarkhos, who is guilty of the worst practices? —This man who has committed a woman's offense with a male body" (Aiskhines, 185).

In a most important passage, Aiskhines goes further and says that men who enjoy this sexual practice are guilty of crimes against nature. Although this phrase appears to be a precursor of the later Christian notion of all homosexual behavior as contrary to nature, the context makes it clear that he is talking about what he regards as nature's proper sexual role for men even in homosexuality, in other words, being on the top in anal sex. In effect, he says such a man should be liable to sanctions, just as a woman who fornicates would be: "If one of you caught a woman in the act, wouldn't you punish her? Then wouldn't you seem stupid to be angry at the woman who commits an offense according to nature, while having as a participant in public affairs the man who violated himself contrary to nature?" (Aiskhines, 185).

In response to this criticism, Timarkhos and his friends protest that Aiskhines himself is known to be the lover of young men, has involved himself in public spats over some of these, and has expressed his love for them in poems. They imply that in his attacks on Timarkhos either he is hypocritical or else he is hostile to same-sex love. Aiskhines in turn hastens to say that he has no intention of impuning homosexuality as such but only when it becomes a purchased commodity. He reassures the jury that he should not be understood as opposed to these affairs:

I do not blame honest love, nor do I claim that those men distinguished by their beauty are prostitutes, nor do I deny that I myself have been and am right now a lover of men. And I do not deny that I have had my share of jealous fights with others as a result of these affairs. As for the poems they say I wrote, some are mine, but I deny that the rest have the character which they will fabricate and give to them. I make this distinction: to be in love with good, decent young men is the passion of a humane and benevolent soul, but the lechery of someone who pays for another with money is the mark of a crude and uncultured man. And I say that to be sincerely loved is a good thing, but to prostitute oneself for money is a disgrace.

(Aiskhines, 136–137)

The appeal here is basically to class values. If one expresses his homosexual love as a gentleman should—without considerations of money, with good taste, with men who are cultured—then such love is a fine thing. But to pay or be paid, to act crudely—these are the signs of a lack of proper upbringing.

The proof that these are not just Aiskhines' personal views but the established values in classical Athens lies in the great amount of space he devotes in his argument to convincing the jury that, no, he really should not be construed as being opposed to same-sex love. If the Athenian jury thought that homosexuality was in itself disreputable or sinful, his argument here would be utterly pointless and self-defeating.

To prove his orthodoxy on this point, Aiskhines refers to a famous incident in Homer's *Iliad*, a book that served somewhat the same function in ancient Greece as the Bible does today in cultures with Christian values. The scene involves the grief of Akhilleus ("Achilles" with the Latin spelling) over the death in battle of his dear friend and youthful companion Patroklos. Although Homer nowhere explicitly says that Akhilleus and Patroklos had a sexual relationship, both the intensity of feeling and the choice of words in Akhilleus' lamentation convinced many Greeks in the classical era that the two had been lovers. Aiskhines tells the jury that he, too, agrees with this sexual interpretation:

I shall speak first of Homer, whom we place in the rank of the oldest and wisest of poets. Although he often refers to Patroklos and Akhilleus, he conceals their love and the name of their affection for each other, since he knows the extent of their feelings to be quite obvious to readers who are educated.

(Aiskhines, 142)

To remind the jury of the close feelings between the two heroes, Aiskhines calls upon the clerk of the court to read to the jury the scene in the *Iliad* where the ghost of Patroklos appears to Akhilleus in a dream and asks for a mingling and common burial of their ashes as a token of their union when they lived:

One thing more I ask—put it in your heart:
Not to put my ashes apart from yours, Akhilleus,

97

> But let the one same earth also cover you
> Within that golden urn your goddess mother gave you.
> Just as we were raised a pair within your house . . .
> Just so, then, let our ashes also lie within a common urn.

(Aiskhines, 149; Homer, Iliad, 23, 82–92)

The text quoted here in the manuscripts of Aiskhines' speech is slightly different in wording from modern editions of Homer, but the basic sentiment is the same in both.

To further buttress his case, Aiskhines moves from poetry to history, directing the jury's memory to the story of Harmodios and Aristogeiton. These were two famous Athenian lovers who assassinated a hated tyrant in the sixth century B.C. and who were greatly eulogized under the subsequent democratic regime. Speaking approvingly of both their politics and their love, Aiskhines says to the court:

> Hence the benefactors of our city, distinguished by their fine qualities, Harmodios and Aristogeiton, were molded by a decent and upright love and inclination (call it what you will), molded into such fine examples that those who praise their deeds never do justice to the accomplishments of these two in their eulogies.

(Aiskhines, 140)

Bringing his argument into the present, Aiskhines mentions to the jury contemporary citizens of Athens who are known to have many different lovers and yet are held in high esteem. These are men whose relationships are based on love and affection, not money, in contrast to the mercenary Timarkhos. Looking right into the face of the latter, Aiskhines mentions with biting sarcasm another Athenian also named Timarkhos who is his exact opposite in character:

> I will mention . . . a boy with the same name as our defendant Timarkhos. Though beautiful to look at, here's how much he's beyond reproach: Recently during the comic plays presented in the deme of Kollytos as part of the rural Dionysia, the comic actor Parmenon recited to the chorus a ribald verse alluding to certain famous prostitutes "like Timarkhos." No one took this verse as referring to the boy, but everyone thought it meant *you*—that's how much the name of your profession has stuck to you!

(Aiskhines, 157)

In view of these examples, Aiskhines clearly does not condemn all homosexuality, but only that which is motivated by a gain of money or where a man takes a physical role associated with women. The orator acknowledges quite openly his own homosexual affairs, even though he is the married father of three children, and praises examples of sincere homosexual love from myth, history, and contemporary society.

Aiskhines proved himself to be a most skillful speaker in this case. By shrewdly appealing to the biases of the jury against prostitutes and woman-like behavior in men—all the while managing to endorse their high regard for "respectable" homosexual liaisons—he succeeded through innuendo and hearsay in utterly destroying the image and reputation of his opponent. When the vote was taken, the jury ruled against Timarkhos. Hence he was found morally unfit to argue any case in an assembly or court and his original indictment against Aiskhines was quashed.

As a result of tactics like these, Aiskhines and his counterparts in other Greek states, all on the payroll of Philip and Alexander, were quite successful in poisoning the political atmosphere in Greece. These provocateurs stirred up factions against factions and cities against cities, exacerbating the Greeks' inability to unite their forces against Macedon. When at last Philip and Alexander appeared at the gates, it was too late. Demosthenes, subsequently in flight from Alexander's successor Antipater and fully aware of the enormity of the political change, committed suicide on October 16, 322 B.C. With his death, the West's first great experiment in democracy came to an end.

The real significance of Aiskhines' speech for our purposes is that it shows the decline in the status of homosexual relations in Athens since archaic times. As previously noted, homosexuality, both male and female, had once been institutionalized in a religious and educational context in those parts of Greece where the most ancient traditions had survived. Through circles of members of their own sex, men and women learned basic social values, acquired skills pertinent to their own sex, worshiped the gods, and enjoyed their first sexual liaisons. But later, in classical Athens, women had come to live a much more restricted existence, and homosexual relations between men had become a mere personal predilection, admittedly respected just like any other personal behavior, but no longer an essential part of the community's educational process or religious sensibility.

This relative decline in the status of Athenian homosexual relations has been hotly contested by a number of recent scholars. For example, Peter Mason, reacting against an earlier work that dismissed Athenian practices as "pseudo-homosexuality," rightly points out that the homosexuality of the time was a matter of genuine passion and not a mere social convention (Mason, p. 61; cf. Devereux). But Mason is wrong to contend that glorification of male homosexuality was on the increase and that this happened as a result of the denigration of women. Such a claim is inconsistent with the evidence cited earlier from Aiskhines, who relentlessly condemns anal receptivity in adult males precisely because he believes it makes men like women, whom he regards as an inferior sex. Aiskhines' speech proves that the denigration of women actually encouraged *negative* attitudes about male homosexuality.

In a similar vein, Bernard Sergent, following up on earlier studies, correctly points out that homosexual initiation rites were pervasive in early tribal cultures, including at one time the early Indo-Europeans (Sergent, pp. 11–12; cf. Bremmer, 1980, p. 290). But he is mistaken to argue that classical Athenian patterns were a continuous development and an expansion of Indo-European practices. Sergent's argument is inconsistent with a number of findings reported in his own study: unlike the ancient Cretans and many other tribal cultures, the Indo-Europeans did not have separate, collective sleeping areas for each sex; most of the early Indo-European root words dealing with sex are negative, having to do with sexual taboos; and no early Indo-European words have survived that designate male partners in a homosexual relationship (Sergent, pp. 47–50). In addition, the ancient Greeks themselves most often pointed to ancient Crete, the land of the *non* Indo-European Minoans, as the historical source of their homosexual practices. This evidence suggests that institutionalized homosexuality disappeared at an early date among the nomadic, militaristic Indo-Europeans.

The most striking evidence against Indo-European continuities on this point is found in the Greek epics. The *Odyssey* and the *Iliad,* written in the eighth or seventh centuries B.C. and glorifying the Indo-European values of the invading Greeks of the fourteenth and thirteenth centuries B.C., contain no explicit homosexual references. At most, as noted earlier, a homosexual theme is indirectly hinted at in the relationship between Akhilleus and Patroklos. Yet we know from other sources that homosexuality by both sexes was widely practiced and even institutionalized in the archaic period. The epics' silence on homosexuality, in the context of a country where it was widely practiced, implies that the cultural validation for such practices did not come from an Indo-European source.

A corollary is that Athenian homosexuality of the classical era was *not* predominantly or exclusively a practice of the upper classes (who were the most tenacious in holding on to aristocratic Homeric values). In arguing for a close association between the aristocracy and homosexuality, Walter Donlon points to the scathing satires of aristocratic homosexual practices by the comic poet Aristophanes (Donlon, p. 164). But the existence and nature of these satires actually prove the opposite, since Aristophanes was himself a conservative who believed in the old aristocratic ideals and disliked the loosening of morals under the democratic regime. He attacks certain aristocrats because he believes they are debasing themselves in their sexual practices to the level of the mob, not because he sees them as having an exclusive historical hold on homosexuality. Moreover, precisely those who were most hostile to the democratic regime and most aristocratic in their moral values and political sympathies—the reactionaries in Plato's circle—were also the ones who first tried to spiritualize (or de-sexualize) homosexual relationships and who finally came to the conclusion that they were unnatural.

Modern readers often misinterpret Plato because he does sound sympathetic to homosexuality when read in the context of contemporary Judeo-Christian values, which are strongly homophobic. But when read in the context of his own time, Plato will be seen ever striving to deflect homosexual passion away from the purely physical to supposed "higher" and more spiritual ends, thus displaying a marked uneasiness with homosexuality's physical aspects. By contrast, as elements in the speech of Aiskhines have shown, the average Athenian juror—who was drawn by lot from the lower classes—thought it was proper to enjoy the physical pleasure of homosexuality for its own sake as long as doing so did not compromise one's masculinity or lead one to become a prostitute.

Scholars who continue to argue that Athenian homosexuality was primarily a matter of the elite misinterpret Plato by seeing him through modern eyes and undervaluing the implications of Aiskhines' speech. Mark Golden for example, a recent exponent of the elitist theory of Athenian homosexuality, does not even mention Aiskhines in his list of principal sources (Golden, p. 312).

The Greek-speaking people who originally invaded and settled in Greece were militaristic Indo-Europeans. As shown by their epics, they had contempt for women, glorified combative qualities in men, and were silent on the practice of homosexuality. After settling in their new homeland, they absorbed many of the pre-Indo-European values and practices of the people they conquered, including a more positive attitude toward homosexuality (a phenomenon later repeated with the Romans). But they continued to disdain those homosexual practices that they associated with femininity. Except in Sparta and a few other places, they did not continue to practice homosexuality in its old Cretan form as a means of education and enculturation, and in Sparta itself homosexuality became totally militarized.

As a result of these changes throughout Greece, the distinction between older lover and younger beloved now took on a new meaning.
Removed from its original religious and educational context and imbued
with the new patriarchal attitudes toward women, this distinction became one of manliness. The activity of penetrating in anal sex came to
be viewed as appropriate to the elder man because he was the more
masculine, not because he was the more knowledgeable or more religiously powerful. The activity of being penetrated was now viewed as
more appropriate to the younger man because he was in an inferior position and hence more like a woman, not because he was the recipient of
the cultural power of his elder partner. Hence for an adult male to enjoy
being penetrated became a disgrace to his masculinity, a thing that made
him like a woman. Such predilections could be expected in boys and
adolescents who had not yet come into fully mature manhood, but not in
real men who were in their prime. This taboo on passivity stemmed from
an utterly contemptuous attitude toward women and anything associated
with women. It was the natural and inevitable result of the patriarchal
revolution and the seed from which all subsequent homophobia in Western society was to grow.

Although K. J. Dover rightly emphasizes the importance of the distinction between active and passive in Athenian homosexual relationships, he errs when he argues that the passive partner—the
eromenos—was generally not expected to enjoy this sexual activity
(Dover, p. 36, n. 18). He maintains that the "good" beloved, the one
who keeps his reputation, does not keep company with the elder, more
active partner because of any sexual desire, but only out of respect and
admiration for the latter's virtues: "Love inspired by admiration and grat-
itude towards the *erastes* [elder partner], coupled with compassion, in-
duces the *eromenos* [younger partner] to grant the "favours" and perform
the "services" which the *erastes* so obviously and passionately desires"
(Dover, p. 53). Likewise, Dover contends that the "good" elder lover
does not really seek to instill sexual passion in his younger beloved but
only nonsexual love (*loc. cit.*).

If the reader will examine the sources that Dover uses to reach these
conclusions, he or she will see that they are all, with one exception, the
writings of the Athenian philosopher Plato (Dover, pp. 52–53). And
the one exception is Xenophon, an oligarchic associate of Plato who
shared many of his class values.

As indicated previously, Plato was an aristocratic extremist who was
highly unrepresentative of the Athens of his time: he was opposed to
democracy, disliked artists, disdained the usefulness of empirical learn-

ing, and viewed the body as a hindrance to self-fulfillment. In his earlier writings, he was more tolerant of sexuality, but still viewed it with great suspicion. His basic attitude was that sexuality, if it is to be worthily experienced, must be refined, elevated, and purified to a higher level so that it leads one away from the physical to higher realms. In his system of thought, the best way to attain this purification is to abstain from actual orgasm, to let oneself be led on by passion only to a certain point, then stop and transform the energy into something more spiritual. His concept of the "good" *eromenos* who does not really enjoy anal penetration is simply the application to Athenian homosexual relationships of this basic system of "Platonic love."

In his later years, Plato became an even sterner moralist. In *Laws*, his last book, he concluded that homosexuality should be suppressed, even though, as he admitted, it was widely practiced and approved of in his time. His argument is that the purpose of law is to make people more virtuous, and since active anal sex makes its practitioner too hungry for pleasure and passive anal sex makes its practitioner too much like a woman, both must be legally suppressed in the name of greater social virtue. In effect, as the following passage shows, Plato simply takes certain presuppositions of the patriarchal mentality to their logical conclusions:

> Come now, suppose we assume that the currently established practice [of homosexuality] is good and not at all bad. In what way would it help us in regard to virtue? Will it instill in the passive partner's soul a habit of manly courage? Or in the active partner a pattern of self-restraint? But who would ever think so? No, quite the contrary, the one who gives in to his own desire for pleasure and cannot overcome it, won't he be blamed for his weakness? And the one who imitates a woman, won't he be blamed for being like her?
>
> (Plato, *Laws*, 8, 836D)

In fact, Plato was the first to develop and articulate a systematic theory that homosexuality is unnatural, as he also states in *Laws*:

> We must consider that when the female and male sex have intercourse for procreation, the pleasure from this seems to be regarded as natural. But when the male sex is with the male or the female with female, it seems contrary to nature, and the shameless behavior of those who first imitated this practice seems due to a lack of self-control regarding pleasure.
>
> (Plato, *Laws*, 1, 636C)

Like all who have adopted these attitudes, Plato finds himself in a contradiction: one on hand, he says homosexuality is unnatural; on the other, it must be outlawed, or else it will spread. But despite Plato, the opposite conclusion would seem to follow: homosexuality would more likely be unnatural if we found we had to pass laws *compelling* people to do it.

Plato never married, and if he followed the implications of his own philosophy, he never reached orgasm with anyone, either man, woman, or himself. He is in fact the father of homophobia, and his thinking, however contradictory, enjoyed a long-time influence when it was later incorporated into Christianity.

Modern readers are often deceived into thinking that Plato's beliefs represent the Athenian values of his time because so much of his work has survived (nearly everything he wrote). But the major reason particular works from antiquity have survived is that medieval monks liked to keep recopying them from age to age. Plato (followed by his pupil Aristotle) is the ancient writer whose ethical system most resembled that of Christianity after it became the state religion of the Roman Empire. In consequence, monks adored him. Sappho, on the other hand, the lesbian poet whom the ancients regarded as the equal of Homer in the beauty of her poetry, has managed to bequeath only a few fragments of her work. Of all the literature created by the ancient Greeks no more than a tiny fraction has come down to us, some lost by accident, some destroyed by fire and war, but most simply filtered out by Christian copyists.

The great irony of Platonic homophobia is that Plato himself was the devoted pupil of Sokrates, whose homosexual feelings for younger men were well known. Although the younger Plato was not nearly so prudish as the older, his early writings nonetheless display a strong bias against any expression of sexuality that does not aim at supposedly higher ends. Despite this bias, he pictures Sokrates on several occasions as being quite down-to-earth and witty about his sexual attraction to younger men. Probably the most famous example of this sexual wit is the quip Sokrates once made about two seeming opposites—philosophy (the use of abstract intellect to lead one to the highest good) and Alkibiades (the dashingly handsome Athenian who was also one of the most unscrupulous and power-hungry men of his time). According to Plato, Sokrates described himself as the "the lover of Alkibiades and philosophy" (Dover, p. 146; Plato, *Gorgias*, 481D).

The key to understanding Sokrates' quip is his concept of philosophy. For him, learning philosophy was not a matter of competitive, career-hungry graduate students poring over books in isolated library stalls, hoping thereby to land decent teaching jobs in prestigious college philosophy departments (the modern style of learning philosophy, which produces the expected technical hacks). No, for Sokrates, philosophy meant critical thinking in the context of intimate personal dialogue and sexual attraction within a circle of same-sex friends. The defining characteristic of Sokratic dialogue was this very circle that was at once philosophical, sexual, and also religious (as witnessed by Sokrates' frequent reference to the inspiration he received from his *daimonion*—his own personal divinity). In fact, Sokrates' circle was probably a continuation and modification within classical times of the ancient religio-homosexual circle of archaic Greece, discussed earlier. In the eyes of his contemporaries, who had lost sight of this old institution, Sokrates' practices seemed like some kind of weird private religion by which he was seducing, both physically and intellectually, the young men of Athens. Hence the two major charges for which he was condemned to death in 399 B.C. were corrupting the young men of Athens and believing in gods the state did not recognize (Plato, *Defense*, 24B). The truth is that Sokrates was guilty of both, but to his credit. He gave such an energy and new sense of direction to philosophy that he bestowed on it a new beginning from which all subsequent Western philosophy has derived some influence. In effect, his circle was to Western philosophy what the cult of Dionysos was to Western theater. And underlying both of these cultural sources was a modification of the ancient religio-homosexual circle.

Sometime after Sokrates' death, Plato wrote his *Republic*, a utopian description of his ideal state, characterized by the rule of philosopher-kings. One common assessment of this work is that Plato wanted to create a state where his mentor Sokrates would be safe. But in this and his subsequent works, Plato actually outlined a state in which Sokrates would have been very quickly done away with. Ironically, in the name of Sokratic learning, Plato turned Sokrates on his head, just as later, in the name of Christian faith, Paul of Tarsus would turn over the teachings of Jesus of Nazareth.

Not only was K. J Dover misled by Plato's theories into a misjudgment about the nature of the feelings involved in Greek homosexual relationships, but his assessment of the physical acts themselves needs correction. Based on an inspection of a number of vase scenes reproduced in his book, Dover argues that the only standard seductive gesture used was for the elder lover to face the younger and touch his chin and genitals; that anal penetration is not depicted between men of different ages; and that the typical sexual act between a man and a youth was for the former to rub his penis between the latter's thighs.

In reaching these conclusions, Dover overlooks the implications of a second seductive gesture also displayed in several of his own illustrations: a man stretching one or more fingers out and placing them either on his own or another man's buttocks. So, for example, an Attic jar (Dover's plate no. B76) shows an adult seducing a youth from the front, in the manner described by Dover. But behind the same youth is another adult man with his right arm outstretched and his finger inserted into the top of the cleavage of the youth's buttocks. Just as the first adult wants to play with the youth's genitals, so the second man clearly indicates he wants to penetrate.

A second example in Dover's book is a vase painting of an orgy scene where a number of men in a circle are anally penetrating women from the rear (plate no. B51). A close look at the picture will show that one of the men, while so penetrating a woman, is also reaching his arm out with pointed fingers and touching the buttocks of the man in front of the woman he is penetrating. Moreover, this same man with the outstretched arm is reaching his other arm behind himself and inserting the fingers of this hand into the top of the cleavage of his own buttocks. Behind this rearward hand appears the erect penis of another man. Anal penetration is clearly implied in both these hand gestures.

Likewise another vase (plate no. B53) shows a man standing behind a youth, and the fingers of his left hand are outstretched and touching the lower back of the youth. Since all other figures in the vase (men and women) are having anal sex, this is clearly a seductive gesture.

Finally, Dover displays a painting of a naked youth reaching forward and inserting the longest finger of his right hand into the anus of the young male in front of him, who is partially bent forward (plate no. R189). Dover calls this "a jocular insult," but in fact it is quite consistent with the other vases just described and represents a seductive gesture proposing anal penetration. The use of the finger for this purpose is understandable, since in anal sex a finger is often first inserted into the anus to massage and relax its muscles, thereby making the later insertion of the penis much easier for both parties.

Seduction gestures from the front are indeed commonly depicted, as Dover claims, but the existence of a second seductive gesture from the rear (together with a large number of vases that show actual anal intercourse) prove that the adult lover often did more than rub his penis between the thighs of his beloved.

Again, although Dover is correct to point out that the typical homosexual male couple are an adult and a youth, he is quite wrong to conclude that "the reciprocal desire of partners belonging to the same age-category is virtually unknown in Greek homosexuality" (Dover, p. 16).

A number of the vase paintings reproduced in his own book quite clearly show men of the same general age enjoying each other sexually, and he himself cites several such depictions in the text (Dover, pp. 86–87). In particular, scenes of Dionysos and his followers are often rich in examples of men of the same age having sex, a theme that runs throughout Dionysian vase painting from the earliest to the latest periods.

In reality, a great number of vases survive from antiquity showing satyrs of every age and bodily appearance involved in a most creative spectrum of sexual acts—with themselves alone, with other satyrs, and with women. Because Dover has mistakenly concluded that the Platonic concept of nonconsummated love was the popular ideal for Athenian homosexual relations, he brusquely dismisses these scenes as those of "ugly, earthy, drunken satyrs, amoral creatures who obey their impulses" (Dover, p. 97). Although there were many in classical Athens, especially in the establishment, who would have shared these sentiments, Dover should not trivialize the old and well-established tradition of breaking through social inhibitions in the context of Dionysian religion. The satyrs, who were often imitated by men in Dionysian rites, represent the affirmation of sexuality for its own sake. Hence they are precisely the beings most likely to exhibit sexual practices regarded as in "bad taste" by Athenians inclined toward Platonic values. Admittedly, depictions of satyrs also often display a marvelous erotic sense of humor, but this fact should not confuse the observer into thinking that the painters intended thereby to discredit them. People with Platonic or puritanical values are usually the least likely to have a sense of humor about sex, especially when it is depicted in art.

A picturesque reference to the free-spirited role of satyrs as well as to the Dionysian openness to same-age sex can be found in a passage of the poet Nonnos. Describing Dionysos' jealousy at seeing his lover Ampelos go with others, Nonnos writes:

> When the boy spent time with the satyrs,
> Or joined with a boy his age to go on the hunt,
> Jealous Dionysos would try to restrain him
> So no one who serves the Passions
> Would divert the desire of the light-hearted boy
> Or draw his favors away from Luaios [Dionysos],
> Since a boy just entering the flower of his youth
> Gives pleasure to one his own age.

> (Nonnos, 10, 243–249)

In this passage, Dionysos is called "Luaios," which literally means "Liberator," an epithet also applied to the Great Mother of the Gods. Its use here is apt, since the Dionysian milieu is one of liberation from the increasing restraints of the patriarchal mentality.

In view of the evidence from Aiskhines, Plato, and other sources, we can see that male homosexuality had a special status in classical Athens. No legal restraints were attached to sexual acts between consenting part-ners, and even homosexual prostitution entailed no criminal sanction as such, although it disqualified its practitioners from the rights of speaking before public bodies (in an old law, rarely cited). Both Greek myth and history, so replete with stories of famous male lovers, were invoked to validate contemporary homosexual activities. Although generally mar-ried, most Greek men spent the greater part of their social life with other males, and homosexual affairs were the expected norm.

Despite this seeming openness by contemporary Christian standards, classical Athenian society had developed a strong taboo, in public opin-ion but not yet in law, against what it regarded as passivity or femininity in men. The prevailing notion in "respectable" society was that males should not enjoy being anally receptive once they clearly entered adulthood, nor should they wear clothing or display gestures commonly associated with women. Among some circles—notably those associated with the aristocratic and antidemocratic Platonists—homosexual love was considered most worthy if not physically consummated. In his last years, Plato himself declared that homosexuality was contrary to nature and as such should be suppressed by the state.

Moreover, the old tradition from archaic Greece of homosexuality institutionalized through same-sex religio-educational circles had all but died out. A vestige of this practice was to be seen among Sokrates and his pupils, but ultimately to his detriment, contributing in fact to his trial and death. In addition, the old dichotomy between older teacher and young pupil in an educational context had been transformed into that of masculine adult and younger, more feminine youth in a pa-triarchal hierarchy, although sexual affairs also existed among men of the same age.

Most significant of all, there had been a stunning decline since ar-chaic times in the status of women. The old lesbian circles were com-pletely gone, and so repressed were women in classical Athens that we have almost no information on lesbianism from this period. Some vases show lesbian scenes (Dover, plate no. R207), but as to the nature of the relationships we can only guess.

Contempt for women, embarrassment at one's own femininity, aver-sion to passivity in sex, disdain for anal receptivity, a growing suspicion toward physical passion—all these traits in classical Athenian male society were consistent and mutually reenforcing. They constituted the pattern of conditioning for the new Athenian man, the man who had removed himself from nature, asserted his supremacy over women, and proved his masculinity by getting the better of other men, both sexually and otherwise. In fact, the male sexual organ had been transformed into a symbol of domination and power (Keuls, *passim;* Dover, p. 104).

This system of male conditioning was both the outcome and prop of the patriarchal revolution. In classical Greece as in the world of today, war was the lord and arbiter of all. Any city-state that did not ground its existence on a powerful army or navy would soon be swallowed up, economically if not politically, by other well-armed states. Who was to be king, whose gods were to be worshiped, who was to be a free citizen, who was to be slave—all these questions were ultimately decided on the battlefield. In its deepest core—beneath all the lovely sculpted columns of the artists, all the idealistic theories of the philosophers, all the public ceremonies of the statesmen—the city-state was an engine for making war. To be raised a man in such a culture meant to be raised with the inclination to fight with other men or at least to idolize those who so fought. And for a man to internalize such values meant to sustain and support the city-state that first encouraged such conditioning.

The problem, of course, with instilling these values is that they run counter to many deeply rooted human capacities. We are not born exclusively masculine or feminine, nor alienated from nature, nor inclined toward perpetual violence to the members of our species. On the contrary, we all have the capacity for a very wide spectrum of human characteristics, as evidenced by the glorious variety in values and behavior found in the world's differing cultures. But when we are raised in a society that deliberately delineates half of the spectrum of human abilities and feelings as taboo (as patriarchal society does by the way it divides "masculine" and "feminine"), every person born into that society is fated to spend a huge amount of energy denying half of his or her personality.

As with historical classes, so with individuals: what is repressed from above returns from below. And so Dionysos appeared in Athens, bringing in his train all the repressed hopes and fantasies of the forgotten and silenced past as well as those of the forgotten and silenced self. How appropriate, then, that he should be the enemy of war, the final madness that patriarchal civilization visits on itself. His character in this respect is derived from Pan, the Arkadian goat-god who lived in the woods with nymphs and satyrs, a deity similar to Eleuthereus, already discussed in connection with the rise of Greek theater. Dionysos' special relationship to Pan is highlighted in the scene of Euripides' *Bakkhai* where Pentheus is raving mad. Here the disguised Dionysos indulges Pentheus in his wild fantasies about his own destructive strength—except when it comes to Pan:

> Pen. Will I be able to bear on my back
> The glens of Mt. Kithairon
> And all the women of Bakkhos, too?

> Dion. You can if you want.
> The mind was unsound you had before,
> But now it is as should be.

> Pen. Do I need to bring a crowbar?
> Or should I put my arms and shoulder
> At the bottom of the peaks
> And tear them up by hand?

> Dion. No,
> You mustn't destroy the nymphs' sacred places
> Or shrines where the sounds of Pan are heard.

> (lines 945–952)

One of Pan's special talents is to strike terror into troops on the battlefield and make them throw down their arms and flee rather than fight (his name is the origin of the English word "panic"). When Dionysos absorbed the cult of Pan, he also took on this antiwar trait, as indicated by the warning of the prophet Teiresias to the battle-happy Pentheus:

> And he has a role in Ares' sphere, the god of war.
> When the enemy has come and arrayed itself to fight,
> At times a sudden fear will come
> And make them run in panic from the field
> Before a spear is even thrown.
> This madness, too, is a gift from Dionysos.

> (lines 302–305)

Not only would Dionysos have soldiers desert their posts in war, but he enjoins on all humans the positive pursuit of peace and the pleasures of life, as the chorus declares before the scene where Pentheus' thugs bring in the arrested god in chains:

> The god that is the Son of God
> Delights in celebrations.
> And he loves the goddess Peace,

110

The bearer of prosperity,
The nurturer of children.
To rich and poor alike
He gave the gift of wine that kills our pain.
He hates those men who aren't concerned
To live their days and treasured nights
In happiness and in joy.

(lines 417–426)

Dionysos would much rather feast, drink, and play with the satyrs than go to war, and his efforts to seduce men away from the battlefield to join his revel is a divine gift to humankind. In this respect, he is in sharp contrast to the war god Ares, the only Greek god who was *not* famous for his homosexual love affairs (Symonds, p. 10). (Although, as we shall see, even Dionysos became a militaristic god when he was finally co-opted into the patriarchal pantheon.)

Such, then, was the nature of the confrontation between Dionysian religion as the bearer of older, sexualized tribal values and the new patriarchal order of the city-state and militarized men. And such as well was the real nature of the conflict between Dionysos and Pentheus, for the former was the embodiment of a prepatriarchal mode of masculinity, derived ultimately from the matricentered culture of the Stone Age, just as the latter embodied the masculine role-playing of the new Indo-European invaders. Hence in the memorable clash between the two in Euripides' *Bakkhai*, the playwright brings more into question than just Dionysos or Pentheus as individual mythical figures. Euripides' greater indictment runs against the very essence of classical Greek civilization, for the latter had violently rejected the androgynous energies of an earlier, more peaceful era (Dionysos) and become totally dependent for its existence on a patriarchal model of masculinity (Pentheus). According to this deeper message of Euripides' *Bakkhai*, such masculinity inevitably and compulsively creates unending violence and war, and therein lies the real madness, not of Dionysos, but of patriarchal civilization.

Ironically, part of the scenario of Euripides' *Bakkhai* was later acted out historically in another memorable conflict over similar issues, this time involving the most famous state in the Mediterranean. This is the story of the coming of Dionysos to Rome and the violent resistance of that city's establishment to his rites. To learn of these events, we must move forward in time to the second century B.C.

V

ROME

❂

IN 186 B.C. the senate of Rome, acting at the urgent request of the city's chief executive officer, banned the private celebration of the rites of Dionysos throughout Italy and authorized a witchhunt to track down and arrest all the religion's leaders. In accordance with this decree, mass arrests and confiscations of property quickly followed. Panic swept Rome and the entire Italian peninsula, as many people fled abroad.

The events of 186 B.C. are recorded at some length by the Roman historian Livy (Titus Livius), who flourished at the beginning of the first century A.D. Livy was a member of the privileged classes of his time and devoted much of his long life to research and study. He strongly believed in the traditional values of the old landed Roman aristocracy and in Rome's manifest destiny, as those classes saw it, to dominate Mediterranean civilization.

Like most ancient historians, both Greek and Roman, Livy wrote creative history: that is, he sought to produce a work that was not just a record of events or an analysis of situations but also a readable *story* that was entertaining in content and pleasing in style. To this end, he often embellished the bare bones of his sources, in particular speeches, with reconstructions of his own. Although Livy's embellishments would not be considered a good scholarly style of history writing by contemporary bourgeois standards, his history nonetheless remains most valuable, partly because he did have a large array of good sources at his disposal, partly because his reconstructions in most cases probably do capture the essential features of what happened, and finally because his embellishments reflect his own personal values and so are a key to upper-class Roman attitudes at the time of his writing.

Livy relates that the rites of Dionysos (the Bacchanalia) were first brought to Rome via Etruria, an area whose inhabitants were long given to religious practices that educated Romans regarded as superstitious. In his account of the introduction of the rites, he stresses several features he finds distasteful: they were brought by a foreigner (a Greek), they lacked the characteristic rationalism of the country of their origin, and they were practiced in private:

> An obscure Greek came first of all to Etruria but without any of those many skills which the most learned nation on earth has introduced for the development of our minds and bodies. He was a sacrificer, a soothsayer, worse than those who deceive people's minds by publicly unveiling a new system of rites, who openly profess their trade and mode of teaching. No, he was an initiator of secret, nocturnal rites [occultorum et nocturnorum antistes sacrorum].
>
> (Livy, 39, 8, 3–5)

This passage is both remarkable and ironic, for it brings to mind the many myths about the first introduction into Greece itself of the rites of Dionysos: a stranger appears, a soothsayer, who brings in new rituals from the East that are a threat to the established order. So, for example, in Euripides' *Bakkhai*, King Pentheus fumes:

> They say some stranger—a sorcerer, an enchanter—
> Has come to the city from the land of Lydia . . .
> That by day and by night he stays with young women
> And shows them ecstatic rites.
>
> (lines 233–238)

The introduction of the kind of rites mentioned by Livy was not unique to Italy, as we have previously seen, but part of a longer series of such introductions coming in waves and invigorated by the repressed religious aspirations of the agrarian underclasses. What is unique in Livy's account, however, is that written history and not myth is the source of our knowledge of these events.

Likewise reminiscent of earlier mythical accounts is Livy's description of the use of wine and the practice of sexual rites (with homosexual overtones): "When wine inflamed their feelings, when the nightly mixing of men and women and young and old abolished all of shame's distinctions, every form of debauchery first began to appear, since everyone found an easy release for whatever was his own sexual preference" (Livy, 39, 8, 6–7).

Livy does, however, add a descriptive element not generally found in earlier accounts: he accuses the celebrants of torturing and even killing some of the participants: "Through deceit they got away with much, and even more through violence. But the violence was hidden, since the sounds of the victims screaming amid debauchery and bloodshed could not be heard above the din from chants of *olololo*, tambourines and cymbals" (Livy, 39, 8, 8).

His account on this particular point is suspect, not only because it is inconsistent with earlier reports, but also because of the Romans' well-known penchant for ascribing murderous rituals to any religious group that practiced private rites. Hence Martin Nilsson is probably right when he says that "his report of their terrible crimes remind[s] us too much of the horrors commonly ascribed to a despised and persecuted religion by their adversaries, e.g. the abominable rites imputed to the Christians or the Jews by their foes" (Nilsson, 1957, p. 15).

From Etruria the rites spread to nearby Rome and inadvertently came to the attention of the authorities through a lovers' quarrel. Hispala Fecenia, an ex-slave and ex-prostitute, discovered that her wealthy lover's family was pressing him to be initiated into the rites of Bakkhos. Horrified, she told him that the parents had no idea of what they were doing. She said as a slave she used to visit the rites and knew that they were scenes of debauchery. Persuaded by Fecenia's entreaties, the lover rejected his parents' plans for his initiation, whereupon they drove him from the house.

Livy's account of the lover's relationship to his family on this issue is unsatisfactory. He mentions a quarrel between the lover and his step-father over an inheritance, suggesting that the stepfather was hoping to use the lover's impending initiation as a means of discrediting him. But it remains unclear how the father intended to accomplish this discrediting. In any case, the upshot was that the lover and Fecenia complained about the rites to Spurius Postumus Albinus, a consul (one of the two chief magistrates at Rome).

Consul Albinus granted Fecenia immunity from prosecution if she would expose the rites and inform on those who participated in them. Having this guarantee, Fecenia said the rites were originally limited to women and were celebrated three days per year in the daytime. At some point, one of the women priests decided to admit men, at the same time moving the rites from day to night and extending the frequency and duration of their celebration to five nights every month. She said that after this transition the rites became scenes of debauchery, although most of the sexual activity occurred among the men themselves:

> Since the time that the rites have been done in mixed company, since men have mingled with women and the license of night has been added, every

114

kind of shameful and criminal act has found its place there. There is more debauchery among the men with each other than with the women.

(Livy, 39, 13, 10–11)

It remains unclear whether Fecenia is here relating a received myth about the distant origins of the Bacchanalia or a historical account of fairly recent Roman developments. Since she mentions the individual Roman names of the first male members of the cult, she would seem to be relating an actual incident. However, the transition from an all-female to a mixed membership probably happened at a remote point in the past, since male members (the satyrs) had long been associated with the cult of Dionysos in Greece and elsewhere. Moreover, Livy previously said that a Greek *man* first brought the religion to Italy. In all probability, this part of Fecenia's testimony is garbled, mixing recent Roman developments with the cult's myths about its ancient past.

Fecenia describes the activities of the cult's leading women in terms reminiscent of the Mad Women of Euripides' *Bakkhai*: "The leading women, dressed like followers of Bakkhos and with dishevelled hair, run with burning torches in hand to the Tiber. They plunge the torches into water and then lift them up still burning, since they contain a mixture of active sulphur and lime" (Livy, 39, 13, 12–13).

Whether prompted by the consul or acting on her own initiative, Fecenia suggested that the rites were rapidly gaining in popularity and becoming a threat to the Roman establishment: "There is a huge crowd now, almost a counter-state [*alterum iam prope populum*], and among them some notable men and women" (Livy, 39, 13, 14).

Using Fecenia's testimony as evidence, Consul Albinus entered the senate house and prevailed upon the senate to enact extraordinary legislation. That body authorized a special inquisition (*quaesitio extra ordinem*), including an armed force, to hunt down priests and leaders of the religion, which it termed a conspiracy against the state; rewards were offered to anyone who would inform on suspected members; the rites of Bakkhos—except for those publicly performed and duly regulated by the state—were banned in Rome and throughout Italy; condemnations of defendants in absentia were allowed; all nighttime assemblies were outlawed; and it was declared a crime to help anyone fleeing from the inquisition (Livy, 39, 14: 6, 7, 9, 10).

To justify these stern measures, Consul Albinus subsequently appeared before a mass assembly of the citizens and delivered a speech outlining the nature of the threat as he perceived it. This speech, although no doubt embellished by Livy, is quite valuable, for it clearly reveals why the Roman establishment, including Livy himself, felt the ecstatic rites of this new god to be such a danger to its system of life.

Albinus declares right from the start that the principal causes of the trouble are women and "men who are just like women," in other words, men engaging in homosexual acts:

> As for what most of them do, if I said there were many thousands of them, you would no doubt be terrified unless I told you just what kind of people they are. In the first place, then, a large number are women—and so there is that source of the present problem—and then men who are just like women— men who debauch and ravish and rave, driven by sleepless revels, wine, night-time clamoring and shouting. The movement still has no power, but it is experiencing a large increase in numbers, growing bigger every day.
>
> (Livy, 39, 15, 8–11)

The reason such men are a threat to the state, Albinus continues, is that in effect they undermine Roman militarism:

> If you knew how young these initiated males were, you would not just pity them, you would blush with shame. Citizens, do you think that young men initiated in this rite should be made soldiers? Should arms be entrusted to those who have been trained in an indecent ritual chamber? Men who have wallowed in their own and in others' debauchery—are they to fight with sword for the decency of your wives and children? It would not be quite so bad that their shameful passions made them effeminate (that would largely be a question of their own disgrace), if only they had kept their hands from crimes against others . . .
>
> (Livy, 39, 15, 13–39, 16, 2)

The implication here is a familiar one: young males are being initiated in the rites of Dionysos by being anally penetrated. This act makes them like women and hence utterly unworthy to carry on the quintessential male activity—warfare. Moreover, not only do they enjoy this act, but they are making converts of others! Obviously, with the change of a few phrases, this passage could easily have been delivered by the Athenians Aiskhines or Plato, whose views were discussed in the last chapter.

Albinus finds in these revellers a most convenient political scapegoat, claiming that they are responsible for all the ills of the time, adding that they will soon be a threat to the established political regime:

> You need to know that whatever wrong-doing . . . has occurred in recent years owes its origin entirely to that ritual chamber. . . . The evil inches

along and grows every day. Already it is too big for private resources to contain. It casts its eye on the supreme power of the state.

(Livy, 39, 16, 2–4)

Albinus hastens to assuage the religious scruples of the Romans, who fear that by suppressing this religion they may be committing an offense against the gods. The manner in which the consul makes this argument clearly shows the degree to which the official state religion had become a creature of the public officials who were its priests:

> I am concerned, citizens, that even some of you may be led astray. . . . A fear enters the mind that we may violate some involved prerogative that is divine. . . . But you have been made immune from this present religion by innumerable rulings of the state priests, decrees of the Senate, and responses of the augurs.

(Livy, 39, 16, 6–8)

Continuing in the manner of Pentheus' diatribes against the barbarian Mad Women, Albinus declaims that the rites come from *foreigners* and "nothing so characterizes a religion as fit for elimination as sacrifice after a foreign manner rather than according to our own" (Livy, 39, 16, 9–10).

Livy reports that after the consul finished his speech there was panic in Rome and many people tried to flee. There were also mass arrests, and a number of men and women committed suicide. Those who confessed only to being initiated without actually partaking in any further wrongs were imprisoned, while those engaged in "debauchery or bloodshed" were sentenced to death (Livy, 39, 18, 4–5) and "more were executed than imprisoned" (Livy, 39, 18, 5).

As a reward for their services as informers, Hispala Fecenia and her lover were paid a large sum of money by the senate. In addition, Fecenia was granted special privileges not usually enjoyed by Roman women at the time: the right to sell or give away her own property without the consent of her father or male guardian; to marry outside her class, including free-born citizens; and to be forever protected by the authorities from any retaliation because of her accusations. Her lover, one Publius Aebutius, was granted exemption from all military service and from the cavalry tax (Livy, 39, 19, 3–7).

The hostile reaction of the Roman authorities to the spread of the rites of Dionysos was a combination of cynical power-politics and genuine fear. The consul Albinus prompted Fecenia as to what he wanted to

117

hear in her confessions and then used the results to alarm both senate and people. His statement that the worshippers of Bakkhos were responsible for "whatever wrong-doing . . . has occurred in recent years" suggests there had been some recent problem or discontent and that he was using the celebrants as scapegoats on which to blame these problems. When public officials resort to such tactics it is often to divert attention away from their own failures or malfeasance.

But the Roman repression of the Bacchanalia was more than just political scapegoating, and Livy's account of the affair was more than an exercise in historical fantasizing. In a recent study of Etruscan religious artifacts, Yves Bomati has shown that Livy was right when he claimed that Dionysian influences first entered central Italy via southern Etruria. The Etruscans originally worshipped a god named Fufluns, who was similar to the Greek Dionysos (Bomati, 1983, p. 87). From the sixth to the second centuries B.C., the cult of this god was absorbed into that of Dionysos, as is shown by the nature of a great number of vases, buckets, mirrors, and other artifacts depicting Dionysian scenes (Bomati, 1983, p. 88 ff). In these artifacts, not only is the Etruscan Fufluns transformed into the Greek Dionysos, but familiar Dionysian figures appear in abundance: Semele, satyrs, Ariadne, Wild Women, perhaps even Pentheus (Bomati, 1983, p. 98). Another Etruscan deity, Phersu, a sort of Lord of the Dead, also absorbed many Dionysian traits in the same period (Bomati, 1986, *passim*).

In creating Dionysian artifacts, the Etruscans did not just borrow motifs at random for artistic purposes but adopted them with a selectivity that shows their interest in Dionysian rites as a mystery religion and in Dionysos himself as the god who presides over rites of passage (Bomati 1983, pp. 102 and 106). After becoming entrenched in Etruria, this seemingly new religion made its way into the heartland of the Etruscans' conquerors, the Romans. The latter, in turn, viewed their Etruscan subjects as exotic foreigners because of their differing religious and social customs. Etruscan women, in particular, had a notably higher status than their Roman counterparts (Warren, p. 229).

The hysterical reaction of the Roman male establishment to the religion seeping into their land from Etruria shows that important psychological factors were at work in addition to political scapegoating. The electrifying impact on the people of the consul's charges about the influence of women and male homosexuality and his argument, so persuasive to the senate, that such practices would undermine Roman military power cannot be explained by mere political expedience. They imply that on some level the Roman establishment really believed its power system was based on a certain personality type: the repressed, disciplined "real man" who was ready and eager to kill other men on orders from above. Moreover, the authorities' response implies that they also knew how tenuous and artificial such a masculine personality type was; otherwise, they would not have feared that these subversive sexual practices would spread like fire if not checked. In short, the situation was as if the senate had said, "If you let our men enjoy sex with other men, they will; and if they do, you won't be able to manipulate them any more as soldiers. What then will become of our power?"

The senate's reaction is understandable in view both of actual Roman history and of their myths about that history. As Livy explains at some length, the Romans traced their nation back to the legendary heroes Romulus and Remus. The myths surrounding the birth and maturation of these two show certain similarities to myths about the young Dionysos, suggesting that they were in part derived from the some common and very ancient mythic stock. For example, the twins were said to be born from a god who slept with a "virgin" (or an unmarried woman, according to the old sense of the word), a birth story quite similar to that of Dionysos. Their virgin mother's name was Rea Silvia, in origin probably a mother-goddess figure related to the Greek goddess Rhea. Their father, to add a typically Roman touch, was Mars, the god of war.

After the birth of the legendary twins, their violent grandfather cast them out into the wilderness to die, where they were discovered and nursed by a wolf. Later a herdsman found them and hid them in a stable. Some of these anecdotal features were also borrowed from a common mythic stock, since Dionysos was likewise associated with shepherds and a stable. Christians would later use similar associations in fabricating the manger myth about the historical Jesus of Nazareth.

At this point, the similarity to Dionysian myths ends. The Romans quickly transformed the twin heroes of herdsmen and shepherds into chiefs of nomadic pillagers:

> Thus born and raised, as soon as they became of age, they did not linger around in the stable or out with the flocks but ranged through the forests as hunters. Having thus strengthened both body and mind, they were already not only encountering wild animals but also attacking brigands laden with booty, dividing their spoils with herdsmen, and together with the latter, as the band of youths grew in size day by day, partaking of both serious and playful pursuits.

(Livy, 1, 4, 8–9)

This passage probably records a dim recollection of the time when the Romans were transformed from a pastoral into a nomadic people. Concomitant with this change was the transformation of wandering shepherds first into hunters and then into warriors. The word for "youths" above is *iuvenes*, which can also mean "soldiers"; hence the phrase "band of youths" can also be translated as "troop of soldiers."

Despite this important militaristic shift in early Roman myth, there seems to have been some openness to influences from Dionysian-type rites in early times, for Livy reports that a certain Euandros left Arkadia and moved to Rome, bringing with him the famous god Pan, whom the Romans variously called Inuus, Lupercus, and Faunus. The first name derives from the verb *inire*, "to penetrate." Some commentators believe this penetration was sexual, attributing the connotation to the god's role as "fertilizer of cattle" (Gould and Whitely, p. 108). They are right about the connotation but wrong about the reason. As we have seen earlier, Pan was a very sexual Greek god, often having sex with both men and women. His Roman counterpart was called "Penetrator" (or, more accurately translated, "Fucker," possibly a relative of the British Puck) because of these liaisons with humans, not just because he increased the fertility of animals. His major festival, the Lupercalia, certainly suggests as much. At this rite, celebrated every year on February fifteenth, nude young men ran down the Palatine Hill in Rome and slapped anyone they encountered with a goat skin they carried (Gould and Whitely, p. 107). These men did *not* wear the goat skin wrapped around their waists, as some commentators believe (*loc. cit.*). Instead, they held it draped over their shoulders with the rest of their body nude, as indicated by the verb used by the ancients to describe their method of carrying it, *amicire*, which is used "exclusively of upper garments" (*amicio* in Lewis and Short; Burton, pp. 37–38, n. 2). So, for example, Justin says:

> At the foot of the hill he [Euandros] established the precinct of Lycaeus, whom the Greeks call Pan and the Romans Lupercus. The nude image of the god is draped with a goat skin *[caprina pelle amictum est]*, and in this style the participants run down the hill today in Rome.
>
> (Justin, 43, 1, 7, quoted in Burton, *loc. cit.*)

This festival calls to mind the traditional Spartan "dance of the naked boys" (*gymnopaidia*).

This old Dionysian influence quickly faded as the real interests of the Romans shifted toward war and empire-building. The old myths tell us that Romulus killed his brother Remus, became sole ruler of Rome, and encouraged a rapid population growth for the new city. The historical implication is that Rome was a violence-prone city from the start and that geographical expansion was early adopted as deliberate policy. The emphasis on rapid population growth as a tool of empire-building is most significant, since societies that push such a policy usually also believe that the sole purpose of sex is to procreate (in other words, to generate more soldiers and workers).

As might be expected, the status of women was quite low in such a society. Legally, the husband had the same authority over wife and children as he had over livestock, including the right to inflict death. Although this power, the right of *paterfamilias*, was in practice tempered by public opinion, women in the early period led a markedly subjugated existence. This situation is clearly reflected in a popular Roman myth: the rape of the Sabine women.

As Livy tells it, Romulus was concerned that there was a shortage of wives for Roman men, which frustrated both their individual desires and the city's policy of rapid population growth. So Romulus decided to seize all the young women of the neighboring Sabine people and dole them out to his men. To this end, he held elaborate public games in Rome to which he invited the Sabines:

> By this time the whole Sabine population had come with women and children. They were invited as guests to different homes. . . . When the day came for the games and all eyes were directed at the spectacle, a force of Roman men suddenly appeared according to plan. At a given signal they burst forth to seize and carry off the Sabines' young women. Most of the women were taken by the men who happened by them. But certain ones of outstanding beauty were allotted to the leading Fathers [Senators] . . .
>
> (Livy, 1, 9, 9–11)

According to the remainder of the myth, the Sabine men—taken by surprise and unarmed—fled home to plot war against the Romans. After quite some time, the day of battle came, but by now the women had become accommodated to their Roman husbands. Hence they wanted to avoid any battle, since whichever side won, they would lose close relatives. Livy paints a memorable picture of their intervention in the battle:

> Then the Sabine women . . . ventured into the hail of missiles, their hair dishevelled and their clothes torn. . . . Moving en masse from the side, they brought the threatening armies to a stop, stopped the violence, here calling on their fathers, there on their sons . . .
>
> (Livy, 1, 13, 1–3)

As a result of the success of this brave endeavor, the two peoples were united into "one whole Roman sovereignty" (Livy, 1, 13, 4–5).

As usual with such myths, this account probably telescopes into one episode a historical process that was long in developing. The Romans were, in fact, a mixture of Latins and Sabines, a commonality born out of much conflict. In addition, Roman men in the early period often did obtain their wives by raping and carrying off women living in the territory of defeated enemies. Many of these same women also quite likely did resign themselves to their new situation and so probably became a stabilizing influence between Rome and its conquered foes.

Roman men of Livy's time were not horrified or embarrassed by the myth of the Sabine women but took it in stride, even with a sense of amusement. Indeed, they used it to explain certain anomalies in Roman customs. For example, when the groom led out the bride at Roman marriages, it was the practice of the attendants to shout, "For Thalassius! For Thalassius!" Livy explains this cry as an echo of the scene where the Sabine women were first being carried off from the games:

> They say that one woman, the most beautiful to look at of all, was seized by the attendants of a certain Thalassius. When everyone kept asking for whom she was intended, they would say over and over, "For Thalassius!" so that no one would rape her. Hence they say this became the Roman marriage cry.
>
> (Livy, 1, 9, 12)

Livy's derivation here is doubtful, but the anecdote reveals something important about the way Romans of his time thought: on some level they sensed that their institution of marriage was similar to rape. Their feelings were well grounded since both they and their ancestors did on a number of occasions get their wives through the right of conquest. By Livy's time, the status of upper-class women had risen, principally because large numbers of Roman men were continually absent in wars of conquest and many had also been killed, with the result that their property and wealth eventually came under the control of their female relations (Pomeroy, p. 177). Nonetheless, nostalgic conservatives like Livy looked back to "the good old days" when women were kept in their place.

The true depth of Livy's condescending attitude toward women can be seen in his account of Romulus' personal visit to the Sabine women right after they were carried off. In the usual male-chauvinist fashion of blaming the victim, he says that "the deed was due to the arrogance of their fathers, since they refused to let their neighbors marry their daughters" (Livy, 1, 9, 14). Romulus then proceeds to lecture them, saying they should stop complaining because they will have the legal status of wives and enjoy Roman citizenship (in other words, unlike many Roman captives, they would not be sold into slavery). No doubt with a knowing smile to other men of his class, Livy concludes this episode thus: "In addition, their husbands flattered them and tried to make amends with passionate lovemaking, which is the inducement most likely to work on a woman's nature" (Livy, 1, 9, 16). In other words, Livy invokes that old patriarchal standby, "All they need is a good lay."

Beneath these old-buddy smirks to male peers there lay a stone face that was capable of witnessing, unmoved, the most inhumane treatment of women. Livy displays such a face in his retelling of another popular myth about women, the story of Horatia.

During a war between Rome and its neighboring city of Alba Longa, Livy reports that both sides agreed to resolve the conflict by a battle between champions: each army was to choose three brothers who would fight until only one of the six remained, and his side would be declared the victor. The battle was duly held, and the victor was a Roman, a certain Horatius, one of whose victims from the other side happened to be the fiancé of his own sister, Horatia. While Horatius was bearing the spoils of battle into Rome, he was spotted by Horatia:

> She recognized the cloak her brother was carrying on his shoulder as the one she had made herself for her betrothed and she let her hair down, tearfully calling the dead man's name. The proud soldier was infuriated that his sister would wail at a great public celebration in honor of his victory. He drew his sword, cursed at the young woman, and stabbed her to death, saying, "Depart with your ill-timed love to your betrothed, you who are mindless of your brothers, living and dead, and of your country. So shall it be for any Roman woman who grieves for an enemy."

> (Livy, 1, 26, 2–5)

The brother was brought to trial for murder, but the jury acquitted him, principally because of a plea from the father of Horatius and Horatia, who said he felt his son had acted properly:

> The trial judges were quite moved when Publius Horatius, the father, declared that he considered his young daughter's death justified and that if he had not thought so, he would have punished his son in accordance with a father's prerogative [as *paterfamilias*].

> (Livy, 1, 26, 9)

We do not know for sure whether this incident actually happened, but the story was repeated to reenforce a lesson to Roman women: You are bound to the men of your family and to the state in all matters, even in regard to the deepest and most sensitive of your feelings.

Rome's patriarchal and militaristic values were enshrined in its religion. In his account of the origins of the Roman state religion, Livy explicitly attributes the foundation of the worship of Jupiter, the Romans' chief god, to warfare. In early times there had been a battle between Romulus, the legendary king, and the Caeninians. Romulus killed the Caeninian king with his own hands, stripped him of his armor, and triumphantly ascended the Capitoline Hill in Rome, where he displayed the dead king's armor on a frame near an oak sacred to herdsmen:

> While making this gift, he marked out the boundaries of an area sacred to Jupiter and added a second name to the god, saying, "Jupiter Spoils-Bringer, I Romulus, victor and king, bring to you the armor of a king, and I dedicate to you this holy precinct that I have just marked out with pride, to be a home for spoils personally taken by my successors from the kings and enemy leaders they kill with their own hands, following my example." Such is the origin of the very first temple that was consecrated at Rome.

> (Livy, 1, 10, 5–7)

Although Romulus was a legendary figure, this myth accurately reflects the fact that Jupiter and the other state gods of Rome were both the corporate symbols and moral sanctifiers of Roman imperialism. The connection of Jupiter's first temple with the herdsmen's oak also suggests, as do other myths previously mentioned, that the road to violent patriarchy for Rome was a process of herdsmen evolving into hunters evolving into warriors.

An indication that at some point in the distant past either the Romans or some of their constituent antecedents may have been less ruthlessly patriarchal is Livy's report of a queen, Lavinia, said to have once reigned in the city named for her, Lavinium (Livy, 1, 3, 1–3).

As a result of the rapid success of Roman imperialism, an astounding amount of wealth poured into the capital, and with it new values. The Romans were now less involved in day-to-day struggles for their immediate survival as a people, and they had both more money and leisure to enjoy life. For many, the stern values of their forefathers began to appear inappropriate. In addition, the belief systems and values of the people they conquered also started seeping into Rome, especially through the slaves who were now imported and sold in large numbers. Many individuals among the privileged classes quickly accumulated gigantic fortunes, and graft and corruption became a way of life among governing circles. A class of "new men," those whose power and fortune derived from conquest or the exploitation of new markets, sprang up to challenge the power of the old oligarchy of landed aristocrats. These new men were joined by poorer citizens and residents in subordinate lands in seeking a bigger slice of constitutional power.

These changes produced a crisis in Roman values that peaked in the early part of the first century A.D. Many in the old landed aristocracy looked back with nostalgia on the prior and simpler values of discipline, order, and self-sacrifice for the state. Among these latter was Livy, who esteemed the old Roman values of stern militarism but who was horrified by the social and economic upheaval produced as a result of this very militarism. And so his great work on the history of the Roman people begins on a cautionary note:

Nor has there ever been a city into which greed and excess have entered so late, nor whose respect for modest measures and thrift has so long and persistently prevailed. In fact, the less there was of wealth, the less also of the desire for it. Only recently have riches introduced greed, and new-found pleasures introduced a hunger for extravagance and a passion both utterly to be wasted and to waste.

(Livy, Preface, 11–12)

The Roman senate's banning of the Bacchanalia thus took place in the context of a patriarchal and militaristic society at a time when its official values were being undermined by new belief systems and practices originating from its conquered neighbors and when the power relations between the sexes in the ruling classes were changing due to economic causes. As often before in the history of Mediterranean civilization, the religion of Dionysos became both the vehicle for expressing the resurgent values of suppressed traditions and a focus for the wrath and fear of the conquerors toward their subjects and toward the power of the feminine. In Livy's account, this conflict is made concrete and historical; in Euripides' *Bakkhai* it is treated poetically and generically.

In the face of the new political and economic complexities, the senate proved itself increasingly inept at governing. In 49 B.C. Gaius Julius Caesar, an aristocrat who aligned himself with the new forces seeking fundamental change, seized power in Rome and became for a brief period dictator. He introduced many reforms long sought by the lower classes, among which was his repeal of the ban on the Bacchanalia. On March 15, 44 B.C., he was assassinated by a group in sympathy with the senate. After a period of devastating civil war, Caesar's grand-nephew Octavianus (later called Augustus Caesar) finally consolidated all power in his hands and ruled as emperor for forty-one years (although carefully observing all outward legal forms).

After the reign of Augustus Caesar, Rome was a different nation. The status of upper-class women rose, and attitudes toward sexuality relaxed. Although male homosexuality had been outlawed by the old senate in 169 B.C. (Meier, p. 180), the law fell into disuse in the new regime, partially because of the influence of Greek values introduced by highly skilled Greek slaves, who became a mainstay of both Roman civil administration and private education. In fact, Rome became a bilingual culture, and all educated persons spoke both Greek and Latin.

The nature of this homosexuality was, however, quite different from before. It had no established place in religion or education, but was a purely private matter. Moreover, sex in general tended to acquire a tinge of cruelty and sadism among the Romans. This characteristic is not surprising, since Rome remained a hierarchical, militaristic, and highly coercive society. Some Roman men who engaged in homosexual relations did so burdened by an unspoken sense of shame or guilt and hence tended to eroticize the infliction of punishment either on themselves or on their partners, a phenomenon that often appears when people feel guilty about their sexual behavior. There were, of course, numerous exceptions to this mentality, the most notable being the celebrated love of the Emperor Hadrian for Antinous.

After Julius Caesar lifted the ban on the Bacchanalia, the rites surfaced again, but they too were different. Previously "the adherents chiefly belonged to the lower classes, plebeians or people in Italy who were not Roman citizens" (Nilsson, 1957, p. 21). Now the upper classes, who had earlier largely disdained the rites of Dionysos, took the god to their breasts.

In the older version of the rites, there was a minimum of hierarchy among the celebrants and the rites were wild and sexual. In the new version, hierarchical offices proliferated and the rites themselves were spiritualized and tamed, although a definite sexual element remained. Under the probable influence of mystery religions and Orphism (first emerging in the sixth century B.C.) Dionysos was turned into a lord of the underworld, to which he was said to have descended and from which victoriously risen (Nilsson, 1957, pp. 40–41). His followers seemed to have connected this new concept of the god to belief in a personal afterlife, and they constructed for themselves expensive stone coffins engraved with lavish Dionysian scenes in a style of art now appropriately called "Dionysian baroque" (Kerényi, p. 381). Although these coffin scenes are often of an erotic nature, including depictions of homosexuality, their thrust has clearly become more spiritual: they represent anticipations of a future life of sensual joy with the god who has become a savior from death. This preoccupation with the afterlife was typical of the age, as the subjects of the Roman military autocracy tended to withdraw their emotional allegiance from a world over which they had little or no political or other control and fantasize instead about a life of bliss to come.

By the end of the Roman era, Dionysos was even transformed into a militaristic deity. Nonnos, writing in Greek in the fifth century A.D., devotes much space in his *Epic of Dionysos* to the battles waged by the god in his invasion of India, patterning incidents after the actual invasion nearly 800 years before by Alexander the Conqueror. Ironically, as we shall see, there *was* a Dionysos in India, but Nonnos has reversed the direction of the god's march of influence.

The patriarchal transformation of Dionysos also affected his mother Semele. As we have previously seen, her name meant "Earth" and she was originally a version of the goddess Mother Earth, with a history of worship deeply entrenched in the agricultural underclasses. The Romans changed the myth to the effect that she had been assumed into heaven, a motif possibly influenced by Christian beliefs (Sandys, p. 89; Nilsson, 1957, p. 130). And so, ironically, the goddess of the earth was finally uprooted from her own element and placed in the sphere of the patriarchal sky gods. In the end, she too, like her divine son, was co-opted.

Among some wealthy Romans, the Dionysian religion lost much of its unique content and became in fact little more than a fad. As the gorgeous mansions unearthed at Pompeii show, some of the rich, probably practicing a kind of mystery religion with initiation rites, decorated their walls profusely with Dionysian murals. But the rites had now become stylish, even elegant—a new taste acquired by "well-to-do people who loved a pleasant and luxurious life" (Nilsson, 1957, p. 146).

These upper-class influences on Dionysian religion had little lasting impact on history, either Roman or otherwise, and did not survive the imperial economic opulence which made them possible. But Dionysos had another impact, one of enormous historical significance, on a new religion that emerged out of Galilee. But before turning to that story, we have to take a side trip well beyond the boundaries of the Roman Empire.

VI

INDIA
AND
BEYOND

◉

SO far this investigation of the worship of Dionysos has restricted itself largely to Greco-Roman civilization and its historical antecedents. There is much more to the story, but the information is hard to get. Many scholars, driven by the desire to specialize that characterizes contemporary research methods, have become so engrossed in studies of some facet of the classical epoch that they have lost sight of the larger picture of which that cultural system was only a part. They tend to scoff at suggestions of influence from outside the Greco-Roman world. Like the university astronomers who were hostile to Galileo, they often even refuse to look at the evidence for a larger picture. A good example of this type of narrow approach is the work of Albert Henrichs, who argues that "Greek religion is largely a conglomeration of local cults, and the history of Greek religion is basically a history of the changes of these local cults . . ." (Henrichs, 1978, 9, p. 154).

A principal cause of this provincialism is the type of institutional training research scholars now receive in bourgeois universities. In most departments of graduate study, the emphasis is on understanding by analysis: cut up the subject matter into pieces until you find one little bit that nobody else has a claim to, stake your claim there, do your research, publish your findings in a professional journal, and congratulate yourself on having made a contribution to the progress of human knowledge.

The problem with this narrow approach is twofold: first, bits of information make no sense unless they are interpreted as parts of a greater context. A newly discovered sub-atomic particle, for example, is intelligible because it is predicted by, consistent with, or subversive to a pre-existing theoretical context (such as the atomic theory of matter). Without such a context, its discovery would be meaningless. To understand is in part to put into a context, for an utterly isolated datum of information is utterly uninterpretable. To refuse to examine critically the context in which one perceives is simply to take that context for granted. And this is exactly what many classical scholars do: they arbitrarily *assume* that Greco-Roman civilization is the most meaningful context for their work and hence refuse even to look at any evidence that would suggest a different context.

In addition to overlooking the contextual nature of the research process, this narrow approach has a second problem: the world itself is interconnected, and especially so in human history. The widespread distribution of similar artifacts in remote times, the commonality of many myths, the ability to travel great distances by means of the technology of the time—all these factors imply that Greco-Roman civilization was not a hermetically sealed unit but in fact interacted with distant societies throughout its history. At the very least, one should acknowledge that the Greeks and the Romans traveled great distances before settling in places now commonly associated with them and establishing their civilizations.

Analysis is extremely valuable, indeed absolutely essential, in furthering human knowledge. But it is only half of the job. The rest is integration—putting the pieces back together to see how they fit, comparing them to other pieces and other systems of pieces, and, at times, experiencing that leap of the imagination which suggests an entirely new way of ordering the pieces or even of defining what a piece is. Sometimes it is precisely such an integrative leap of the imagination that brings the greatest breakthroughs in human knowledge. In the sixteenth century A.D., all the known facts about astronomy could be explained by assuming that the solar system revolved around the earth. Corpernicus' genius was to reinterpret these known facts by a much more elegant and simple system—the theory of the revolution of the earth around the sun. Of course, not every new theory is correct or useful. The way to determine such correctness is by re-examining the old evidence and looking at any new evidence. But many classical scholars refuse even to take a peek at things outside their old theoretical groove.

Recently a whole new view of the worship of Dionysos, and indeed of the historical context of Greco-Roman civilization, has been provided by Alain Daniélou, in his book *Shiva and Dionysos* (translated from the

French by K. F. Hurry, London, 1982). Daniélou demonstrates that the ancient Indian god Shiva is strikingly similar to Dionysos, not only in the concept of the god himself, but also in the nature of his rites and followers and in the historical context of his first appearance and subsequent repression. Having lived for some time in India, Daniélou has availed himself of a number of ancient religious texts that have never been readily accessible in the West and that show Indian religious evolution to be more complicated than most Westerners have previously thought.

According to Daniélou, a number of peoples coming from the Southwest and speaking the Dravidian family of languages (as distinct from the Indo-European family) settled in India from before 4000 B.C. and thereafter. Their religious traditions provided the seedbed from which grew the subsequent worship of Shiva. In the early Bronze Age, two of their important deities were Pashupati (the Lord of the Animals) and Parvati (the Lady of the Mountains), reminiscent of similar deities in Crete. The ancient appearance of this religion in India was part of a great cultural movement, first appearing in the sixth millenium B.C., which extended from Portugal in the West through Europe to India and Southeast Asia and showing in many places the common features of the cult of the bull, snake, and phallus, the royal symbol of horns, depictions of yoga positions, and the building of funeral chambers (Daniélou, pp. 20–34). From approximately 3000 B.C. to 1800 B.C. "the three great sister-civilizations of Mohenjo Daro [now in Pakistan], Sumer and Knossos developed along parallel lines, extending over the whole European continent on one side, and central and east India and southwest Asia on the other" (Daniélou, p. 34).

Beginning in approximately 1800 B.C., a great series of events occurred that was to change all subsequent human life. Out of the Caucasus mountain range (now in the southwestern Soviet Union) there poured wave after wave of patriarchal invaders speaking various dialects of the Indo-European family of languages. For hundreds of years they swept in pulses into Europe and India, everywhere bringing great destruction and havoc and introducing a stern new religion based on a pantheon of sky gods. Wherever they settled, they mingled with the indigenous population and formed a two-tiered society, with the new warlords and their sky gods on top and the native peasant masses with their old agrarian and animistic deities underneath. In many places, new hybrid nations eventually formed, incorporating strong undercurrents from the older religious tradition, but displaying an Indo-European dialect as the new official language and patriarchal domination as the new principle of social organization. Everywhere the status of women fell, sexuality was increasingly repressed, and permanent warfare was established as a way of national life.

In Italy, the invading *Latini* brought the Latin language and founded Rome; in the southern Balkan Peninsula, the *Akhaioi* and their allies brought Greek; and in India, the invaders introduced the antecedents of Sanskrit. This exploding cancer of patriarchal violence continued well into historical times, for, as Daniélou aptly observes, both the so-called European "discovery" of the Americas (with all its devastation) and the "colonization" of Africa were but recent extensions of the same basic imperialist thrust launched by the bearers of Indo-European languages and culture (Daniélou, p. 25).

In India, the older religious traditions were integrated in various degrees into the new patriarchal religion of Vedic Brahmanism. Hindus eventually codified this religion in a series of holy books, the *Vedas* and the *Upanishads*. A number of these record pre-Aryan traditions, especially the *Atharva Veda*, the *Shvetashvatara Upanishad*, and the *Mundaka Upanishad*. Other textual collections that describe the rites of the older religion can be found in certain *Puranas*, especially the *Shiva Purana* and the *Linga Purana* (Daniélou, pp. 42–43).

Based on these and other sources, as well as on old cult practices that have survived in some areas until the present day, Daniélou has concluded that the god Shiva inherited many of the same traits from the old Dravidian culture that Dionysos in Greece inherited from the Minoan. Among other things, Shiva was associated with the form of a bull, wore the same saffron-colored robe as Dionysos, was worshipped in a religious tradition that knew of the double-ax and the labyrinth, and was revered as the giver of intoxicants (especially his drink *Soma*) and as the lord of the dance.

Dionysos and Shiva also shared many common epithets, such as *Bromios* (Greek for "The Raving One") and *Bhairava* (Sanskrit for "The Terrible One"); *Eriboas* and *Rudra* (both meaning "Howler"); and *Kouros* ("Young Male") and *Kumara* ("The Adolescent").

In Greece, Dionysos was regularly associated with Mt. Nysa, and many localities claimed to be the site of this Nysa. In fact, wherever Dionysos had a center for his cult, the ancients were likely to locate a Mt. Nysa nearby. When Alexander the Conqueror invaded India, his men discovered several mountains there as well named Nysa, and one of the Indian epithets of Shiva is *Nisah* (Daniélou, p. 135). Shiva was likewise thought to have his haunts in mountains.

In all probability, the name *Dionysos* itself means "The God of Nysa," from *di*, an old Indo-European root meaning "god" and *nys*, the root which appears in the name of his special mountain. Hence "Dionysos" may literally mean the God of the Mountain. This derivation is appropriate in view of the famous mountain dances—*oreibasiai*—held in Greece in the god's honor. In the Theban version of his myth, Dionysos is also especially associated with a mountain, Mt. Kithairon, located near Thebes. In Euripides' handling of this myth, the wild followers of Dionysos are repeatedly described as moving from one mountain to another, like so many way stations, in their journey from the East. So, for example, in his opening monologue in *Bakkhai*, Dionysos identifies both the beginning and the end of his recent journey with mountains, Mt. Tmolos and Mt. Kithairon (lines 55–63). When the chorus make their first appearance in the play, they call on the god to come to them—down from the mountains:

> Bring Dionysos down from Phrygia's high peaks,
> Yes, down, down, to the very highways of Greece,
> The Raving One!

(lines 85–87)

The Greek followers of Dionysos were called *Bakkhai*, and the followers of Shiva in his role as leader of the ecstatic dance were known as *Bhaktas* (Daniélou, pp. 51, 100). The Korybantes and Kouretes—young male dancers associated by the Greeks with Dionysos—correspond to Shiva's Ganas (Daniélou, pp. 36, 89, 99).

As with Dionysos, so with Shiva, homosexuality and transvestism are important parts of the god's rituals. All forms of sexuality are considered to represent the god's power and are enjoyed, not for any procreative goal, but for their own sake: "From the point of view of Shivaite mysticism, as is also the case with Dionysiac orgiasm, erotic ecstasy is not a means of reproduction, but purely a seeking after pleasure" (Daniélou, p. 57).

Shiva himself is often depicted as effeminate (but nonetheless quite powerful), a characteristic reflecting both his rituals and their participants:

The hermaphrodite, the homosexual, and the transvestite have a symbolic value and are considered privileged beings, images of the *Ardhanararishvara* [Shiva as hermaphrodite]. In this connection they play a special part in magical and Tantric rites, as they do also in shamanism.

(Daniélou, p. 66)

In Tantric yoga, a system of meditation involving sexual practices and dating back to the earliest times, forms of male anal intercourse are practiced as a method leading to enlightenment (Daniélou, p. 123). As the lord of Tantric yoga, Shiva was closely associated with ritualized anal sex in India as was Dionysos in Greece.

Shiva was also famous for his homosexual loves. According to one myth, the god Brahma was born from the sperm that Shiva deposited in the male god Vishnu (Daniélou, p. 95). In another account, one of Shiva's ejaculations of sperm turned into the Ganges River, out which emerged Skandra ("Jet of Sperm"), the god of beauty and the patron of homosexuals (Daniélou, pp. 95–96). As with Dionysos, Skandra was later transformed by patriarchal influences into a war god, and his penis became a symbol of power and domination (Daniélou, p. 96).

A number of myths tell of resistance by the authorities to the cult of Shiva and of the god's punishment of them for this affront. For example, Daksha, a Vedic king, refused to offer sacrifice to Shiva, complaining that the god was naked, wore dishevelled hair, revealed sacred texts to people of low birth, used intoxicants in his worship, haunted cemeteries, and ruled over the spirits of darkness. Daksha also reneged on his previous promise to give his daughter to Shiva as a wife. As a result of his resistance, the king was cursed by the bull, the animal personification of Shiva. His daughter eventually killed herself, and a terrifying spirit came and cut off Daksha's head, the same fate suffered by Pentheus at the instigation of Dionysos (Daniélou, pp. 47–48).

After the Aryan invaders established themselves in India, they created a rigid caste system, which was reflected in the established religion. The cult of Shiva, however, continued to remain open to members of the lowest castes, since they were historically its major adherents. Periodically, as with Dionysos in Greece, the cult of Shiva became the vehicle for the expression of the values and needs of the lower classes: "The reappearance of Shivaism or Dionysianism represents a return to an archaic and fundamental religion, kept alive underground despite invasions and persecution" (Daniélou, p. 37).

Daniélou does not point to any significant body of myth that puts special emphasis on the title "Son of God," as happened in the stories about Dionysos. If his omission mirrors an actual situation in the myths, then we have here an important difference between the two deities. By staking his divine status on the claim to be Zeus's son, Dionysos implies that Zeus is the principal source for determining divine status: to be a god means somehow to be connected to the family of Father Zeus. But to give this power to Zeus is to recognize that the patriarchal religion has in effect become the only legitimizing religious tradition. The absence of such a thrust on Shiva's part and his demand to be accepted as a god on his own terms imply that the victory of patriarchal religion in India has not been as extensive as it was in Greece. In fact, this seems to be the case, for Daniélou claims to have personal knowledge of existing Shivaite religious cults that still practice the oldest of rites on their own terms, including human sacrifice and cannibalism (Daniélou, pp. 169–170).

Another difference between Dionysos and Shiva, according to Daniélou, is the nature of their relationships to a mother-goddess figure. While Daniélou agrees that Shiva was associated with such a goddess (Shakti) from ancient times, he implies in one passage that Shiva was the principal member of the pair and that Shakti was a mere manifestation of Shiva (Daniélou, p. 76). But this assertion runs counter to the implications of another of his own arguments, for he claims that the Shivaite religion itself emerged out of a prior religious stratum centered on a Great Goddess and a male deity (Daniélou, pp. 24, 27, 49, 77). Moreover, in the oldest level of this previous religion, the goddess is depicted as giving birth to the bull-shaped predecessor of Shiva (Daniélou, p. 114).

In fact, the evidence cited by Daniélou himself clearly shows that Shiva was originally derivative and secondary to Shakti. With the triumph of the patriarchal invasion, there would naturally be a tendency for him to eclipse the goddess and even appropriate to himself her cult, which apparently also happened with Dionysos and the Great Mother. Hence the anomaly in ancient Greece of a sacred band of Mad Women fiercely asserting their independence and yet worshipping a male god. Originally their principal if not sole object of worship was probably the Mother. Both Shiva and Dionysos, although carrying on many pre-patriarchal traditions after the male invaders' conquests, nonetheless represent a relative eclipse of the religious status of women from the point of view of the Stone Age and the early Bronze Age.

A principal failing of Daniélou's work is his apparent lack of interest in the history of women's spirituality. Aside from a few general references to the cult of the Mother Goddess, he analyzes neither myth nor artifact in regard to women's rituals or sexuality. His book is also marred by a puzzling racism that manifests itself near the end: "Whether in the animal or human world, the mixture of races degenerates individuals, who distort the harmony and beauty of creation since they no longer possess the characteristic virtues of either race" (Daniélou, p. 217).

It would be difficult to imagine any statement more contradictory to the original religions of both Dionysos and Shiva in view of their characteristic emphasis on breaking down artificial social conventions. If such attitudes are prominant in modern Shivaism, as Daniélou implies, they are most likely a reflection and absorption of caste values from the dominant Vedic tradition.

Daniélou's argument for the existence of a Dionysos-type deity in India is consistent with a number of passages from ancient Greek writers. The historian Diodoros of Sicily, though writing in the postclassical period of the first century A.D., nonetheless had access to sources dating back to much earlier times. He says that a number of "learned Indians" report that a god they identified with Dionysos entered India from the West with an army and that he was a founder of cities and a creator of cultural innovations. This tradition is reminiscent of Daniélou's account of the ancient immigration from the Southwest of the cultured Dravidians and their god Shiva. In Diodoros' account of the Indian story, the figure of Dionysos probably stands for both the god and the people who worshipped him:

They say that thereafter he gave part of the store of crops he had accumulated to the Indians and he gave them the invention of wine and other amenities for living. And in addition he became the founder of noteworthy cities by drawing towns together into suitable locations. He instructed them in how to worship the divine and introduced laws and courts.

(Diodoros, 2, 38, 5)

The reason for identifying this incoming god with Dionysos lies in the Indians' description of his characteristics in battle: "They related that he also led around with the army a multitude of women and that he would use tambourines and cymbals when drawn up against the enemy's lines" (Diodoros, 2, 38, 6).

Apparently the rites of this god became well established, for Diodoros reports that, as in Greece, many places had local tales about him:

They say that in India to this day the place the god happened to be born in is known as well as the names of his wars in the language of the local people and that many other significant proofs remain of his Indian birth, which it would take too long for me to relate.

(Diodoros, 3, 63, 5–3, 64, 1)

Diodoros says the Indians claim that after Dionysos became settled there, he advanced with an army to the whole world, showing people how to cultivate the grape (Diodoros, 3, 63, 4). He adds that a few

Greek myths tell various stories about Dionysos' coming to Greece on an elephant, a typically Indian animal (Diodoros, 3, 65, 7–8, 4, 2, 6).

The poet Nonnos, writing quite late in the fifth century A.D., relates at some length an account of Dionysos' invasion of India and his battles there. Although some of his sources may refer to the original Dravidian immigration, he seems to base much of his account on the short invasion into India at a much later date by Alexander the Conqueror.

Diodoros recounts stories of the worship of Dionysos in many other lands besides India. These myths demonstrate both the interconnected-ness of ancient civilizations and the international nature of a Dionysos-type god. A good example is his account of a set of myths from Lybia, a country which had many cultural interactions in antiquity with Egypt, Crete, and Greece (Diodoros, 3, 68, 1–3, 73, 6). According to these myths, there was a Lybian culture hero or god, Ammon, who had the head of a ram. Although married to Rhea, the daughter of Ouranos (Heaven), he met and fell in love with the goddess Amaltheia, often pictured as a goat, who was an earth-mother goddess and from whom was derived "Amaltheia's Horn" (the horn of plenty). "Stricken by desire, he made love to her and fathered a son [Dionysos] of remarkable beauty and strength" (Diodoros, 3, 68, 2). To protect Amaltheia and their son from the jealousy of Rhea, Ammon sent the two to the city of Nysa in Crete, an island then renowned for its rich vegetation, beautiful cities, and the good health of its people. There the child was raised, hidden away in a secret cave. Ammon became the king of Crete, and Kronos, Rhea's brother, came with an army of Titans to make war against Dionysos. Leading an army of Cretans and Amazon women, Dionysos defeated the Titans and captured (and subsequently freed) Rhea and Kronos. After this victory, Dionysos advanced to conquer Egypt and many other lands, including India.

A number of familiar Dionysian themes are found in this Lybian myth, but with some interesting variations. As usual, Dionysos is here the son of an earth goddess, has horns (as do both his parents), is raised in a secret cave in Crete (the so-called "Cretan Zeus"), and is associated with a place named Nysa. In the war against those who would repress Dionysos, Amazons have replaced the Mad Women, which may mean that women were sometimes warriors in archaic Cretan and Lybian culture. The myth also suggests that the worship of Dionysos originated in Lybia, moved to Crete, and spread from there to Egypt and eastwards to India.

A Greek poet, writing in the sixth century B.C. and imitating the style of Homer, confirms that Dionysos was quite at home in Egypt and its environs. In a surviving fragment of his work he claims—like many others in speaking of some local cult of Dionysos—that he has found the true location of Nysa, the god's legendary original home. In this fragment, he addresses Dionysos by the name Eiraphiotes, whose exact meaning is unknown, although the word seems to mean "young goat" in some dialects:

> Some say it was on Mt. Drakonos, others on windy Ikaros,
> Others in Naxos, that you were born, Divine Son, Eiraphiotes,
> And others that by deep-running Alpheios River
> Pregnant Semele bore you for Zeus, who delights in thunder.
> Yet others would say you were born in Thebes, my Lord,
> But all are wrong. The father of gods and men gave birth to you
> Far from men, concealing you from white-armed Hera:
> There is a certain Nysa, a lofty mountain full of trees,
> Outside Phoenicia, near waters of the Nile . . . [fragment ends]
>
> (Pseudo-Homer, *Hymn to Dionysos*, 3, 1–9)

Although the poet is wrong to claim this Nysa as the "real" one, his poem shows that both the god and his legendary mountain were a familiar story in Egypt in the sixth century B.C.

Writing at a much later date, Diodoros of Sicily refers back to the fragment of this poet (whom the ancients mistook for Homer because of the style of his writing) and relates it to another myth about a Dionysos in Egypt and in many other countries:

Then they say Zeus took up the babe [Dionysos] and gave it to Hermes and told him to take it to the cave in Nysa, which was situated between Phoenicia and Egypt, and to give it to the nymphs to raise and diligently to bestow the best of care on it. So having been raised in Nysa, Dionysos obtained his name from Zeus [Dios] and Nysa. And Homer testifies to this in his hymns when he says:

> There is a certain Nysa, a lofty mountain full of trees,
> Outside Phoenicia, near waters of the Nile.

They say he was raised by the nymphs in Nysa and was the inventor of wine and the teacher of vinticulture to men. He travelled over nearly the whole world bringing much land under cultivation and so obtained everywhere the greatest honors.

(Diodoros, 4, 2, 3–5)

According to the writer Plutarch, the Greek Dionysos is the same as the Egyptian Osiris, who was associated with the Egyptian great-mother goddess Isis. These two were the chief agricultural deities in Egypt and the most popular of all the Egyptian gods among the lower classes. Lavish and spectacular processions and celebrations were held in their honor from remotest times. Plutarch's book on the identity of Osiris and Dionysos is noteworthy because he dedicated it to a friend, a certain Clea, who was both the leader of a group of Bakkhic women at Delphi and an intiate in the secret rites of Osiris (Plutarch, Moralia, 364E). Plutarch states that Clea herself personally knew that the private rites of the two gods were the same and points to a number of parallels as well between their public practices.

Some scholars discount Plutarch's opinion on the identity of the two gods because he wrote at a late date (first century A.D.) when many differing Mediterranean cults were beginning to blend together. But the Greek historian Herodotos, writing nearly five hundred years before, notes: The Egyptians do not all worship the same gods in common except for Isis and Osiris, who, they say, is Dionysos" (Herodotos, 2, 42).

According to this passage, Egyptians and not just Greeks make the claim for a common identity for the two. In addition, the passage refers to the fact that many cults had not yet become homogeneous in Egypt, let alone throughout the Mediterranean.

Diodoros reports similar myths to the east of Egypt in Arabia. There as well we find stories of the familiar Nysa and a concept of the god as a culture-bringer to many different nationalities:

> There [in Mt. Nysa in Arabia] they say the boy was raised by nymphs and named Dionysos from his father and that place. He was of outstanding beauty and at first spent his time with bands of dancing women in every sort of delicate joy. Then he assembled an army from the women and, fitting them out with ivied staffs, led an expedition throughout the whole world. . . . Moreover he established festivals everywhere and created artistic contests . . .
>
> (Diodoros, 3, 64, 6)

A deity reminiscent of Dionysos was also found throughout much of Europe in the religion of the Celts. Although they were part of the Indo-European invasions of that continent, the Celts assimilated many of the early traditions of the peoples whose lands they occupied. They entered Europe from the East in approximately 1500 B.C., and by 500 B.C. had created a national Celtic culture (although divided among many tribes) that extended from Turkey through Europe to the British Isles. As I have shown in an earlier work, one of their chief deities was a horned god who was associated with animals, seasonal cycles, and sexuality, including homosexuality (Evans, p. 18 ff).

In the eighteenth century of the present era, a depiction of this horned god was discovered under dramatic circumstances in Paris. Construction workers doing repairs under the main altar at Notre Dame Cathedral uncovered a Celtic stone altar dating from the time of the Roman occupation of Gaul. The altar was cubical in shape and was engraved with the picture of a male deity wearing deer antlers. The god's name as inscribed in the stone was Cernunnos, which means "The Horned One" (Bober, p. 28 ff). After the triumph of Christianity in Europe, churches were often built on the sites of ancient pagan temples, and the Cathedral of Notre Dame apparently was built on one such site originally dedicated to Cernunnos.

Another striking and well-known depiction of this horned god is a silver bowl found in Gundestrup, Denmark. It shows a male deity wearing deer antlers, holding a snake in one hand, and surrounded by animals. The god sits in a cross-legged yoga-like position, a posture frequently found in his depictions and one that is similar to the seated yoga position found in statues of traditional Indian gods.

The ancient geographer Strabo reports that a god whom he identifies with Dionysos was once worshipped by Celtic women on an Atlantic island off the coast of Gaul (France). He relates that no men were allowed to visit the island and that the women, although married, spent only part of each year visiting their husbands, who lived elsewhere (Strabo, 4, 4, 6). These women were called *Namnetes,* and the French city of Nantes is named after them (Detienne, 1986, p. 69).

Women had a higher status among the Celts than among their Roman conquerors, and goddesses played a prominent role in Celtic religion. Among the most important were y *Mamau,* "the Mothers," a tripartite version of the great-mother goddess, called *Matronae* and *Matres* by the Romans. After the triumph of Christianity, churches dedicated to the Virgin Mary were built on sites previously sacred to the Celtic Mother Goddesses (Markale, p. 17).

Celtic men were renowned for their homosexual activity, as Diodoros indicates in a colorful passage:

Although they have good-looking women, they pay very little attention to them, but are really crazy about having sex with men. They are accustomed to sleep on the ground on animal skins and roll around with male bed-mates on both sides. Heedless of their own dignity, they abandon without a qualm the bloom of their bodies to others. And the most incredible thing is that they don't think this is shameful. But when they proposition someone, they consider it a dishonor if he doesn't accept the offer!

(Diodoros, 5, 32, 7)

As a result of the studies of Daniélou and of others discussed in previous chapters, we may conclude that a certain cultural and religious continuity existed from remotest times over an enormous geographical expanse, from Portugal on the Atlantic through Europe, Asia Minor, Arabia, and into India, and likewise including parts of North Africa, a linear distance from tip to tip of nearly five thousand miles. Although there was, of course, great variation in political, social, and economic conditions in these areas, nonetheless a persistent commonality in each culture was the myth of an important male horned god associated with vegetative and animal powers, sexuality, and cult practices of an orgiastic nature. His names are as various as the nationalities where he is found: Dionysos, Bakkhos, Pan, Eleuthereus, Minotaur, Sabazios, Inuus, Faunus, Priapus, Liber, Ammon, Osiris, Shiva, Cernunnos. But underneath these many names the same basic god-type persists: the lord of the agrarian underclasses who evokes the emotional, nonrational aspects of human consciousness; asserts natural continuities between animal, human, and divine; validates erotic pleasures as ends in themselves; and serves as a focus for aspirations and values preceding and contrary to the patriarchal revolution.

The same god-type is also frequently associated in a significant way with a great-mother goddess, who likewise has many names: Semele, the Great Mother of the Gods, Demeter, Artemis, Diana, the Goddess, Our Lady of the Beasts, Amaltheia, Isis, Shakti, y Mamau. Everywhere she represents the power of nature to engender and support the life of plants, animals, humans, and gods. Like her male counterpart, she is often worshipped in rites of an orgiastic nature. She also echoes a time when women had much greater religious, political, sexual, and economic power.

Not only are these two deities regularly associated with each other, but they often persist as the most popular gods among people from the lower classes, even when the political establishment puts great money and effort into propping up the official war gods and the gods that personify the authority of clan and state. In some cases, the Great Goddess and the horned god also become the focus for an assault against the basic world-view of the established religion.

The reason for these commonalities is not hard to find. In the earliest

140

times, humans everywhere in the areas in question survived by foraging, hunting, and farming and were organized socially into tribes. Such common material circumstances tend to engender common ways of feeling and thinking about nature, sex, and the role of human beings in the cosmos. (Just as people who are born and raised in concrete urban sprawls and survive by working in offices and factories also tend to develop certain basic attitudes about nature, sex, and what it means to be a human being.)

After the patriarchal revolution in these areas, the upper classes created the new institutions of city-state and nation-state and sanctified them with the gods of the patriarchal pantheon. But since even the invaders themselves once had agrarian gods and goddesses, these latter deities became a new guise for the old religion of the conquered underclasses and hence tended to take on a much greater importance than they previously had in the eyes of the conquerors who brought them. In those areas where Indo-Europeans came to power, the new gods would be everywhere similar, since the whole Indo-European explosion originated from the same general location in the Caucasus Mountains. Hence the Indo-Europeans themselves at some point in their remote past must have had a horned god and a Mother Goddess who were both associated with agrarian pursuits. These proved to be the very gods in every conquered area that the lower classes latched on to and used as vehicles for affirming their old beliefs. In sum, the religious commonalities from Portugal to India were due first to the common agrarian interests and pursuits of the conquered and then to the common origins of the various Indo-European invaders and their gods.

The persistence of this anciently established agrarian religion had an enormous impact on the cultural development of Europe much later. As I have shown in my previous work on the origins of European "witchcraft," this old religion survived the fall of the official patriarchal gods of Greece and Rome and was practiced in various broken-down forms until well into the Christian era (Evans, *passim.*). Although by 1000 A.D. paganism had largely died out in Europe among the privileged urban classes, it continued in the lower rural classes hundreds of years beyond this date. Scholars who say Europe was no longer pagan after 1000 A.D. are right in regard to urban intellectuals and political leaders but overlook the beliefs of the great majority of the rural population. For a long time there were in fact two Europes: the minority of orthodox kings, priests, and aristocrats who held all the political and economic power, and the great mass of the poor, uneducated population who had attachments of various kinds to older religious traditions.

Although organized Christianity has always been extremely hostile to sexuality in religious rites, homosexual practices in any context, and a religious leadership role for women, it was unable for a long time after the fall of Rome to impose these views on the majority of the agrarian population of Europe because of the general breakdown in political and legal authority characteristic of the early Middle Ages. This lack of action by the early medieval church should not be confused with a policy of tolerance, which some scholars mistakenly say prevailed in this period. The orthodox church always had repressive values, but it did not always have available the necessary political machinery to carry them out.

By the year 1100 A.D. the Christian upper classes were in a position to consolidate their political power, build up large armies, and create a widespread system of courts and prisons. As a result, practices that Christian authorities had long let pass for lack of an efficient means of control now became the objects of an organized onslaught.

The first memorable clash between orthodox Christians and the practitioners of the older religion occurred in the context of "heresy." For quite some time, Christian and pagan elements had been fusing in certain religious and cultural movements, and a number of interesting hybrid religions arose where people worshipped both Christ and various versions of the Great Goddess and the horned god (Evans, p. 52 ff and p. 63 ff). By the thirteenth century A.D., some of these hybrids had developed their own ideology and were practicing rituals with a sexual content, giving prominent leadership roles to women, exerting political control over their own geographical areas, showing tolerance to homosexuals and Jews, encouraging artistic freedom, and even speaking their own dialects. The popes at Rome, who by now had become quite powerful, defined these movements as "heresies" and created the Office of the Holy Inquisition to wipe them out (Evans, p. 90 ff).

Triumphant in their initial battles against heretics, Christian authorities eventually decided to apply their efforts directly against the broken-down strains of the old agrarian paganism, since these had been important sources of cultural inspiration for the newer heretical movements. Many peasants and even members of the urban underclasses continued to pay homage to the goddess and the horned god (sometimes disguised as saints) or engage in pagan-derived rituals, all the while giving lip-service to Christianity. As in Greco-Roman times, so in Christian Europe, the goddess had taken on many names, depending on the locality: Diana, Hulla, Berchta, Faste, Selga, Abundia, Satia, Befania, Frau Venus (Evans, p. 64 ff). The horned god likewise had many apparitions: Herne the Hunter, Harlequin, Berchtold, Derndietrich, Quatembermann, Kwaternik (Evans, p. 69).

The church declared that these deities, both male and female, were so many demons in the service of Satan. Moreover, the church took the typical traits of the old horned god—horns, hooves, a close identification with sexuality—and gave them to the Devil himself, who has been popularly depicted in this manner ever since (Evans, p. 27).

By the sixteenth century A.D., Christian authorities—both Protestant and Catholic and supported by nearly every major intellectual and cultural leader of the time—declared that these archaic peasant traditions were "witchcraft," and that their practitioners were involved in an unholy conspiracy with Satan to overthrow Christian civilization. The hysteria of priests, ministers, and leading intellectuals was empowered by the inquisitorial legal methods devised by lawyers and judges. Persons accused of witchcraft were considered guilty until proven innocent (which was rare) and were tortured until they named "accomplices." As a result, many people perished (estimates vary from hundreds of thousand to millions) simply because a neighbor had a grudge against them or someone happened to disapprove of their way of life. Independent-acting women and men suspected of being homosexuals became favorite targets in these pogroms (Evans, p. 89).

The first modern scholar to suggest a historical connection between witchcraft and the archaic agrarian religion of Europe was Margaret Murray, whose ground-breaking book, *The Witch-Cult in Western Europe,* was published in 1921. Since the publication of her book, Murray has often been criticized by both Christian and secular researchers in the field. The former argue that the witches really did worship the Devil, and the latter, that the whole concept of witchcraft was simply an hysterical illusion dreamed up by the Inquisition. The flaw in both these views is their scholarly provincialism: they ignore the vast amount of evidence throughout Europe, India, and North Africa pointing to the entrenched existence over millennia of an alternate prepatriarchal religion of the agrarian underclasses. The repression of European witchcraft is of the same general type as the Roman senate's banning of the Bacchanalia and Pentheus' arrest of Dionysos. They are all examples from the history of patriarchal domination of the establishment's effort to put down a return of the repressed fueled by ancient agrarian traditions and deep-seated human needs.

Margaret Murray was an Egyptologist by training and familiar with ancient Eastern Mediterranean religious traditions. This background provided her with the needed breadth of vision to see European witchcraft in a fuller context. Her book does contain a number of factual errors, is lacking in sufficient detail on certain crucial points, and fails to trace important connections between religious phenomena and those related to politics and class considerations. Nonetheless, such faults are not uncommon in any pioneering work and should not obscure the real value of her book in providing a whole new theoretical context for European witchcraft.

The violent reaction of European Christian authorities to lingering influences of the old rural religion is ironic since some of the most essential Christian doctrines were originally molded by that very paganism, and nowhere more so than in the church's concept of Christ himself. Let us turn, therefore, to the story of how Dionysos was eventually co-opted and Jesus of Nazareth turned into a Dionysian-type god.

VII

DIONYSOS
AND
CHRIST

❋

THE concept of Dionysos as developed in ancient Greek religion and particularly in Euripides' *Bakkhai* was destined to play a major role in the formulation of myths that turned the historical Jesus of Nazareth into a god. In the case of Euripides this situation is most ironic, for, as previously discussed, he displays a critical attitude toward Dionysos in the second half of his play.

Euripides had no intention of contributing to a new religion based on an expanded concept of Dionysos. Readers are sometimes misled on this point because of the positive way the playwright depicts Dionysos in the first half of the play when he is oppressed by Pentheus. But in the second half of the play, after the murder and dismemberment of Pentheus, Dionysos wears a second face: that of the implacable, spiteful god who shocks human capacities for sympathy.

The manner in which Euripides turns the tables can be seen in the scenes where Kadmos, the grandfather of Pentheus, and Agaue, the latter's mother, mourn for the slain king. Although Pentheus has been presented all along as a violent and thoroughly obnoxious personality, his death brings genuine grief to his family, and Euripides spares no effort in presenting these feelings. His point seems to be that violent vengeance, even when seemingly well deserved, is always a tragedy.

After both Kadmos and Agaue deliver their lamentations, Dionysos himself suddenly appears, no longer disguised as a vulnerable and effeminate man, but in his glory as a god. In this aspect, he is totally insensitive to the suffering of the two and vindictively taunts them. Agaue, aware she has been utterly defeated by the power of the god, rises first to plead and then to judge and condemn:

> *Agaue.* We've wronged you, Dionysos, and we beseech—
>
> *Dion.* Too late, too late you've come to know me.
> When you should have, you did not.
>
> *Agaue.* I know. But in your vengeance, you're too harsh.
>
> *Dion.* [Shouting]
> But didn't you abuse me, though I was born a god?
>
> *Agaue.* [Firmly and with dignity]
> It ill befits the gods
> To mold their wrath on men's.
>
> (lines 1344–1348)

At this point Euripides makes Agaue the real hero of the play and puts into her mouth his own belief, evident in many of his works, that all the gods, including in the end even Dionysos, are just as wretched in their behavior as human beings, indeed, even more so, for they lack the one redeeming human characteristic: the ability to recognize and condemn cruelty.

As previous chapters have shown, Euripides' *Bakkhai* is a trenchant critique both of patriarchal civilization and of Greek religion, first exposing the utter hypocrisy of the religious establishment in trying to deny and disown Dionysos and then condemning the moral vacuity of all the gods, including Dionysos. The play is really an eloquent appeal for Euripides' own humanist values, saying in effect: "Beware of the dehumanizing consequences of patriarchal civilization and of all religion. Fulfill yourself by leading a balanced life that integrates reason and emotion."

How ironic, then, that such a work should ultimately contribute to the mythological development of one of the world's most distinctly patriarchal religions. But so it did and in a number of important ways.

The most obvious influence of Euripides' *Bakkhai* on Christian mythology lies in its concept of Dionysos as the suffering Son of God. Although Greek myths had traditionally viewed Dionysos as the Son of God, Euripides' play made the question of this relationship into its central motif. As soon as Dionysos steps out onto the stage, he announces:

146

> I am Dionysos—the Son of God!—
> And I have just arrived here in the land of Thebes.

> (lines 1–2)

Although the Greek here literally reads "the Son of zeus" (*Dios pais*), this phrase had the same heavy impact in the ears of Euripides' audience as the phrase "Son of God" does in English, since Zeus was the father and king of the gods and the legitimizing source for any being's claim to divinity. Dionysos makes a defiant announcement of his title—practically spitting it out—as indicated by its prominent place in the word order of the play's first sentence (*Heko Dios pais*).

Not only is Dionysos the Son of God, but he was conceived in the body of a mortal woman impregnated by God. He himself has taken on human flesh to walk the earth as a god incarnate. As such, he is not recognized as a god, even by his closest followers, and suffers at the hands of those who know not what they do, as he says to Pentheus:

> You don't know what you're saying,
> Or what you're doing,
> Or who you are.

> (line 506; reading *pheis* for *zeis*)

Albert Henrichs argues that there is no Greek evidence for the concept of a suffering Dionysos until the later development of Orphism (Henrichs, 1984, p. 222, n. 35). But the whole meaning of Euripides' *Bakkhai* depends on the reality of Dionysos' unjust suffering at the hands of a violent Pentheus, who first has the god arrested and put in chains and then seizes his thyrsos, cuts off his hair, throws him in jail, and threatens to kill him. That Dionysos felt wounded by this violence is indicated by the fury of his retribution and by his words rejecting Agaue's plea for mercy:

> But didn't you abuse me, though I was born a god?

> (line 1347)

The Greek verb used here is a form of *hybrizein*, which means to abuse, outrage, or do violence to.

To some commentators, even this evidence is not convincing because the Greek gods were immortal and impervious to suffering by their very nature. But this argument overlooks the fact that Dionysos was a god-man, partaking both of the divine nature of his father and of the humanity of his mother. As such, he bridged the gap in his own person between the divine and the human and was capable of the experiences of both. This dual nature of Dionysos was underscored by the fact that in Greek myth he personally took part (in mortal disguise) in his own rites, the only Greek god to do so (Auger, p. 60).

Dionysos is also the god of wine and so gives that substance a sacramental character. To drink wine in the rites of Dionysos is to commune with the god and take his power and physical presence into one's body. And when wine is sprinkled at Greek sacrifices, the god himself is physically present on the altar, as Teiresias says:

> Being himself a god,
> He is poured on our altars as an offering to gods.

(lines 284–285)

Dionysos also miraculously supplies wine to those of his followers who are in need of something to drink, as the herdsman testifies of the Mad Women on Mt. Kithairon:

> Another took and sank her staff to earth,
> Through which the god sent forth a spring of wine.

(lines 706–707)

And regular festivals in ancient Greece celebrated Dionysos' miraculous powers of turning water into wine (Dodds, p. 164).

The description of Dionysos in Euripides' Bakkhai had an enormous impact on the popular Greek concept of the god. The play was disseminated just as Orphism, which was an outgrowth of Dionysian worship, was spreading and a few decades before the conquests of Alexander of Macedon. As a result, the play became a well-known fixture wherever Orphism gained new adherents or the conquests of Alexander spread the influence of Greek language and culture (Jeanmaire, p. 155).

Euripides' popular depiction of the god anticipated the Christian concept of Christ as God incarnate in human form, a man-god conceived by a mortal woman from the impregnating action of the Holy Spirit, just as it foreshadowed the image of the miracle-worker who turns water into wine and who is physically present in wine sacraments conducted in his honor. Christian mythology likewise had its Son of God appear in divine glory after the conclusion of his sufferings, just as Dionysos in Bakkhai revealed his true form after triumphing over his enemies. Miraculous birth, suffering deity in mortal form, sacramental value of wine, final manifestation in glory—all these essentials in the later myth of Jesus' divinity appeared in Euripides' *Bakkhai* nearly five hundred years before the Greek-writing authors of the New Testament composed their books.

The historical cult of Dionysos left many other legacies to Christian mythology. As a descendant of the Minoan bull-god, Dionysos was particularly associated with stables and shepherds. Hence the irony of Pentheus' locking up Dionysos in the stable—he puts the god right in his own element, thereby inadvertently increasing his power. Significantly, the first eyewitness report to Pentheus of the god's divine power comes from a herdsman, just as the first to learn of the divine birth of Christ from the angel of the Lord are shepherds in the field. In another allusion to the divine-stable motif, the infant Jesus is placed in a manger. The shepherd's crook, often seen in ancient paintings as a symbolic implement of the priests of Dionysos, later became the crosier of Christian bishops, who were themselves known in Latin as *pastores*, meaning "shepherds."

One of Dionysos' favorite animals was the mule. A famous ancient painting shows him riding in a triumphal procession on the back of a mule while satyrs hail him waving ivy branches (Kerényi, plate 54A). This scene calls to mind the description of Christ entering Jerusalem on the back of a donkey and greeted by throngs waving palm branches.

Dionysos, at least originally, was famous for his hostility to war and was hailed as the prince of peace. So, in writing about the myths of Dionysos in Arabia, a land not far from Judaea, Diodoros says:

> Moreover, he established festivals everywhere and created artistic contests and in general resolved the conflicts of nations and states, and in place of domestic strife and war he laid the grounds for concord and great peace. The coming of the god was proclaimed everywhere, and because he dealt fairly with everyone and contributed much to making civil life more humane, people thronged to meet him and greeted him with great joy.
>
> (Diodoros, 3, 64, 7–3, 65, 1)

This myth is echoed in Christ's role as the long-awaited Prince of Peace and the healer of nations. In addition, Dionysos is hailed as a savior and liberator. He liberates "the instinctive life in man from the bondage imposed on it by reason and social custom," as Christ was thought to liberate humanity from the burden of sin (Dodds, p. xx).

A number of ancient myths also tell of Dionysos' descent into the underworld and his successful return from the dead, although this tradition is not mentioned in Euripides' *Bakkhai*. It was common enough, however, to be lampooned in Aristophanes' play *Frogs* and later became a leading tenet of Orphism. Christianity echoed this motif in its dogma of the Son of God's descent to and return from Hell.

A number of anecdotes told about early Christian leaders also seem to be borrowed from stories about Dionysos. One such anecdote calls to mind Dionysos' arrest in *Bakkhai*. After King Pentheus orders his guards to hunt down and seize the new god, his henchman appears with Dionysos in chains. The henchman explains to the king that his prisoner was unexpectedly easy to catch and then adds that he has witnessed a miracle among the followers of the god who are already in jail:

> Besides, those Raving Women you detained,
> The ones you seized and bound in chains in jail,
> They're gone, escaped, skipping off along the meadows
> And calling on their raving god.
> Their chains by themselves fell off their feet,
> And the keys moved the door by a hand not human.

(lines 443–448)

Compare this scene to the story of the freeing of Peter from prison as told in the book of *Acts:*

> During the night . . . Peter was sleeping between two soldiers, fastened with double chains, while guards kept watch at the door. Suddenly an angel of the Lord stood nearby and bright light shone in the cell. He tapped Peter on the side and woke him. "Hurry, get up!" he said. With that, the chains dropped from Peter's wrists.

(*Acts* 12: 6–7; trans. by *New American Bible*)

In both cases, followers of a new god, unjustly imprisoned, are miraculously released from chains by the intervention of their god and hurry off to continue practicing his worship. A notable distinction between the two cases is the introduction of a disparaging remark about Jews by the Christian author. Although Peter himself was Jewish, the author of *Acts* has him say: "Now I know for certain that the Lord has sent his angel to rescue me from Herod's clutches and from all that the Jews hoped for" (ibid., 12:11).

Another well-known anecdote about a Christian leader also appears to be based on a scene in *Bakkhai*. The disguised Dionysos, seeking to dissuade Pentheus from his persecution of the new god's followers, says:

> Better to offer him [Dionysos] sacrifice
> Than get enraged and kick against the goads,
> A man against a god.

(lines 794–795)

Compare this scene to the description of how the new Christian god allegedly appeared to Saul (later Paul) on the road to Damascus and urged him to stop his persecutions of Christians: ". . . I saw a light more brilliant than the sun shining in the sky at midday. . . . All of us fell to the ground, and I heard a voice saying to me in Hebrew, 'Saul, Saul, why do you persecute me? It is hard for you to kick against the goad'" (*Acts*, 26:14; *New American Bible*).

The Greek expression used in these passages is *pros kentra laktizein* ("to kick against the goads"), probably an old proverb derived from farm life. Although *Bakkhai* and *Acts* use different grammatical forms of the verb, the meaning of the phrase is the same in both: to resist the new god is like kicking against the sharpened cattle prods used by herders, an appropriately coined metaphor in the case of a god, like Dionysos, who was originally a bull.

In subsequent years, Christians lost sight of the manner in which their predecessors had been influenced by Euripides' *Bakkhai* in forming their basic doctrines. In the fourth century A.D., during a temporary revival of interest in the Greek classics, Christian theologians rediscovered the play and, struck by parallels between it and the gospels, came to the conclusion that God had providentially used Euripides to help prepare the way for Christian belief.

Using Euripides' *Bakkhai* as a model, Gregory Nazianzos, bishop of Constantinople in the fourth century A.D., wrote a dramatic trilogy, *The Passion of Christ*, in which he recounted the life, death, and resurrection of Christ using a large number of lines taken directly out of Euripides' play (Tuilier, p. 58). Until fairly recently, scholars were under the mistaken impression that this *Passion of Christ* was written much later, in the twelfth century A.D. (Brambs, p. 18). However, André Tuilier has shown through linguistic and historical analysis that it was written earlier by Gregory (Tuilier, pp. 38, 58).

In his *Passion of Christ*, Gregory makes Christ, the Virgin Mary, and John (the so-called "Beloved Disciple") the three main characters, putting into their mouths lines once spoken by Dionysos, Agaue, and others in Euripides' *Bakkhai*. He also creates a chorus of women, in this case attendants of Mary, patterned after Euripides' chorus of Mad Women.

151

In a prologue to the play, Gregory explicitly acknowledges this debt to Euripides:

> Since you have listened to poems with a pious ear,
> And seek to hear now pious things but in a poet's way,
> Give heed: for now, as would Euripides,
> I shall tell of a passion that redeemed the world.
> Here you will find the mysteries fully told,
> For they come from the mouth of a maid and virgin mother
> And the initiate beloved of his teacher . . .
> And these then are my drama's roles:
> The Ever Holy Mother, the chaste initiate,
> And attendant maidens of the Mother of the Lord.

> (Gregory, prologue)

Gregory's play proved to be an early forerunner and the most sophisticated anticipation of a new literary genre, the medieval morality play. Through Gregory, Euripides continued to exert an oblique artistic influence on subsequent Christian art.

Although early Christian writers were heavily indebted to Euripides' *Bakkhai* and other myths pertaining to the cult of Dionysos, they did not blindly copy these elements but transformed them into something genuinely new. To understand the full significance of this transformation, we need to look at the general context of religious change taking place between the sixth century B.C. and the first century A.D. A number of crucial developments in this period served as steps along the religious path leading from Dionysos to Christ.

An early turning point in this change of religious mood was the appearance within the Dionysian religion of a new tradition: Orphism. In the sixth century B.C., an Athenian religious innovator by the name of Onomakritos composed a number of seemingly bizarre poems and pretended they were written by Orpheus, a legendary poet of great antiquity. Onomakritos claimed that Orpheus had lived even before the time of Homer and hence, he argued, his work was of greater authority than the Homeric poems. Onomakritos used this claim to validate some basic changes he introduced into Greek religion and in particular into the worship of Dionysos. In making these changes, Onomakritos did in fact draw on a number of variant, archaic myths that had not been incorporated into the Greek religious mainstream, but he gave them a new meaning. Onomakritos' creation at first seems quite odd, something apparently far removed from Christianity, yet it proved to be a key stepping-stone in transforming the myth of Dionysos into that of Christ. To understand how this was so, we need to look in some detail at his myths.

According to the poems written by Onomakritos and attributed to Orpheus, Dionysos was born to Persephone, the goddess of the underworld, after she had been seduced by Zeus. After his birth, Dionysos climbed up onto the throne of Zeus and acted as a sort of infant lord of the universe. Shortly thereafter, the Titans (a race of gods with wild, animal-like qualities) disguised themselves by smearing their bodies with chalk and plaster. They came to Dionysos in this guise and offered him a number of toys, including a mirror. While the infant god was engrossed with looking at his own image in the mirror, the Titans pulled out a knife and stabbed him to death. Next they cut him into small pieces, which they first boiled, then roasted on a skewer. After this cooking ritual, the Titans ate all the pieces of Dionysos except for his heart. In retaliation for this monstrous crime, Zeus blasted the Titans with his thunderbolt, and from their ashes the human race emerged. Dionysos himself was eventually regenerated from his uneaten heart.

Although writing a thousand years after the time of Onomakritos, the poet Nonnos was nevertheless deeply influenced by Orphism, and his work shows the lasting impact Onomakritos' speculations had on Greek and Roman mythology. Nonnos' own work, *The Epic of Dionysos*, incorporates his personal retelling of Onomakritos' legends along with many other stories about Dionysos and is one of our best sources for understanding the nature of the Orphic shift in Dionysian religion.

Nonnos calls the Orphic Dionysos by the name Zagreus, an old Cretan name often used for the god by the Orphics, and gives the following vivid account of his conception by Persephone and Zeus (the latter acting in the disguise of a snake):

> Zeus, once coiled in counterfeit form,
> Had wrapped like a playful snake
> Around her enticing curves,
> Then ravished Persephone's innocence,
> While she was then still young.
> . . .
> And gently he licked the maiden's body
> With his head for copulation,
> And from that heavenly serpentine union
> Persephone's womb swelled up with a growing child.
> And then she brought forth Zagreus,
> An offspring with horns,
> Who climbed on his own
> To the throne of Zeus in heaven
> And twirled in his little hands the lightning's fire.

Within the infant hands of a newborn master
The bolts of thunder became as toys.

(Nonnos, 5, 567–570; 6, 162–168)

Nonnos proceeds to relate, in his own baroque style, the Orphic story of the death of Dionysos:

As the Titans slashed him apart with a knife,
The god Dionysos clung to the last of his life
As a source from which to rebound,
Continuing to change his form,
As he passed from shape to shape.
At first he looked like a youthful and crafty Zeus,
Shaking his goat-skin shield,
Then like aging, thick-kneed Kronos,
When he makes the rain to pour.
Now like a baby of motley shape,
Now like a youth in fury
Whose first-blooming down
Casts a shade on the lines of his face.

(Nonnos, 6, 174–181)

In his final death throes, Dionysos appears in many animal forms, and finally as a bull:

And the spirited bull fell to the ground.
The butchers took turns with the knife
Slicing the god's bull-body.

(Nonnos, 16, 204–205)

To harmonize the newer Orphic myths with existing traditions, Nonnos has Zeus regenerate Dionysos in Thebes, which allows him to incorporate the now familiar story of Semele:

And Semele was reserved for a more glorious marriage,
For high-ruling Zeus already intended
To bring into being a new Dionysos,
A bull-shaped copy of the original god,
Since he missed his ill-fated son Zagreus,
The boy Persephone bore
From the bed of snake-like Zeus,
She who is wife of the black-robed, underworld Lord.

(Nonnos, 5, 561–566)

154

Although these Orphic myths may seem like incoherent hallucinations, they are quite significant when viewed in terms of their cultural context, as Marcel Detienne has cleverly shown in his work *Dionysos Slain*. For example, an important detail in the myth of the killing of Dionysos is the order of cooking of his body parts: they are boiled, then roasted. But as Detienne has discovered, the established process of cooking a sacrificial animal in Greece was the exact opposite: first parts of the animal are roasted, then other parts are boiled. After the animal is slain, the *splangkhna* (liver, lungs, spleen, kidneys, and heart) are roasted on a spit as an offering to the gods, who are thought to savor the aroma; next the *sarx* (remaining edible body parts) are boiled for human consumption (Detienne, 1979, pp. 74–75). In addition, a pretense is ordinarily maintained that the animal victim consents to its sacrifice: the priest leads it calmly to the altar, then pours grains of barley and wheat in its ear, causing it to shake its head, which is taken as a sign of consent (Detienne, 1979, p. 73). In the slaughter of Dionysos, not only is the order of sacrifice reversed, but the god vehemently resists his death.

The significance of the cooking details in the Orphic myth of Dionysos' sacrifice is that they are an attack, almost a parody, on the whole Greek concept of sacrifice. By reversing the expected order of cooking, by applying the process to an infant, and by having bloodthirsty Titans play the role of priest, this Orphic myth shocks conventional Greek notions about religious sacrifice. It is as if the myth were to say: "Change just a few details in our rites of sacrifice, and look how grizzly and absurd the whole business appears." The implication is that the rites as actually practiced *were* rather grizzly and absurd.

The Orphics believed that the worst moral offense was to kill, and as a result they rejected the eating of meat and the sacrifice of animals. Since the whole concept of the established Greek religion was based on sacrifice (in other words, the community was defined as those persons who shared in common sacrifices to the city's gods), the Orphics rejected both the established religion and its legitimizing function for the political establishment.

In the older version of Dionysian religion, the rite of *omophagia*, the eating of raw animal flesh, denied the established city-state religion by affirming participants' links with untamed animal behavior otherwise regarded as below human dignity. In a similar manner, Orphic vegetarianism denied the established religion by following a moral mandate held to be higher than conventional human behavior. The former practices "escape the human condition by way of bestiality, taking the lower route among the animals," while Orphism "proposes the same escape on

155

the divine side, taking the upper route" (Detienne, 1979, p. 88). Behind both these divergent Dionysian options lies a common bond: a sense of alienation from the world-view of the Greek politico-religious establishment.

Albert Henrichs has challenged Detienne's analysis of Orphism, claiming that the latter confuses myth and cult and ignores the many types of more traditional Dionysian sacrifice (Henrichs, 1984, pp. 210–211). But as discussed in chapter 1, Henrichs overstates the distinction between myth and cult, virtually ignoring the former as a guide to the meaning of Greek religion. The Orphics devised a new myth because they had a new message, and Detienne correctly points out how elements in this new myth referred to and inverted existing practices. The coexistence of more traditional practices in the religion of Dionysos—both before and after Orphism—does not invalidate Detienne's argument. To the Greeks themselves, judging by their own words, the features that were most characteristic of Dionysian practices are the ones discussed by Detienne.

Some scholars deny the very existence of Orphism as a distinct religious tradition, saying that at most there existed only a scattered body of speculative writings without rituals and that some of the most important representations—such as the killing of Dionysos—did not develop until much later. So, for example, Albert Henrichs says that the earliest use of the term *hoi Orphikoi* ("the Orphics") did not occur until 150 B.C. (Henrichs, 1977, p. 21). But Henrichs' argument underestimates the importance of the fact that Plato, writing much earlier in the fourth century B.C., speaks of *hoi amphi Orphea* ("the followers of Orpheus"). The words *hoi amphi*, when followed by a personal name, are the standard Greek phrase used to indicate an established religious or philosophical school (see *amphi* in Liddell-Scott-Jones). So, for example, the school of the Sophist Protagoras was called *hoi amphi Protagoran* (*loc. cit.*). In speaking of "the followers of Orpheus," Plato clearly implies that they were an established group with well-defined beliefs. He even contrasts their view of the nature of the body to that of a different group who, making a pun in Greek, called the body (*soma*) a tomb (*sema*): "But it seems to me that the followers of Orpheus prefer just the name 'body' [*soma*, not *sema*], saying that the soul is being punished for whatever misdeeds were committed, and it has the body as a restraint, in the manner of a prison . . ." (Plato, *Kratylos*, 400C). Nowhere in this passage does Plato imply that the Orphics had no rites; he merely limits himself to a discussion of their beliefs because of the philosophical thrust of his own book.

Several early sources mention the use of both books and rites in Orphism. For example, in Euripides' play *Hippolytos*, Theseus makes Hippolytos into a pretended Orphic and uses the occasion to denounce the religion:

> Well, then, make your boasts
> And ply your trade in meatless foods.
> Take Orpheus as your lord
> And hold your Bakkhic revels.
> Revere your scripture's vapors.
> I'm on to you!
> I say to all in public,
> Beware such men.
> They hunt their prey with holy books,
> Scheming what is shameful.

> (Euripides, *Hippolytos*, 952–957)

This passage implies that Orphics existed, practiced vegetarianism, held rituals of an ecstatic nature *(bakkheue)*, revered a set of scriptures, and made converts.

Although writing later, Plutarch mentions that Philip and Olympias, the parents of Alexander the Conqueror, first met when they were both initiated into an Orphic cult in Samothrace in the North. As noted in chapter 1, Euripides imples in his *Bakkhai* that the rites of Dionysos were practiced with greater freedom in the North. Plutarch observes that ". . . all the women of the area have long been under the sway of the Orphics and the secret rites of Dionysos and known by the names of *Klodones* and *Mimallones* and engage in practices like those of the Edonian women and the Thracian women around Mt. Haimos (Plutarch, *Lives*, *Alexander*, 2, 7–8).

Plutarch adds that snake handling was a part of the cult's practices, as shown by this description of Alexander's mother: "She would drag out large tamed snakes for the band of celebrants, and the snakes would often crawl out of the ivy and the ritual winnowing baskets and curl around their wands and garlands, thus scaring off their husbands" (Plutarch, *Lives*, *Alexander*, 2, 9).

Later Greek commentators themselves agreed that the Orphics were a long-established religious tradition with definite beliefs and practices. Pausanias, the second-century A.D. traveler who personally investigated the religious practices of many different countries, said concerning the founder of Orphism: "Onomakritos took the name of the Titans from Homer and invented rites for Dionysos and fabricated the story that the

157

Titans by their own hands were the cause of Dionysos' suffering" (Pausanias, 8, 37, 5).

The notion that the Orphics had beliefs but not rituals is unlikely on the face of it. Contrary to certain modern writers, the Greeks of the classical period rarely if ever made a sharp distinction between myth and rite, since they were but two different expressions of the life of the cult. In addition, Orphic theology placed a strong emphasis on the need for personal purification. Having developed such a view, the Orphics would have been highly illogical had they not practiced at least some kind of purification rite. The notion of Larry Alderink that Orphism is merely "a mood or a spirit which animates selected literary texts" (Alderink, p. 19) is refuted by Plato, who explicitly says in *The Republic* (364E) that the Orphics used their books in ritual practices.

The reason that Orphism has confused some recent commentators is that it was an *incipient* religion in the classical period. It was gestating in the context of the established Dionysian religion in the same way that Christianity in the first century A.D. was born in the context of established Judaism. But just as it would be wrong to dismiss incipient Christianity as a religion, so it would be wrong to dismiss the Orphism of this period.

Eventually Orphism established itself over large areas: recent discoveries of Orphic scripture, recorded on thin gold sheets, have been reported in Italy, Thessaly, and Crete (Henrichs, 1982, p. 154).

The Orphics changed Dionysian religion by introducing the concept of moral purification as the essence of spirituality. They argued that human beings were originally descended from the Titans who had killed and eaten Dionysos. Hence human nature was twofold—a divine element inherited from the eaten flesh of Dionysos and a wild, animal-like element from the Titans. By participating in the Orphic life—reading their scriptures, practicing their rites, abstaining from meat and acts of violence—followers strengthened and purified the divine element, allowing it to gain mastery over the Titanic element in their souls (Detienne, 1979, p. 83).

The Orphics changed Dionysos himself by emphasizing his role as the lord who conquers death. Although certain myths from Greece and elsewhere had depicted Dionysos as the one who returns from the dead, such a belief was not of overriding importance in the mainstream of Greek Dionysian religion in the earlier, classical era. Later, Orphics made Dionysos' return from the dead the central motif of their religion.

The Orphics, who were still on the religious fringe at the time, probably attributed their scriptures to Orpheus because of his own famous descent to and return from the underworld to retrieve his dead Eurydike. Moreover, Persephone, the mother of Dionysos in Orphic accounts, was the Queen of the Dead and the wife of Hades. Each year she moved back and forth between the living and the dead, spending winter with her husband in the underworld and the other seasons with her mother Demeter above, on the earth. By emphasizing Dionysos' connections to Persephone in the context of poems attributed to Orpheus, the Orphics made their notion of Dionysos' own return from the underworld seem better grounded in traditional Greek myths.

The Orphics' belief in Dionysos' triumph over death was connected to their own hope for an afterlife. By purifying the divine element in their souls, they hoped to attain a lasting, divinelike life with their lord who had conquered death.

The Orphics eventually changed the worship of Dionysos into a male-dominated religion. Originally, as we have seen, the most ancient antecedents of Dionysianism probably existed as separate men's and women's religious circles, each worshiping a god of the same sex. With the subsequent decline in the status of women, the Mad Women in historical times ended up worshiping Dionysos. Although a male god, he was known for his effeminacy, homosexuality, and transvestism, as were his circles of male followers. Eventually men joined the women's circles themselves (as did Kadmos and Teiresias in Euripides' *Bakkhai*), and with the advent of Orphism finally took control. Marcel Detienne has gone so far as to believe that women were excluded from Orphic rites (Detienne, 1979, p. 92, n. 138); but he is mistaken here, as indicated by the passage about Alexander's mother quoted earlier from Plutarch.

By introducing these changes into the religion of Dionysos, the Orphics were moving in the direction of creating a salvation religion. As we have seen, previous myths about Dionysos stressed the notion of the suffering of the Son of God who was born from the union of a mortal woman and the Father God. To this notion Orphism now added the concepts of the return of the Son of God from the dead and the hope of a life to come. In addition, Orphism changed the purpose of religion from the collective celebration of the joys of life to purification of the soul, introduced the principle of the priority of written scripture as the defining trait of religion, and greatly reduced the leadership role of women. Orphism also anticipated the myth of original sin in its notion that all human beings were descended from the violence-prone Titans. All of these innovations were moving in accordance with the spirit of the times—an ever greater emphasis on asceticism and masculinism in the Greco-Roman world—and were clearly another major step in the direction of Christianity.

Despite these changes, however, the Orphics still retained a significant imprint from the former Dionysian religion: like their predecessors, they continued to see an essential connection between sexuality and religion. The proof of this connection is the abundance of sexual imagery found both in their myths and in visual depictions influenced by Orphism. As mentioned previously, openly sexual themes, including themes of homosexuality, occur on many elaborately carved stone coffins in the Roman period (Kerényi, plates 140–142). Their owners, well-to-do people influenced by Orphic beliefs, looked forward to a happy afterlife that included sexual practices from this life. In addition, Phanes, a deity prominent in some Orphic creation myths, was depicted as a hermaphrodite.

The later Orphics made a prominent use of sexual artifacts in their rituals, the most famous of which was the *likhnon,* a fruit-filled winnowing basket with a large phallus sticking up out of its center. This device was *not* used here principally as a symbol of the fruitfulness of the earth, but as a symbol of Dionysos' power to provide his followers with a joyous afterlife: "The little we know about the ideas of the Dionysiac mysteries of the Roman age shows no trace of a vegetation god; they were concerned with the ascent of Dionysos from the Underworld and they looked after the burials of their members" (Nilsson, 1957, p. 44).

In short, the purification that Orphics required in this life did not require abandoning commonly established sexual practices. But sexual imagery was being used less as a celebration of sex itself and more as a metaphorical symbol, as Orphism shed its earlier Dionysian character and moved in the direction of becoming a salvation religion.

Orphism was only the most prominent example of a number of salvation religions that rose to positions of influence in the Roman Empire. Another, the Eleusinian mysteries of the goddesses Demeter and Persephone, showed a similar shift away from celebrating the agrarian world-view and toward the anticipation, through secret purification rituals, of a happy existence in the life to come. A third important example, because of its later influence on Christianity, was Mithraism, which spread rapidly in the Roman army in the first and second centuries A.D. Originating in the empire's eastern provinces, this religion was centered on the god Mithra, whose birthday was celebrated every year on the winter solstice (which, due to the precession of the equinoxes, occurred in Roman times on December twenty-fifth). Mithra may originally have been a horned god, because the supreme sacrament in his mysteries was the slaughter of a bull on top of an elevated grating. His devotees stood beneath the grating and were thought to be purified by being splashed in the bull's blood. Not only did Mithraism bequeath December twenty-fifth to Christians as the traditional birthday of their god, but also the motif, given a metaphorical twist by Christianity, of being "washed in the blood of the lamb." In contrast to the annually dying and resurrecting vegetation gods, Mithra broke through the birth-death cycle and would never die again; hence he was called *invictus* ("invincible") (Bianchi, pp. 11–12).

In the first and second centuries A.D., these various salvation religions mutually influenced each other. Many myths and rites were traded back and forth between them, with the result that their lines of demarcation were blurred.

When Jesus of Nazareth was born into Roman-controlled Judea in the latter part of the first century B.C., a well-defined mythological matrix existed in classical civilization. This matrix had emerged from the old agrarian religion of Dionysos (especially as articulated in Euripides' *Bakkhai*) and had been further developed by the Orphics. Together with influences from other pagan salvation religions, this matrix stamped on the consciousness of the age a number of variations of the following standard theme: the Son of God has been born from the union of the Father God and a mortal woman; he has come as a liberator of the human race; he has died and risen from the dead; the purpose of religion is to cleanse oneself from the moral imperfection, inherent and otherwise, of the human condition; the mechanism for this moral cleansing is participation in certain sacraments; the effect of this cleansing is a continued life after physical death.

In addition to this mythological matrix, a strongly ascetic and authoritarian tradition emerged from the writings of the Athenian philosopher Plato. These ideas, together with certain Stoic notions, were absorbed and modified by Philo Judaeus, the greatest Jewish philosopher of classical antiquity, who flourished in the early part of the first century A.D. and who wrote in Greek. Philo developed and gave classic expression to the doctrine of "the Logos," by which term he meant, alternatively, God's mind, the totality of God's creative powers, the intelligible structure of the universe, and the means whereby God created the world (Randall, p. 115). Philo developed this doctrine in the context of a long-standing debate, ultimately derived from Plato, as to

161

the nature of the relationship between God, the rational order of the universe as perceived by human intellect, and the material world. To Philo, the rational order of the universe was causative of the material world and identical with God's mind. This entity—God's mind as world order—he called the Logos.

A third crucial pre-existing factor that influenced popular beliefs came from Jewish history and religion. The centuries prior to Jesus' birth had seen Alexander conquer Judea, the Greek ruler Antiokhos Epiphanes occupy the Temple at Jerusalem and install an altar to Zeus, the Jews revolt under the leadership of Judas Maccabeus, the Jewish King Hyrcanos rebuild the Jewish state, the Roman general Pompey intervene after a Jewish civil war, the Roman general Anthony conquer the eastern Mediterranean, including Judea, and Augustus Caesar consolidate Roman control through his client king, Herod. After the death of the latter, Augustus reduced Judea to the status of a province ruled by a Roman governor.

As a result of the Roman occupation, many Jews looked back to previous revolts and fervently hoped for the coming of the Messiah who would be their political and religious liberator, throwing off the Roman yoke and re-establishing an autonomous Jewish state.

These three factors—the Dionysian matrix, Philo's platonic conception of the Logos, and the Jewish expectation of a Messiah—all helped determine how Jesus was perceived. The first two in particular became all the more influential the further removed people were from actually knowing Jesus.

Some twenty to sixty years after the death of Jesus of Nazareth, a number of religious writers composed a series of books claiming that it was Jesus—not Dionysos or Zagreus or Mithra—who was the incarnate Son of God and that he was born, died, and rose again to save humankind from sin. Their works have come down to us under the name of the New Testament.

Although many Christians of the present day still believe that the authors of the New Testament were close personal associates of Jesus, a long history of biblical scholarship has proven otherwise. *None* of the writers of the New Testament knew Jesus personally. Most New Testament authors do not even claim to have been associates of Jesus. The few who do have been shown to use the apostles' names falsely. Furthermore, all the writers of the New Testament wrote in Greek, while Jesus and his associates were Jews who spoke Aramaic.

The four gospels and the letters of Paul of Tarsus constitute the core of the New Testament. Of these, the four gospels were all originally published anonymously, and it was not until approximiately 200 A.D., 170 years after the death of Jesus, that church tradition assigned them to certain specific authors (Aland, p. 5). The four gospels originally appeared along with a number of other gospels, each with a competing account of Jesus' life and teaching, and were not widely reckoned as more authoritative than the rest until this same date of approximately 200 A.D. (Childs, p. 18). Most of the competing gospels have not survived.

Of the four gospels, three (those attributed to Matthew, Mark, and Luke) purport to give a historical account of Jesus' life. The oldest is Mark, written sometime after 70 A.D., at least forty years after the death of Jesus, by someone who never knew him, and aimed at a non-Jewish audience. Most of the historical account of Jesus' life in the other gospels is borrowed directly or indirectly from Mark or from another anonymous source, which has not survived, called "Q" (from German *Quelle*, meaning "source"), which apparently was a record of Jesus' sayings, not an account of his life (Tyson, p. 154). Mark is thus the principal historical source for all subsequent knowledge of the facts of Jesus' life.

Biblical scholars have long noted that a curious anomaly in Mark is picked up and reflected in the other gospels. Although the author sincerely believes that Jesus is the Messiah and writes to convince others of the same, he nonetheless repeatedly mentions incidents implying that Jesus himself did not want people to think so. Mark also reports a number of interesting anecdotes concerning Jesus: his family thought he was insane; both he and his followers were sometimes unable to heal people; he was crucified with a recently arrested group of political subversives; his body disappeared from his tomb a few days after his burial. On the latter point, Mark reports that several women found Jesus' tomb empty and that a young man dressed in white told them that he had risen. Despite this young man's affirmation, however, it is a remarkable fact that Mark contains *no* account of any appearances of the risen Jesus. His gospel ends with the women leaving the tomb in fright. The account of Jesus' risen appearances that is printed in most modern editions of Mark is now known to be a later addition by unknown persons who felt uneasy with the gospel's actual ending (Childs, pp. 92–93).

In view of these and numerous other textual considerations, many independent biblical scholars have concluded that Jesus himself never claimed to be the Messiah, the Son of God, or any other special type of being:

These gospels produce an overwhelming impression that although Christians were convinced that Jesus was the Messiah, he was not remembered as having taught this about himself. In respect to the claims of Jesus about himself there is a dissimilarity between him and early Christianity.

(Tyson, p. 252)

The letters of Paul of Tarsus, which constitute the second major part of the New Testament, began to appear ten to twenty years after the death of Jesus and, in fact, created the basis of Christian theology (some were actually written by followers of Paul). This same Paul never knew Jesus when he lived, was originally an opponent of Jesus' followers, became a Christian only after claiming to have had a miraculous vision of Christ, spent most of his time trying to make converts in lands outside of Jesus' homeland, and aroused hostility on the part of Jesus' immediate successors in Jerusalem. Moreover, his writings contain only a few references to the actual sayings of Jesus and are mostly concerned to show what Paul believed about Jesus, not what Jesus believed about God or religion. Hence they are of little value in providing information about the historical Jesus.

The one exception to this distance of the New Testament from Jesus' life and teachings is the letter commonly attributed to James (actually Jacob). Although debate continues on the actual date of James, most scholars agree that the letter was produced by the small circle of followers that Jesus personally founded in Jerusalem; hence tradition claimed that it was written by Jacob, Jesus' brother, who led Jesus' followers after his crucifixion. Textual analysis shows that James is similar to "Q," the early anonymous source used by several of the gospels (Childs, p. 477).

The short letter of James is remarkable in that it contains no evidence for a belief on the part of its author in the resurrection of Jesus or in Jesus as the redemptive Son of God. In fact, it is not concerned with teachings *about* Jesus at all but with the teachings *of* Jesus. As they appear in James, these teachings can be summarized as follows: the rich are oppressors, and their power and wealth will pass away; forgiveness promotes healing; faith in God can only be proved by acting with love and justice toward other human beings. Most scholars also detect in James a veiled rejection of the doctrines of Paul.

The nontheological thrust of James has long been a bone in the throat of dogmatic Christian theologians. Martin Luther thought that it was so inconsistent with the concept of a redeeming faith in Christ that he wanted to eliminate it from the Bible. Ironically, it probably reflects

164

the actual beliefs of the earliest Christian community better than any other surviving document.

How did it happen that, with the possible exception of the letter of James, no account has survived from the immediate circle of followers founded by Jesus in Jerusalem? The answer, which was to have staggering consequences for the future development of Christianity, lies in a fluke of history. In 70 A.D., after a Jewish rebellion, Roman troops led by their general Titus (soon to become emperor) entered Jerusalem and destroyed both the city and the temple. Again, in 135 A.D., after another Jewish rebellion in the partially restored Jerusalem, Roman troops entered and sacked the city and forever banished all Jews from living there.

As a result of these two catastrophes, members of the original community founded by Jesus were either killed or scattered. Although a later tradition claimed that some escaped to the Greek city of Pella, this story is a confusion of the actual events and incorrect (Lüdemann, p. 170ff). In fact, after the events in Jerusalem, the influence of Jesus' original circle of followers forever came to an end.

As Gerd Lüdemann has correctly pointed out, the death of the first-generation followers of Jesus, followed by the absence of any organizational continuity from them, created an identity crisis for early Christianity and a historical gap that could not be bridged:

> Who and what Christian community can lay claim to be the true successor of the apostles? . . . More generally, the whole body of pseudonymous writings in the New Testament tried to bridge the gap between the present and apostolic times by using the name of one of the apostles.

> (Lüdemann, p. 172)

The historical gap following the death of Jesus' original followers made it easy for subsequent writers to claim almost anything they wanted to about Jesus. None of his contemporaries were left who could challenge such new claims.

An example of how far some writers were prepared to go can be seen in the fourth gospel, falsely attributed to John, an early associate of Jesus. This gospel, actually the work of several hands, begins by identifying Jesus with "the Logos" of Philo, as discussed earlier:

> In the beginning was the Logos,
> And the Logos belonged to God,
> And the Logos was God . . .
> And the Logos became flesh
> And lived among us . . .

> (John, 1:1–14)

In this passage, translators usually render "Logos" as "Word," a practice that stems from early Latin translations of the gospel. Modern translations have continued this tradition because it stresses continuity with the concept of the creative Word of God as it appears in the Old Testament book of Genesis. This concept is indeed echoed in the opening lines of the fourth gospel, but to translate "Logos" by "Word" obscures much of its meaning, since it refers to and modifies the complex Platonic and Stoic concept of Logos as developed by Philo. To convey the full implications of the opening lines of the fourth gospel, they should probably be translated by something like the following: "In the beginning was the Cosmic Order that is the pattern for the world's creation. The Order was a part of God, and the Order was God . . . The Cosmic Order became flesh and lived among us . . ."

The author of the fourth gospel is here challenging other Platonists who had argued that the Cosmic Order (the rational structure of the universe) is a mere creation and not part of the divine nature. In contrast to this view, he maintains that the Cosmic Order existed as a part of God before the creation of the world and that Jesus is the savior of that world because he is its very order of existence made flesh.

However the word Logos is to be translated, the opening lines of the fourth gospel show the great extent to which speculation about the role and identity of Jesus had departed from the actual facts of his life. Most of Jesus' listeners were poor, uneducated people who knew little or nothing about the abstract debates of Greek philosophers. Jesus did not speak to them in Greek but Aramaic, not in abstractions, but in parables, not with quotations from Plato or Philo, but with stories from the Old Testament and their own daily lives.

To get a concrete idea of how far removed the New Testament is from Jesus, imagine for a moment that after Mohandas Gandhi died in India in 1948 all his immediate followers were wiped out and that nothing of his own writings survived. Then imagine that in 1968 an Englishman by the name of Paul, who never knew him, began circulating letters claiming that Gandhi had risen from the dead and was the world's savior from sin. Next imagine that after 1988 a number of conflicting short stories appeared out of London, written anonymously by people who likewise had never known Gandhi, claiming that he was the Son-of-God, born from a virgin. Finally, imagine that around the year 2118 four of these stories were declared to be the gospel truth for all future beliefs about Gandhi. Imagine this process, and you will be close to visualizing the emergence of early Christian beliefs about Jesus.

Some traditional Christians still insist that there is no parallel between their concept of Christ and the Son-of-God motif that emerged out of the ancient salvation religions. They claim that a crucial difference between the two is that the story of Christ is historical whereas the stories about Dionysos or Zagreus or Mithra are purely mythical. George Ring insists on this difference, saying:

> Reliable testimony establishes the Savior's death and corporal resurrection in the same class of historical facts as, let us say, the revolt of the thirteen colonies from the rule of Great Britain. The personalities and adventures of Dionysos Zagreus and his compeers are the spawn of mythological fancy.

> (Ring, p. 228)

The fallacy of Ring's argument is that he has confused evidence pertaining to the existence of the historical Jesus with subsequent mythological claims made about the significance of Jesus' life. Biblical scholarship has indeed shown that a religious reformer named Jesus most probably lived and taught in Judea and was crucified by the Romans. But this same biblical scholarship has also shown something else: the claim that Jesus was the resurrected Son of God is not based on evidence from his immediate circle of followers but on the later beliefs of people who never knew him. In effect, the writers of the New Testament took and modified existing salvation theology about the Son of God and applied it to the historical Jesus of Nazareth. Of course, one can still accept and believe in traditional Christian teachings as a matter of faith, on the grounds that the writers of the New Testament were divinely inspired in making this application. But one cannot claim, as George Ring does, that such beliefs are historical in the sense that conclusions about the thirteen colonies are.

The concept of Christ that emerged a generation after the death of the historical Jesus was molded by mythological and philosophical traditions that had nothing to do with his life, applied by people who never knew him, recorded in a language he never used. The rapidity with which these traditions attached themselves, like so many barnacles, to his name reveals a pervasive and deep-seated craving of many people in Greco-Roman civilization: they wanted a divine force to descend from the sky and be their savior.

The craving of people of that epoch for a savior was accompanied by a thoroughgoing alienation from their own civilization. The intensity of both such a craving and such an alienation increased perceptibly among inhabitants of the eastern Mediterranean after the conquests of Alexander and his successors. Democratic government and political independence disappeared, while dynastic, authoritarian states were everywhere established in their place. After a period of protracted and bloody war, the power of the Greek dynasts who succeeded Alexander was supplanted by that of the Senate and People of Rome. Again after a period of convulsive civil war, the power of the ruling oligarchs within Rome passed into the hands of one man, the emperor.

Under the rule of the Roman emperors, freedom of speech was curtailed, and meaningful political involvements disappeared. The arts deteriorated into fadish imitations; creative scholarship degenerated into specialized technical application; and the economy became increasingly dependent on consumption by the huge military establishment and the emperor's retinue. The result was that people no longer had a sense of control, direction, or purpose to their lives. Increasingly they began to fantasize about a more rewarding life in the afterworld. In the late classical period, with the onset of the early Middle Ages, the physical world itself seemed to be crumbling. Alienated and powerless, people yearned for a Son of God who would come to give their lives meaning and save them. The dreadful irony is that when at last they thought he had come, when they gave their allegiance to those who acted in his name, they only discovered with the passage of time that they had succeeded in trading a political suffocation for one that was ecclesiastical.

Not everything reported of Jesus of Nazareth in the gospels arose from external mythologies. If we peel away accretions due to the longing of the Jews for the Messiah, the Platonists for the Logos, the adherents of mystery religions for the Son of God, a few glimpses remain of something quite extraordinary. We find a man who teaches that the way to fulfill our religious obligations is by loving each other as our own selves; that the kingdom of God is neither a political entity nor a future life but a state of mind; that the wealthy can only be spiritually fulfilled by giving their wealth to the poor; that we can heal ourselves through faith, forgiveness, and prayer. We find a man who withdraws with embarrassment and anger when people hail him as the Messiah, who tells people who believe he has cured them that their own faith is the cause, and who organizes his own close followers into a circle where all resources are shared in common. Beyond these few features, we know very little else, except that he was executed as a religious and political subversive.

It should at once be obvious that no coercive civilization—whether that of ancient Greeks and Romans, medieval Christians, or modern capitalists and communists—could long survive if such values became widespread. Since the inception of the patriarchal revolution, all social and political order has been based on institutionalized violence: the police within the state, the army without. Likewise all economies have been based on exploitation: conqueror over captive slaves; lord of the land over serfs; capitalist corporation or socialist state over workers. None of these political and economic orders can be maintained without large numbers of people who are motivated to compete, dominate, fight, and kill. To live by love would mean to refuse to perform these socially necessary functions. Under such conditions, no privileged hierarchy—whether of state or church or party or corporation—would be able to maintain its privileges or power. They would all be swept aside.

The establishment of Jesus' time no doubt sensed on some level the revolutionary implications of his teachings, and that was probably one reason he aroused such hostility both from the Torah-bound Jewish fundamentalists and the sedition-fearing Roman conquerors. A similar awareness on the part of an increasingly hierarchical Christian church was likewise an incentive for them to play down the scanty remnants of his teachings on love and emphasize instead the abstract theological thinking of Paul and the early church fathers. It has always been so very convenient for the church's own status, power, and wealth to proclaim as the central tenet of Christianity the doctrine that Christ is the incarnate Son of God who died to redeem humanity from sin. What would have become of them over the ages if they uncompromisingly defined themselves by the definition Jesus gave: "Go and give all that you have to the poor, and come and follow me"?

The immensely convoluted and gilded theology that the church has contrived to place around the person of Jesus seems almost like a way of protecting itself from the explosive implications of what were probably his most genuine teachings. And so the typical Christian concept of him has become like one of those overwrought Byzantine icons: so much intricate peripheral filigree that one easily overlooks the nearly smothered center face.

The merit of Jesus' teaching was that it saw through the dominant conventional pretenses of his day, both political and religious, both Jewish and non-Jewish, and was inspired by a genuine and eloquently stated compassion for other human beings. The failure of his teaching was the failure of all philosophies that hope to transform the world by sincerity of feeling alone: they are unable to transform themselves into lasting political and economic realities. The initial power of such philosophies is usually limited to small groups of founders who inspire by personal example. After the death of the founders, the movement is either wiped out or else co-opted and turned into something utterly alien to what was originally intended. Perhaps Jesus himself sensed this failure. The gospel attributed to Mark reports that at the time of his crucifixion he made only one statement, and that right before he died. The author quotes his words here in Aramaic, the longest of the very rare instances in the New Testament where Jesus is actually heard in his own language: "And at about mid-afternoon Jesus cried out with a loud voice, *Eloi, Eloi, lama sabakhthanei,* which means in translation, 'My God, my God, why have you abandoned me?'" (Mark, 15:34).

The death that Jesus suffered on the cross was of his body. His spiritual crucifixion was yet to come: the mangling of his teachings by the church that emerged in his name. Initially his personal disciples continued the traditions that he founded, centering themselves in the city of Jerusalem, but soon tensions emerged between them and the entourage of Paul of Tarsus, who was turning Jesus' teachings into a salvation religion and rapidly making many non-Jewish converts. As we have seen, as a result of persistent political resistance by the Jews, Roman troops destroyed Jerusalem in 70 A.D., and from that date all significant influence from the original followers of Jesus came to an end, never to be revived. Henceforth all theological developments in Christianity would be the outgrowth of the thinking of Paul and the Greek-writing authors of the New Testament.

The new church theology latched onto and modified the Dionysian matrix as handed down by Orphism and the salvation religions. Jesus was declared to be the Jewish Messiah, the incarnate Logos, and the Son of God, all in one. The Orphic concept of the Titanic taint in human nature was magnified into the doctrine of original sin: to be born human was to be born in sin; only by belief in the divinity of Christ could one be redeemed from this sin.

The concept of moral purification was greatly expanded: to abstain from violence was no longer enough; one must also renounce the flesh as such (in other words, view all sensuality as a potential trap set by the Devil). The concept of the afterlife was likewise purged of sensuality: no more baroque Orphic fantasies of lovely revels and perfect bodies. Heaven now meant the beatific vision of God in his glory. Christians also invented the concept of Hell as a place of eternal torture and punishment for those who rejected Christian beliefs and lifestyles. Hence they found themselves in the awkward position of saying both that God is love (a remnant of Jesus' beliefs) and that God intends to damn the great majority of the human race to eternal torture.

In a striking departure from the Dionysian tradition, Christians made a sharp distinction between sexual practices and religious rites. From now on, sex had the taint of the Devil and would not be allowed in acts

170

of worship, as had been the case in the rites of the old agrarian paganism. This cleavage between religion and sex had enormous historical repercussions, especially in regard to the church's attitudes toward lesbianism and male homosexuality. The main reason Paul of Tarsus so trenchantly condemns same-sex love is its association in his mind with the old pagan religious rites, where, as we have seen, it had a well-established role. In his letter to the Romans he says that homosexuality is a curse that God inflicts on people because of their participation in such rites:

> They [the pagans] exchanged the glory of the immortal God for images representing mortal man, birds, beasts, and snakes. In consequence, God delivered them up in their lusts to unclean practices. . . . Their women exchanged natural intercourse for unnatural, and the men gave up natural intercourse with women and burned with lust for one another.
>
> (Romans 1:23–27, trans. by *New American Bible*)

Christian theology reenforced the decline in the status of women. In the old rites of Dionysos, women were the principle leaders. In the newer rites as practiced by Orphism, men became the leaders, although women still had significant functions. Paul argues that in Christianity women must be completely eliminated from any leadership or teaching roles:

> A woman must listen in silence and be completely submissive. I do not permit a woman to act as teacher, or in any way to have authority over a man; she must be quiet. For Adam was created first, Eve afterward; moreover, it was not Adam who was deceived but the woman. It was she who was led astray and fell into sin. She will be saved through child-bearing, provided she continues in faith and love and holiness—her chastity, of course, being taken for granted.
>
> (Tim. 1: 11–15, trans. by *New American Bible*)

In other words, women must keep their mouths shut and continue having babies, an extraordinary change in values from the religion of the original Mad Women.

Christianity intensified the tendency toward hierarchical structure that first appeared in Orphism and the later mystery religions. In the earliest period in Judea, Christians formed loose communal groups where organizational power and worldly possessions were shared in common. After the destruction of Jerusalem and the spread of Paul's new version of the religion, hierarchies began to appear. By the fourth century A.D.,

171

when Christianity became the state religion of the Roman Empire, the church had become a rigidly hierarchical corporate body possessed of enormous wealth and political influence. Corresponding to the church's growing hierarchical structure, power, and wealth was its new, higher theological status: whereas previously it had been sufficient for Christians to believe in the divine mission of Christ, it now became equally important to believe in the divine mission of the church as a corporate body. Grace may have been earned for humanity by Christ's sacrifice, but it could only be dispensed at the hands of the properly consecrated (and therefore controlled) corporate officials of Mother Church. This new emphasis in church theology was eventually captured in the famous phrase *Extra ecclesia non est salus*, "Outside of the church there is no salvation."

The Christian religion made a decisive break from the rural world and its values and hence from the historical source of the rites of Dionysos and the later mystery religions. From the very first days of its spread outside of Judea, it was an urban religion. In the time of Paul, it drew most of its new converts from the lower middle classes of eastern Mediterranean port cities (Evans, p. 42). Eventually, after the period of its persecutions, the religion became fashionable, and the urban wealthy converted in large numbers. Throughout this period it maintained a suspicious attitude toward the rural poor, especially rural slaves, who continued to resist the new religion and practice various forms of the old agrarian paganism. So associated with non-Christian rituals did these rural people become that the word for pagan in several European languages is derived from the Latin word *paganus*, which means "country dweller."

As mentioned previously, Christians took the physical traits of the agrarian horned god and attributed them to the Devil, where they have persisted to this day. In a sense, therefore, the Christian concept of the Devil is a survival of the old horned god, but conceived as a sinister being. Likewise the Christian concept of Christ was a development and transformation of the figure of the suffering Son of God as it had been developed in the Dionysian tradition. Hence two major personages in Christian mythology both owe their genesis to the male deity of the old religion of the agrarian underclasses (as suggested earlier in this century by Wilfred Schoff's article "Tammuz, Pan and Christ"). In effect, Christians took the last version of Dionysos as it was developed by paganism and split it in two, giving the "good" traits to their concept of Christ and the "bad" traits to their concept of the Devil. This split reflected in turn their view that the world was the scene of a cosmic struggle between pure good and pure evil.

The net effect of all these changes was a revolutionary shift in Western religious consciousness. Christians finally cut themselves off from nature-oriented sensibilities and relegated sex and women to an inferior status. The religious experience itself—so elusive of control and definition and even wild and subversive in the Dionysian tradition—was now safely channeled and controlled through the sacraments of a hierarchical, authoritarian, male-dominated church.

After Christianity became the dominant religion of Europe, the values and practices that the church forbade continued to live on but underground in the countryside. After the great persecution of "heretics" and "witches" in the Middle Ages and Renaissance, even the underground virtually disappeared. The magnificent religious tradition of Dionysos, once a dominant spiritual sensibility in Mediterranean and European civilizations and the catalyst for so much amazing cultural innovation, had passed from the earth.

VIII

DIONYSOS
AND
US

○

THE patriarchal revolution of Europe's Bronze and Iron Ages, later reenforced by Christianity's revolutionary shift in values, is mirrored in similar historical developments in many other places on the globe (Daniélou, Ferguson, McCall). From Europe through the Middle East to India and the Far East, the story has become a familiar one: early tribal cultures—relatively peaceful and agrarian and having positive attitudes toward sexuality and women—are transformed, often by conquest, into violent patriarchies. At a certain point in the culture's movement toward hierarchy and class domination, a quantum leap in values occurs, after which patriarchal attitudes are codified in an established religious or philosophical system.

Modern industrialism has now taken root in many such cultures, either emerging indigenously or having been imposed by violence. The tendency in all such societies, regardless of whether they call themselves capitalist or communist, has been to absorb and perpetuate entrenched patriarchal attitudes.

The worldwide patriarchal system has everywhere been promoted by, and worked to the advantage of, men, or rather those men who find themselves most adaptable to its conditioning and most likely to be satisfied by its rewards. And it has everywhere worked to the disadvantage of women and those men who display characteristics judged by the prevailing value system to be womanlike.

The fact that there have been men like Mohandas Gandhi, who tran-

174

scend and subvert patriarchal value systems, and women like Margaret Thatcher, who identify with and reinforce their worst aspects, proves that identification with patriarchal role-playing is not just a matter of sex: nature has not decreed that our personal politics or social values shall be determined by our gender at birth. Nor has it determined that all human societies must be ruled by men. Nonetheless, because of intense and persistent conditioning, most people born into a patriarchal culture take its basic values and assumptions for granted. Likewise, since the whole thrust of the patriarchal system is to accumulate power at the expense of others, the world's most powerful societies during the past few thousand years have all been patriarchal.

Despite these long-standing patterns, within the past two hundred years global changes have taken place that undermine the appropriateness of patriarchal life, if indeed a system that has caused so much violence and suffering could ever be called appropriate. Because of a number of related revolutions in technology, the unlimited quest among nation-states for power at the expense of others now threatens the existence of all states. Already the U.S., the USSR, China, India, and several European states certainly—and Israel and the Union of South Africa probably—possess nuclear weapons. Within the next few decades, many medium and small-sized states will join this privileged circle. Clearly the kind of aggressive, violence-prone international politics that have been an accepted way of life since the Bronze Age must be changed if the human race is to have any worthwhile future.

Changes in technology have also resulted in gross overpopulation of the planet. Human beings have been reproducing themselves at such an explosive rate during the past two hundred years that a great many animal and plant species have been pushed into extinction. The earth, the sea, and the air are becoming ever more filled with the toxic waste products of burgeoning human societies, resulting in irreparable damage to the planet's ecosystem and a steady deterioration in the quality of human life. In addition, the inequities and ineptitude of patriarchal governments have impeded the fair distribution of food and other goods to millions of hungry new mouths in the world's poorest regions, thus aggravating massive episodes of famine and increasing the likelihood of war. Clearly it is time to challenge the traditional patriarchal ethic that says the purpose of sex is procreation—breeding new soldiers, workers, and consumers as rapidly as possible in order to increase the power and size of one's own political and economic system.

Euripides' Bakkhai and the old agrarian religion from which it emerged are valuable resources in the face of the current global crisis because they remind us that human beings once had alternative value systems. Even more, they can be a basis for us in criticizing contemporary patriarchal conditions and in laying plans for social reconstruction. Of course, we cannot turn back the clock and return to conditions in the late Stone Age before the rise of patriarchy, and even if we could, who would seek to live under circumstances where the average human life span was about forty years? Nonetheless, Euripides' *Bakkhai* and the ancient traditions that produced it give us a chance to step outside of our culture, as it were, and to see and evaluate it with fresh perspectives. Their value in this respect is nowhere more evident than in our need to rethink sex-roles.

Planet Earth has a male problem. From generals threatening purported national enemies with siloed missiles (poised like so many nuclear phalluses), to rapists prowling for prey, to husbands beating their wives and children, to packs of male teenagers harassing women and gay men on inner-city streets, the planet in general and America in particular are caught in the web of a global male problem. Throughout the past several thousand years, the overwhelming majority of history's grossest acts of violence, from the battlefield to the home, have been and continue to be committed by men.

The root of the planet's male problem today, as it was in the case of King Pentheus in ancient Greece, is contempt for women and anything conventionally associated with women. A man with such contempt is frighteningly insecure because, again like Pentheus, he always struggles to repress within himself that half of his personality which dominant values have labeled "feminine."

One can manipulate a patriarchal man into doing anything, however absurd, irrational, or violent, by convincing him that to do so validates and proves his masculinity. The American advertising industry understands this fact quite well, as witnessed by its ads for cigarettes (Smoking will give you a butch image like the Marlboro man, never mind the cancer) and the Marines (Are you man enough to take it?). If men were secure in their masculinity, such ads simply would not work and would soon cease to be used. The extent to which a nation's advertising industry sells products by hyping them as proofs of manliness is a sign of how insecure that nation's men are about their masculinity. As anyone can tell by a casual look at television, newspapers, and other media, the masculine-image hook is one of the most commonly used devices to sell products in America.

Why are American men so insecure about their masculinity? A major factor is their inability to deal with their own natural homosexual capacities and needs. Although regarded by patriarchal religions as unnatural, homosexual behavior is in fact widespread in nature and becomes more common in mammals the closer a species approximates to humans (Ford and Beach, p. 139 ff). Moreover, as we have seen earlier, there have been times and places in ancient Mediterranean civilizations where homosexuality either served as the basis of education and religion or else was commonly practiced and accepted in personal relationships. If homosexual acts are unnatural, how can these facts be explained?

I also know from my own personal experience, like every other gay man who has been sexually active for a long period of time, that there are large numbers of American men who give every appearance to their wives, children, and closest friends of being exclusively heterosexual and yet have hidden lives of regular sexual encounters with other men.

A notable indication of the violent self-repression of homosexual feelings, especially among young unmarried men, is the popularity of "fag-bashing" in America. A very common, although often unreported, practice in many American towns and cities is for young males to gather in small packs and drive by or near gay hangouts. When they see someone they believe is gay, their reaction usually consists of screaming out "Faggot!" and then hurriedly driving off, or else of jumping the person en masse and battering him. Sometimes they stab their victim to death—on occasion with a degree of passion matching that found in sex itself. Mainline newspapers rarely indicate the great extent of this practice, but the gay press abounds with documented cases, and most active gay people can recount many such stories concerning either themselves or their friends.

If a heterosexual man were sure of his sexual identity and feelings, would he be motivated to go out of his way to abuse or kill gay men to show how masculine he is? Why would he care at all? The prevalence and intensity of these attacks by young American men is an indication of the prevalence and intensity of their own homosexual feelings and the extreme lengths to which they are prepared to go to prove to themselves and their peers that they are, after all, "real men."

The pervasive presence of homosexual feelings of various degrees among American men is one of the best-kept secrets of our times (although documented in such works as the Kinsey studies). Yet these men are everywhere told that having such feelings will make them like women, who in turn are held to be inferior beings. Is it any wonder then that patriarchal men must constantly strive to prove their manhood? And so they do, by buying products that are associated with "real men," going out of their way to make anti-gay remarks, and engaging in "fag-bashing." And so, too, they do by competing against other men in sports, business, and war. This compulsive need of men constantly to prove to themselves and others how unfeminine they are I call the "patriarchal psychosis"—"patriarchal" because it emerges from and is supported by a society where men dominate women and "psychosis" because it is severely injurious to the life function both of individuals and of civilizations.

Women constitute the principal victims of the patriarchal psychosis. Men with strong heterosexual feelings find themselves in a double bind: they are sexually attracted to a class of humans whom they also believe are inferior. Hence their sexual relations are often characterized by a need to dominate and control. The most extreme form of this phenomenon is rape, where men eroticize the need to violate and hurt those they regard as inferior. In rare instances, men so loathe the women who are the objects of their sexual feelings that they become serial killers of their sexual partners, a situation also likely to occur when they are convinced that their sexual feelings are loathsome in themselves; hence the need to degrade, hurt, or kill the persons who stimulate such feelings. This syndrome can also be found among intensely self-hating gay men.

Although a great many American women report histories of being beaten or raped by men, the most common manifestation of the patriarchal psychosis is far more subtle: the stifling lack of emotional reciprocity that most American women suffer with their male sexual partners. Since most American men regard spontaneity, playfulness, tenderness, and emotional vulnerability as "feminine," they spend a great deal of psychological energy repressing any outward display of these qualities for fear that someone will see "the woman within." As a result, they become quite clumsy and inept in situations where the ability to express these qualities is absolutely essential: interpersonal relationships. Hence the classic problem among American heterosexual couples: the husband feels obliged constantly to show he is in charge and yet is an emotional dodo, while the wife must pretend to be passively feminine, although doing most of the emotional work needed to keep the relationship alive. As a result, most American women never experience a sense of emotional fulfillment in their marriages. In time many lower their standards and simply acquiesce to a life that is emotionally stultifying.

The patriarchal psychosis has also taken its toll within gay male relationships, since the great majority of American gay men are acutely anxiety-ridden about their masculinity, just like their heterosexual counterparts. An evidence of this anxiety is the extreme lengths to which many American gay men now feel they have to go in order not to be taken for "sissies." This tendency can be seen on the streets of many of the nation's gay ghettos: compulsive body-building, wearing denim and leather uniforms with Armylike short-cropped hair, deliberately adopting stiff body postures and lumbering styles of walking. The upshot of this conformity is that a new gay stereotype is being created that is almost a satire on masculinity, looking very much like the male fantasies found in American comic books in the 1950s. Among such gay men there is often an extreme hostility to feminine-identified men and transvestites. The prevailing notion seems to be, "I may be gay but at least I'm not a queen."

Many gay men have also internalized homophobic values. Although going to gay-pride marches during the day, they nonetheless display intense self-hatred in their sexual practices at night. A significant minority of present-day American gay men become sexually aroused by the fantasy of hurting, or being hurt by, their sexual partners. In effect, they use sex as a kind of punishment by mutual consent, punishing both themselves and others for being gay. This eroticizing of self-hatred is evidenced in the present-day gay media by an abundance of fantasy themes depicting domination, bondage, humiliation, and even torture. For not a few American gay men, the ideal fantasy lover is big, hard-faced, muscle-bound, short-haired, and otherwise "straight-appearing" (a phrase that often turns up in the personal-ad section of gay newspapers). So intense is their self-deprecation that they have fallen in love with the image of their worst homophobic oppressors.

Anxiety-ridden about their masculinity and driven by eroticized self-hatred, many American gay men have proven to be easy victims of unscrupulous gay entrepreneurs and fantasy merchants. The latter, as owners of the network of gay bars, baths, and "book stores," have until recently effectively defined the social context of urban gay life. During the past twenty years, the establishments they run have proliferated and most often have been characterized as dark, poorly ventilated, filthy firetraps exploding with ear-splitting music. Into such an environment have thronged, week after week, year after year, untold thousands of self-punishing gay consumers, desperately looking for "tricks" and "numbers" and often addicted to alcohol and drugs.

The net effect of such social conditions over decades has been a significant lowering of the immune system of virtually the entire urban gay male community. Whatever may have been its original source, the AIDS virus that appeared in the early 1980s found a most receptive soil in which to grow—a ghetto of men looking for sex, most fleeing homes in repressive middle-American towns, many self-destructive, and all in the clutches of a sleazy gay business establishment hungry for the huge profits to be reaped from the new sexual permissiveness.

Of course AIDS has been contracted by many gay men who have had nothing whatever to do with these social patterns, and AIDS would still be a major problem if these conditions had never occurred. But the internalized homophobia of gay consumers (deriving from established patriarchal values) and the greed of gay business owners (mirroring typical capitalist attitudes) were significant aggravating factors in the initial rapid spread of this disease in the urban gay male ghetto. This situation was made even worse by prudish American attitudes in talking about sex: if frank sex education, including techniques of safe anal sex, had been a part of mainstream American culture, the use of condoms, which prevent transmission of the AIDS virus, would have been a commonplace.

In the midst of the grave crisis of life and death in which the American gay community now finds itself, a re-examination of its values and institutions is underway. Moreover, there has been an extraordinary outpouring of love, caring, and principled commitment by large numbers of gay men toward those infected with AIDS. The net result of these changes is a long overdue redefinition of what it means to be gay. It is now no longer taken for granted that gay identification requires conformity to an oppressive masculine stereotype, that sexual liberation means compulsive "tricking," and that gay liberation itself is nothing more than making the world safe for gay capitalism.

In addition to hatred and fear of femininity, there is another side to the planet's male problem. By defining masculinity in terms of a competitive struggle for power and hierarchical status, the patriarchal psychosis reenforces a basic destructive behavior pattern: objectification. This is the practice of viewing others as mere objects or things to use and dispose of for one's own purpose without giving due regard to their feelings or rights. The most obvious example is sexual objectification, as when men seek to relieve their sexual needs by using women without any regard for the latter's needs, rights, or feelings. When those who practice sexual objectification also have an edge in power over their desired objects (as men do in a patriarchal society), the objectification often expresses itself through physical coercion or violence. Hence the prevalence of wife abuse and rape in America and other patriarchal societies.

But there are many other kinds of objectification besides sexual. In economic objectification, entrepreneurs and corporations act to increase

180

their wealth by treating their workers as mere economic resources and by devastating the environment. In political objectification, whole nations are regarded as objects for strafing, bombing, and acts of government-sponsored terrorism. In ecological objectification, the planet itself becomes either a mere resource for exploitation or a giant toilet in which to dump all of humanity's wastes.

Men who spend much of their energy in objectifying behavior—whether in sex, business, or politics—often end up objectifying themselves; they begin using their own bodies as disposable objects in the pursuit of orgasms, money, or power. This self-directed objectification comes easily to them, for they have become accustomed to treating everything in their environment as a disposable object. First the objectifying process becomes habitual, then compulsive, and finally obstructive to all demands from the outside world for respect or reverence. In a way it becomes like an addiction, an ego-building rush for the objectifier.

Objectifying behavior, when it is compulsive, can lead to the self-destruction of its practitioners, for they burn out their own bodies and psychic energy sources, just as they consume those around them. Hence arises the irony that a behavior-pattern originally adopted to increase the pleasure, money, or power of one's ego can end by destroying it.

Nations, like individuals, can also base their existence on objectification. A society whose economy, politics, and sexual life are run by men anxiously trying to prove their masculinity and accustomed by habit to treating other individuals and nations as so many disposable objects is a society primed for conflict and self-destructive behavior. And a world consisting of nations so run is a world bent on psychological suicide, environmental catastrophe, and war. Hence it follows that to have the possibility of world peace we need more than a limit to the arms race, although such a limit would certainly help. Peace will never be well grounded on Planet Earth until the patriarchal psychosis, together with its compulsive habit of objectification, is replaced by a more rational and humane way of behaving and thinking.

Beneath the patriarchal man's contempt for women, alienation from his own femininity, and compulsive objectifying behavior lies a certain basic way of relating to the world: the I–it type of relationship, where "I" is the male ego and "it" is everything else reduced to a usable and contemptible thing. In the eyes of patriarchal men, the world in effect is divided into four categories: real men, bitches, faggots, and mere things.

The opposite of the patriarchal psychosis is the I–you type of relationship, where the other that one encounters has a legitimate claim in some degree to respect or reverence. But to bestow such a recognition on these others means in some way to invest part of one's feelings in them, to empathize with their circumstances, to step outside the narrow boundaries of one's own ego and give of oneself. In short, the opposite of the patriarchal psychosis is the ability to love.

To live as a human being requires both the knowledge of how to use the world as a resource and the capacity to give of oneself in love. Without the first skill, there would be no survival; without the second, no life worth living. But using the world as an object can be harmful when it becomes compulsive and entrenched as an end in itself. In that case, when taken to extremes, it is destructive and hence defeats its original purpose: to promote survival.

In the patriarchal psychosis, objectifying behavior is taken to grossly disproportionate extremes. The self is reduced to an ego ever in competition with other egos. The world is reduced to a collection of lifeless objects over which competing egos fight. Among individuals the result is alienation from the wonder of life and loss of the ability to love; among nations, perpetual violence and war; throughout the planet in general, ecological catastrophe.

In the twentieth century, all the accumulated contradictions of the past six thousand years of patriarchy seem to be coming to a head, aggravated and accelerated by suicidal developments in the technology of warfare and by the gross overpopulation of humans. If our lives as individuals and nations continue to be characterized by competitive aggression, alienation from nature, the procreative ideal of sex, hostility to the feminine, and an inability to love—if all these continue to prevail, then the world of the twenty-first century will be an uninhabitable wasteland.

Our hope in the midst of the present global crisis is the construction of foundations for a postpatriarchal civilization. Movement in this direction is already well underway. One of the most important examples is the rise of the modern women's liberation movement. For some time now, feminist women have been in the forefront of challenging patriarchal attitudes and practices in regard to sex roles. The virtue of the women's movement has been to reaffirm and validate the right of women to an equal share in political, economic, religious, and sexual power. Its weakness is that it sometimes seems to believe that equal access to the existing power structure is enough. If women become generals, presidents, and corporate leaders, while the heart of the present system of domination remains unchanged, we will still have all the deadly defects of patriarchy, only with women being as culpable as men. The mere placing of women in the patriarchal hierarchy of power will not change the nature of that hierarchy.

Another promising sign is the gay liberation movement. At their best, lesbians and gay men have dramatically challenged the sexist role-playing that is at the very heart of the patriarchal psychosis and have succeeded in making an immense improvement in the quality of life for many gay people. But the movement has also had its weaknesses, in particular the tendency of many gay men to internalize self-destructive fantasies of patriarchal masculinity. What real advance will have been made if gay men simply gain the right to sleep with other men while continuing to embody and perpetuate other patriarchal faults?

All the progressive movements of the past few decades—black civil-rights organizing, unionization, ecological reform, anti-imperialism—have helped raise questions about the inequitable distribution of power in America and elsewhere. But these movements have generally failed to challenge the patriarchal psychosis itself. Moreover, the way such organizations run themselves internally often reflects the same principles of personal interrelation that are found in establishment groups. Simply to demand a bigger piece of the pie is no longer enough; the recipe itself needs to be transformed, as do we ourselves.

In the foregoing chapters of this book, we have seen evidence for the historical persistence of another kind of recipe for social organization. Throughout much of classical antiquity, those human capacities and feelings denied by the patriarchal psychosis found a refuge in the Dionysian tradition. For some 1,700 years—from the end of Minoan civilization around 1200 B.C. to the final fall of Rome around 500 A.D.—the god Dionysos continued to speak in some degree both for the half-forgotten shadows of the pre-Indo-European inhabitants of Greece and for the suppressed visions of the Mediterranean's underclasses. Even as late as 1700 A.D., broken-down strains of the old religion, surviving in scattered pockets of Europe, continued to echo Dionysian themes until they were finally annihilated by the onslaught of patriarchal industrialism. Although distrusted by the Greco-Roman religious establishment, co-opted and then persecuted by the Christians, and finally overwhelmed by industrial institutions and values, the Dionysian tradition managed for nearly three thousand years to embody in some degree an alternative vision of the nature of human experience.

The essence of the Dionysian tradition is the affirmation of the whole self through ecstatic ritual. Patriarchal civilization takes one facet of the person—the rationally calculating ego—and identifies it with selfhood. All other aspects become either demons (as in Christianity) or subversive unconscious forces (as in modern psychologism). In the Dionysian tradition, emotions, fantasies, and sexual longings are summoned forth and embraced as inherent parts of the self.

Patriarchal civilization pits the calculating ego against other egos and views this confrontational situation as the essence of social interrelation. In the practice of the Dionysian mysteries, the essential unit is not the isolated individual but the group-in-action, which manifests its collective energy through the throbbing patterns of song, dance, and orgiastic sex among its individual participants. In these shared patterns of rhythmic energy, one's sense of self overlaps with that of others, and the felt barrier between "me" and "the world" dissolves.

In patriarchal civilization, the ego grows at the expense of the rest of the world by taking away from others and incorporating the gain within its own boundaries. The Dionysian tradition aims at ecstasy—stepping outside of the limits of one's ego. By participating in the god's rituals, individuals enter an altered state of consciousness, break through ego boundaries, and let themselves dissolve into the world. On returning to their ordinary mental states, they sometimes find that the old boundaries of ego-definition have been stretched and altered and that they are slightly different persons. They transcend objectivity not only by giving themselves into the world but by participating in the process of their own self re-creation.

The Dionysian tradition sharply diverges from patriarchal civilization in its use of hallucinogens. In societies influenced by patriarchal values, the use of mind-altering substances is usually forbidden or stigmatized. As a result, people who seek to experiment with them have to maneuver around both the legal system and a network of negative value judgments, a situation that gives to these substances the aura of a tabooed self-indulgence. Drug users lack a supportive ritual context for an enlightened use of their drugs. They may also be driven by the self-destructive feelings characteristic of the patriarchal psychosis. If so, they can easily fall prey first to compulsive drug use and then to addiction. Hence patriarchal societies tend to be schizophrenic in their attitude toward such drugs: officially they have an absolute ban on their use, yet large segments of the population continue to use them compulsively and self-destructively in secret.

In the Dionysian tradition, mind-altering substances (a category into which wine was originally placed) are openly used in accepted, traditional, structured rituals aimed at self-growth. Not only does no taboo attach to such use of these substances, but an elaborate system of myth and ritual guides the user according to the cumulative experiences of generations of previous users. As a result, the extremes both of puritanical denial and of self-destructive addiction tend to be much less common. Users are given the incentives, skills, and supportive ritual context to enjoy their hallucinogens to positive effect. By way of contrast, the traditional approach of patriarchal societies—to condemn all hallucinogens regardless of type or source, to suppress information on rational drug use, to penalize any apprehended drug user—has simply not worked and in fact has often corresponded to a long-term increase in drug addiction.

My own personal encounter with Dionysos began in 1972 when I left New York City with my lover Jacob in search of a more humane and nature-oriented existence. Since 1969, I had been quite active in the gay liberation movement in New York while also attending Columbia University as a graduate student in philosophy. During that time I had seen action in many demonstrations (and several riots), been arrested in a number of gay sit-ins, and been involved in the internal political struggles of the fledgling gay movement. Some time before leaving the city, my friend Leo Martello, a modern-day witch, suggested to me that there was a connection between feminism and the history of witchcraft, and I began to read about the people called "witches" in the Middle Ages. It was as a result of this research that I first encountered the Dionysian tradition, at least intellectually. I came to the conclusion that an old agrarian underground religion long existed in Europe and that it had a traditional place in its rites for lesbians and gay men. I first published these conclusions in an article in *Out* magazine in 1973 and later in articles in *Fag Rag* in 1974, and they became the basis of my book *Witchcraft and the Gay Counterculture* (1978).

After leaving New York in 1972, I felt a deep-seated longing to find a way to relate communally to other gay men outside the context of gay bars and gay political organizations. Might there be a way to draw into one force energy from the Dionysian tradition, the sense of wonder at the magic of nature, and the creative sexuality of gay men?

After my lover Jacob and I finally settled in San Francisco in 1974, I had a number of discussions on this question with Murray Edelman and other good friends. As a result of these discussions, a group of gay men gathered in my apartment at the corner of Haight and Ashbury on October 17, 1975. We decided that we would try to recover a sense of our countercultural spiritual heritage, our common connectedness with nature, and the untapped aspects of our sexual power. We called the new group "The Faery Circle," and our first ritual was to sit in a circle, hold hands, and chant.

Subsequent rituals proved to be more elaborate. On one occasion we decided to spend Halloween night at a remote beach near San Gregorio, California. About twenty of us arrived near the site after nightfall, by which time the fog was sweeping in, filling the air with thick curtains of salty mist. Because it was so dark and misty, we had trouble making out the narrow footpath that descended the steep cliffs down to our destination. We lit a few torches and with their help slowly worked our way down. I could barely make out the features of anything more than a few feet away, and because of the narrowness of the path felt as though I were walking on a thin line in the middle of the air. To my right I could hear the ocean roll and hiss, a great serpentine presence stretching out far behind and to the front. We inched our way down the rocky slope in a long line, like so many ants crawling along the sharp backbone of some long-slain beast. Veils and robes floated in the wind while finger cymbals chimed softly; our torches sparkled in the salty spray.

The beach was cold, dark, and damp—in fact, utterly unpleasant. I thought, Christ, what am I doing here? We built a small fire and sat around it, but the flame was more for effect than warmth, since the large size of the circle kept us too far from it to experience any heat. We did our usual chanting, and I began to feel more comfortable and relaxed. I felt an urge to lift my hands forward and up, and when I did so, was surprised to feel a warm presence in my palms, which entered my hands and traveled up my arms, making me feel warm and comfortable within. In retrospect, I believe this warmth was nothing more than a faint sensation from the distant fire, but having become so relaxed from chanting, I focused on it entirely, and so it filled my consciousness. The experience reminded me of the extent to which my experience of the world depends on how I focus my attention on it.

A celebrant who called himself Loki rose and walked around the circle, calling on the four directions of the planet to be our witnesses and protectors. In effect, he reminded us that we had created a special space—not only our own little geographical piece of beach for spending the night, but a space in consciousness somewhere between the fantasies of dreaming and the realities of ordinary waking life. Here we would be safe to explore experiences and feelings that elude the definitions and concepts taught us by the dominant culture.

Someone rose and called upon the Goddess, the Queen of Heaven, to descend and take possession of our bodies. The purpose of this invocation was to remind us of the ancient traditions of a great-mother goddess, here identified with the moon, and to encourage us to shed our male identities and mental baggage and open ourselves to the power of the

186

feminine in ourselves and in the cosmos. To further this goal, many circle members wore dresses.

Another rose and called on the Horned One to come forth and join the dance that was to come. This invocation called to mind the Dionysos-type god often associated historically with the Great Goddess in the old religion. To call on him meant to reaffirm our connection with animals and to remember the importance of sexuality in religion.

Since this was Halloween night—a holiday derived from the old Celtic festival of Samhain, where the dead were remembered and celebrated—we called upon the gay dead to rise and join our rites. The purpose of this invocation was to remember the great antiquity of gay traditions and to memorialize those gays killed at the hands of Christians, Nazis, and other oppressors.

And then we danced—pulsating and shaking up and down, hurling ourselves around and over the fire, playing music on recorders, tambourines and finger cymbals, shouting and howling. And when the initial pulse of the dance's energy spent itself, we formed a long straight line, one end of which began to turn around upon itself with the rest following, like a giant jelly roll. We kissed and hugged and fondled and groped in one big sexy mass, and I suddenly realized that it made no difference at all to me how anybody looked. I felt as though the group as a whole had become a living entity, and *he* was the one I was having sex with, and all the participants were just so many appendages of that collective body. I realized that my usual type of sexual behavior—responding only to those within a certain range of age, weight, and so on—was but a tiny part of the spectrum of my own sexual possibilities. The limited nature of my usual sexual tastes, I later reflected, was probably due to constant reinforcement patterns from established media and institutions in the bourgeois gay ghetto. When I removed myself from these reinforcement patterns, as in a rite of the Faery Circle, my sexuality became less structured and more playful.

When we had spent ourselves late that Halloween night, we again invoked the four directions of the planet and closed the circle. The ritual was complete. As the fire flickered out on the beach, we each dozed off to sleep, lulled by oceanic hymns and reconciled to an ancient human heritage.

The significance of the Faery Circle's ritual at San Gregorio was that it was an exercise in spiritual and sexual self-determination. Religion in consumerist America has become a canned commodity much like any other: we have the choice of different labels, but all the brands are basically cranked out by the same patriarchal machine. The Faery Circle's ritual was an attempt to identify spiritual needs and to articulate them outside of the hackneyed Judaeo-Christian tradition and with a sense of humor and subversiveness. The participants in the San Gregorio rite likewise rejected conventional sexual attitudes—both of the gay and straight communities—and sought to let the erotic angels fly free of tired patriarchal fantasies.

By appealing to the Great Goddess and the Horned One, the faeries were also grounding themselves in an alternate, but very ancient, spiritual tradition which for thousands of years resisted patriarchal encroachments. Does this appeal then mean that faeries believe the Goddess and the Horned One are in some sense "real"? The answer is both yes and no. None of humanity's gods, including these two, are real in the sense that a rock or a hammer are real. But just as a painting, or a theatrical performance, or a political ideal can move people to action and so have very tangible consequences in the physical world, so too the gods lead their believers to act in very real ways.

We create the gods out of our spiritual needs, just as we create an elegant (or grotesque) political ideal out of our political needs. To me, one of the most endearing traits of faery spirituality is its sense of playful inventiveness and its ability to incorporate campy self-satire into its rituals. The Goddess and the Horned One have been useful gods at some faery rituals, but the essence of faerydom is not any particular god or even the general concept of god, but rather the *process* of ecstatic growth through self-created ritual. So I, for one, believe in the Goddess and the Horned One, and I also consider myself to be an atheist.

By way of contrast, a group of about a dozen faeries once conducted a ritual strikingly different from the preceding one, this time in the mountains outside of Jenner, California. As the previous Halloween celebration at the beach incorporated elements of European "witchcraft," so the rituals in the mountains near Jenner reflected certain practices of the Southwest Native American Indians. A group of faeries had done research on the use of peyote in Indian rituals, and we decided to hold a traditional (albeit modified) peyote ceremony on one cloudless, full-moon night in late summer.

As evening approached, we found a fairly level spot with an open view of the sky and surrounded, at a moderate distance, by underbrush and trees. Jonathan, the member of our circle who was the most knowledgeable about this rite, constructed a small altar in the middle of the circle made out of packed earth in the shape of a crescent moon. On and around this altar he placed our supply of peyote buttons—dried segments

188

of the strongly hallucinogenic peyote cactus. They looked somewhat like pieces of dried apple, although darker and tougher and containing little furry spots. These small spots had to be removed before the peyote was eaten because they contained the poison strychnine.

Within our circle we dug a smaller concentric ditch called "the road," which had an important physical function, for it was here that participants would vomit after eating their peyote buttons. Peyote most often causes an intense but short-lived nausea soon after being eaten, and vomiting is an established part of its usage, at least in the ritual tradition we were following. One of the members of the circle was designated as the Road Faery—whenever anyone vomited in the road, the Road Faery would cover the vomit with soil, holding a smoking cedar branch in front of the person's face for its pungent, cleansing fragrance and giving him a drink of water mixed with vinegar.

We chanted and blessed the peyote buttons and distributed them around the circle. The largest button of all, the Grandmother Button, was not eaten, but kept in an honored place on the altar throughout the ritual.

Jonathan explained that after we ate the peyote, a rattle would be handed around the circle. When the rattle came to each person, he would chant or sing whatever vision he was having, accompanied by the person on his left, who would play the drum. When the person who was chanting finished his song, he would hand the rattle to the one on his right and in turn play the drum for the latter's song. And so the rattle would be continually passed around the circle from sunset to sunup with only a short break in the middle of the night.

I took about eight or nine small to medium-sized peyote buttons and carefully plucked out the little furry white spots. Jonathan had indicated that the way to get the best results was to chew each button thoroughly until it became soft and juicy before swallowing. I put a button in my mouth and began chewing, and it was truly the most godawful thing I have ever tasted. Nevertheless I ate them all. To my surprise I was only mildly nauseated and never even vomited, which was probably not good, since I retained any toxins in the peyote.

The song-and-rattle ritual began, and for about half an hour I felt absolutely nothing unusual. I began to wonder whether I could honestly endure eight hours of listening to twelve men sing out of tune. And then I felt a smooth, warm wave of relaxing energy pass over me, like the effects of a few marijuana puffs. I knew something was happening.

All at once my field of vision dissolved, and in front of me I saw an enormous peyote button, and from every place where I had plucked out a little white spot there was a skull staring at me. I remember thinking to myself, Uh-oh, I think this is going to be heavy.

The big peyote button vanished, and my vision returned to normal. Then my left hand began to vibrate back and forth on its own. The twitching moved up my wrist and left arm, then entered my shoulder, and I felt it move across my whole body to the right. At this point I was twitching and convulsing uncontrollably all over and slobbering at the mouth. I felt as though I must be having an epileptic seizure and was afraid that I would bite off my tongue.

When possible, I glanced around the circle, and the others were looking at me. Their skin appeared to turn ashen, they all had strange smiles, and their faces began to sag as though made out of melting wax. From the corner of my eye I could see that there were strange beings, animal-like and ghostly, racing around the circle behind our backs.

The hallucinations and jerking seemed to come in long waves, interspersed with short periods of relative lucidity. I was able on a few occasions to sing when the rattle came to me, and I was startled to hear my voice—it was not just one voice but seemed like the sounds of a choir.

In the worst periods of my hallucinating, I felt myself sink and dissolve into the earth. The visions I had were of jumbled, monsterlike faces moving erratically. I remember thinking to myself, If I could just die, this would all be over.

To the others in the circle, my appearance did not seem as dire as it felt to me, and in any case they were all absorbed in their own trips. Besides, after intermittently ranting for some time, I was beginning to become a nuisance. My friend Soula, who was sitting nearby, yelled out something to the effect of, "Get over it, girl!" His shout proved to be a turning point, for I could feel the episodes become less intense.

At a certain point, I felt a heavy presence lift up and off my body as suddenly as the peyote's effect had first come on. As though someone had taken his hand and run it across the strings of a harp, I felt a harmonious and beautiful settling into place both of myself and of the things and people around me. I was stepping into the world for the first time—cleansed, refreshed, serene, and joyous. I looked up at the nearly full moon shining in the sky—a jet had just gone over and had left a trail of white through both sky and moon, like the stroke of a painter's brush on an azure canvas. I was amazed at how clear, beautiful and balanced this simple scene appeared.

Other people in the circle had very different experiences. One person became a teller of hilarious stories (as they seemed at the time, anyway), accompanied by the most amazing whistling and sound effects. Another relived a moving episode from his childhood relationship with his parents and so vividly that they seemed to be physically present. My own trip, although initially painful, was one of spiritual growth. In some sense I experienced a kind of death and rebirth cycle that helped me overcome the fear of my own death.

Since the early days of the Faery Circle in 1975, a spontaneous spiritual movement has independently arisen among many gay men who live in rural America or who have an interest in relating more closely to a natural environment. Known as the Radical Faery Movement, it aims at redefining gay identity in a way that transcends the patriarchal fantasies and bourgeois lifestyles of the urban gay ghetto. Many men have contributed to the emergence of this movement, most notably long-time gay activists Harry Hay and John Burnside and author Mitch Walker (*Visionary Love*).

A similar process of cultural self-determination has also been underway for some time among feminist women who have formed ritual circles for mutual nurturing, spiritual and sexual self-discovery, and communication with natural powers. Many of these women have found the ancient religious tradition of the Great Goddess to be a powerful resource in breaking through patriarchal attitudes and practices in religion. Their activities have helped stimulate a brilliant renaissance in women's spiritual literature, as witnessed by the works of Starhawk (*The Spiral Dance*), Judy Grahn (*Another Mother Tongue*), and many others.

These new spiritual developments in the feminist consciousness of both women and men, though quite novel in the context of recent American history, nonetheless have a most ancient cultural tradition to draw on, as the preceding chapters of this book have shown. They also bring hope for a needed transformation of future human life.

The established concept of how human beings must behave—butch, competitive, violent men dominating passive, feminine women and a dead nature—is not necessitated by the order of the cosmos, but is a lopsided and arbitrary reenforcement of certain human capabilities. Ever since the triumph of the patriarchal revolution, the natural and at times necessary human capacity for violence has been made the single principal basis of political and social organization and singled out as the defining behavior of humans who happen to be born male. Likewise playfulness, passivity, and emotional sensitivity—themselves also all natural and necessary human characteristics—have been degraded and identified with humans who happen to be born female. Finally, the ability to conceive of nature as a conceptual object has been ripped away from all natural feelings of love, respect, and reverence toward the cosmos and made into a religion in its own right. The cumulative effect of these concepts has been to support and augment the political, economic, and sexual power of privileged elements in the patriarchal hierarchy. It has also, acting in concert with that hierarchy of patriarchal power, brought the planet to the edge of its ability to survive.

We need a new definition of what it means to be a human being. To that end, we each need access to the full range of our human capabilities, not cutting off half of our humanity in the name of becoming "real men" or "real women." And that means we must find, resuscitate, and embrace our deepest inner feelings and break through the rigid, externally imposed definitions that keep them encased in a crippled knot of inner psychic tensions. We must also break through with our feelings to the world—to animals, plants, the earth, the stars—reestablishing our natural awe and love for the magnificence and beauty of the cosmos. To break through the old self and to open up to the contingency and vulnerability of real growth, to take a decisive step into the risky formlessness of the re-creation of self—such is a process of revolutionary ecstasy: revolutionary, because transcending every external authority's definition; ecstatic, because transcending ourselves.

In the nineteenth century, the German-born philosopher Friedrich Nietzsche, invoking the tradition of Dionysos, also called for a transcendence of self and an overcoming of the restrictive mentality of Western rationalism. In his first book, The Birth of Tragedy, published in 1872, Nietzsche described three different modes of human consciousness: the Dionysian, which he identified as the basic drive of life to break through all dogma, morality, and imposed definition; the Apollonian, which he regarded as the tendency to articulate feelings and perceptions into individually defined artistic forms; and the Socratic, which seeks, as he saw it, to dominate the world through abstract reasoning.

Nietzsche believed the Dionysian and Apollonian elements could play off each other in a creative tension and so create great works of art. But he viewed the Socratic element in modern times as grossly out of proportion, giving rise to naive optimism in the name of science and sterility in the name of art. He called the outcome of this lopsided Socratic approach "Alexandrine culture," after Alexandria, the celebrated center of Greek scholastic learning in ancient Egypt, and condemned it with these words:

192

Our whole modern world is entangled in the meshes of Alexandrine culture, and recognizes as the ideal the *theorist* equipped with the most potent means of knowledge, and laboring in the service of science, of whom the archetype and progenitor is Socrates.

(Nietzsche, p. 137; Haussmann's translation)

In *The Birth of Tragedy*, Nietzsche identified himself by implication as a Dionysian and called on the Germany of his time to rejuvenate itself by reaffirming Dionysian traditions. In particular, he advocated the creation of new German myths and heroes and praised the music of Richard Wagner as embodying the spirit of Dionysos come again.

Nietzsche was right to see Dionysos and Apollo as potential complements and not as necessary antagonists. Their complementarity was reflected historically in ancient Greece, since the Oracle at Delphi was dedicated to *both:* in the winter months, Dionysos was the Oracle's patron deity, and Apollo during the rest of the year. And Nietzsche was right in regard to the creative process, since both emotional inspiration and rational form are necessary to create works of art. But Nietzsche was wrong to attribute the lopsided rationalism of the West to Sokrates. As we have seen, Sokrates' philosophical school was a continuation of the ancient tradition of sexualized learning, something very close to the spirit of Dionysos and one of the main reasons he was condemned to death by his more "rational" peers in Athens.

Nietzsche was misled on these points because he confused the spiritualized and intellectualized portrait of Sokrates in the writings of Plato with the historical Sokrates. Plato, and not Sokrates, made a sharp distinction between the body and the mind and regarded everything nonintellectual as an impediment to self-fulfillment. In composing his dialogues, Plato put the words that furthered this view into the mouth of Sokrates, just as Paul of Tarsus later erected his own salvation religion in the name of Jesus of Nazareth. In reality, the West's great hostility to the Dionysian tradition does not derive from Sokrates but from Plato. Hence the real cultural dichotomy is not Dionysian versus Apollonian or Socratic, but Dionysian versus Platonic.

Objections of a much more serious nature can also be raised against Nietzsche. Ofelia Schutte has recently shown that certain elements in his later thought, often downplayed by admiring commentators, in fact represent patriarchal assumptions taken to their logical extremes (Schutte, p. 188). For example, Nietzsche believed that both democracy and the emerging women's movement should be crushed and that the existence of widespread slavery was justified to maintain an elite of ruling philosopher-artists. Nietzsche's language often displays a love of hard, masculine images, and he uses the words "effeminate" and "effeminacy" as pejorative terms.

The later Nietzsche called for creation of the Ultra-Man (*der Übermensch*), a superior type of male who would seek to distance himself, in the language of Schutte's summary of his views, from "the herd, the slave, the wife, the effeminate" (Schutte, p. 185). In fact, this is the familiar patriarchal concept of the "real man," but now systematized and made into a philosophy of life.

Although Nietzsche disdained nationalism, anti-Semitism, and what he regarded as the boorishness of German culture, his later works—in particular *The Will to Power*—became the chief philosophical sources for German and Italian fascism (Stern, p. 25). The final format for *The Will to Power* was prepared by his sister, Elisabeth Förster-Nietzsche, an anti-Semite who had moved to Paraguay with her husband to help form a racially "pure" settlement (Stern, pp. 22 and 24–25). After her husband committed suicide, Elisabeth Förster-Nietzsche returned to Germany and looked after the now vegetating Nietzsche, who went insane in 1888, apparently as the result of advanced syphilis (Stern, pp. 28–29). After the death of her brother in 1900, Elisabeth Förster-Nietzsche moved to Weimar and established the Nietzsche Archives, where she later received an admiring Adolf Hitler (Stern, p. 33).

Despite the fact that Nietzsche continued to call himself a Dionysian, much of his later work actually reflects the spirit of Pentheus, the legendary enemy of Dionysos. Common to both Pentheus and Nietzsche is the concept that the quest for power constitutes the road to self-definition, and they both display a marked hostility to women, effeminacy, and the rights of the masses. Nietzsche was later embarrassed by many of the Dionysian sentiments he expressed in *The Birth of Tragedy*, and he added a preface to subsequent editions virtually repudiating the work.

Ironically, Nietzsche seemed to mirror in his own personal life the mythic cycle of Pentheus in Euripides' *Bakkhai*: a preliminary fascination with Dionysos; then a *de facto* rejection of the god and a glorification of patriarchal values; finally a madness that persisted until death.

One can easily read some of Nietzsche's later writings as a justification for the implicit, but never openly acknowledged, values underlying the conduct of ruling elites in modern patriarchal societies. Although communist commissars continue to give lip service to the dignity of the working masses and the importance of the historical struggle on their behalf, and although leaders in bourgeois countries never fail to praise in public the ideals of individual freedom and the democratic process, the stark fact is that all the leaders of all the world's nations act by a set of values determined by the will to power. War, government-sponsored sabotage and terrorism, cut-throat competition for markets and spheres of influence, diplomatic intrigue, spying, media manipulation and control—these are everywhere the means whereby the nation-states of the world survive and grow. In the pursuit of power by these means, the world's political leaders continually demonstrate their actual contempt for human life and dignity, as a casual glance at any day's newspaper will show. In the eyes of these leaders, the prime consideration is ever to get and hold onto power, both for themselves and for their respective politico-economic systems, and by whatever means available. Just as Machiavelli in the sixteenth century candidly outlined the real principles by which Renaissance princes conducted their politics, so some of the later writings of Nietzsche, cutting through all moral pretense, highlight and validate the will to power as the principal motive force in human affairs.

By contrast, Nietzsche's first work, *The Birth of Tragedy*, was the last significant attempt in the West to build a philosophy of life based on Dionysian foundations. No major school of modern Western philosophy has succeeded in following through on Nietzsche's first tentative steps in this direction.

The anti-Dionysian thrust of modern philosophy is widespread. Among communists, the proper role of philosophy is regarded as mere amplification and application of the basic insights of Marx, Engels, Lenin, Stalin, and Mao. In Third World areas where communists lead an actual armed insurgence against colonial government and imperialism, such a philosophy can be a well-honed tool in bringing about desperately needed political and economic changes. But in the established and bureaucratized communist regimes themselves, this philosophical approach has generally degenerated into a set of dogmatic and sterile shibboleths that serve to stifle all innovative thinking.

Similarly, in English-speaking countries of the bourgeois West, various strains of "logical positivism" and "analytic philosophy" have become the dominant philosophical trends. Originating in the early twentieth century as a reaction against the wildly speculative and unverifiable claims of German idealism, these new movements were at first brilliantly creative and liberating, helping to clear away much of the cluttered intellectual debris of idealism and providing new insights into the use of both technically formulated languages in the sciences and the ordinary language of nonscientific pursuits. However, although these new philosophies disdained what they called "metaphysics," they often reintroduced elaborate metaphysical categories into their own systems while refusing to acknowledge that they were doing so (Putnam, p. 29). By denying their own metaphysical biases, positivists and philosophical analysts were less intellectually forthright than the idealists they criticized, since the latter frankly acknowledged that *every* system of human thought begins with certain unproven definitions and postulates. The real difference between the old idealists on one side and the new positivists and analysts on the other is not the presence or absence of metaphysics, but rather the question of which metaphysical assumptions are to be judged, by whatever criteria of judgment, "better."

As with dogmatic Marxism in communist countries, positivism and analytic philosophy have become a kind of established religion in many of the philosophy departments of Anglo-American universities. The effect has been to dampen philosophical ingenuity and innovative thinking. Moreover, a number of positivists and analysts themselves now find that they are unable to solve basic theoretical problems caused by their own presuppositions and methods. A feeling is emerging in some academic quarters that positivism and analysis have played themselves out and that the time is right for a new spirit in philosophy.

A small, but hopeful, breath of fresh air appeared in American philosophy in 1985 with the publication of *Post-Analytic Philosophy*, a collection of essays by contemporary philosophers looking for a way out of the dead end of positivism and analysis. As part of this collection, Cornel West, a black philosopher at Yale Divinity School, voices an eloquent appeal for a new role for philosophy as a critique of patriarchal civilization:

In the eyes of many, we live among the ruins of North Atlantic civilization. . . . Possible nuclear holocaust hovers over us. Rampant racism, persistent patriarchy, extensive class inequality, brutal state repression, subtle bureaucratic surveillance, and technological abuse of nature pervade capitalist, communist, and neocolonial countries. The once vital tradition of bourgeois humanism has become vapid and sterile. The emancipatory intent of revolutionary Marxism has been aborted and discredited. The shock effect of catastrophic nihilism is now boring and uninteresting. As we approach the end of the twentieth century, the rich intellectual resources of the West are in disarray and a frightening future awaits us.

(West, p. 259)

Unfortunately, West's tentatively proposed solution—a return to an updated and enlivened form of American pragmatism—is disappointing, for it fails to acknowledge both the provincialism of that tradition and the intellectual promise of alternative "non-

196

philosophical" ways of thinking. An example of the enthnocentricity of neopragmatism can be found in the writings of Richard Rorty, a prominent modern exponent of that school, who argues that the basic world-view of bourgeois Western liberals must continue to set the standards for permissible philosophical discourse:

> We should say that we must, in practice, privilege our own group, even though there can be no noncircular justification for doing so. . . . We Western liberal intellectuals should accept the fact that we have to start where we are, and that this means that there are lots of views which we simply cannot take seriously. . . . It is just the way *we* live now.
>
> (Rorty, p. 12)

The fallacy of Rorty's view is that it discounts the wondrous complexity and richness of intellectual accomplishments from other cultural traditions. It also discounts within the modern West itself the many voices that have something of philosophical significance to say but who are not white, straight-identified, bourgeois, or male.

In the face of the current worldwide patriarchal crisis and the sterility of contemporary American philosophy, a worthy source for new reflection can be found in the many rich and varied historical outgrowths of the Dionysian tradition as well as in the many traditions of non-white cultures embodying Dionysian-type world-views. Maenadism, Orphism, Greek tragedy, medieval "heresy" and "witchcraft," the belief systems of Africa and those of Native American Indians—all are treasure troves of insights that can help in the task of transcending the tired thinking of an ossified patriarchal world and its shriveling rationalist deities.

Of course, none of these traditions is in itself "philosophical," but then neither is mathematics or ordinary language. Philosophy begins with systematic reflection on the implications and presuppositions of a given subject matter. If we can reflect on the ordinary use of the English language, can we not also reflect on the cultural traditions of ancient Greece, the religions of Africa, the heresies of the Middle Ages, or the myths of the original inhabitants of North America?

One of the major impediments to broadening the scope of American philosophy is the limited personnel make-up of American university philosophy departments, which are generally dominated by white, ostensibly heterosexual males with bourgeois lifestyles and values. A wider spectrum of philosophers would encourage a wider spectrum of philosophies. And a wider spectrum of philosophies would help us see beyond the intellectual limitations of patriarchy.

Driven by the six thousand-year history of its own contradictions, the patriarchal world is everywhere in the throes of grave upheavals and perhaps on the verge of its own self-destruction. But in the midst of all the ugliness and violence of our age, something new and better also is struggling to come to birth—a more balanced way of living and a more open definition of what it means to be human. Amid the scenes of this worldwide tragi-comedy, the vision of Euripides and the dance of Dionysos yet remain as sources for wisdom.

APPENDIX

THE GOD OF ECSTASY

❂

A NEW TRANSLATION FROM THE ANCIENT GREEK OF EURIPIDES' PLAY *BAKKHAI*

CONCEPT OF THE PLAY

The following is a complete, new translation of Euripides' play *Bakkhai*, originally written in 406 B.C., with comments pertaining to the production done at the Valencia Rose Cabaret in San Francisco in December 1984.

In the Valencia Rose production, the play was conceived as a critique of patriarchal role-playing. Modern costumes and characterizations were used to emphasize parallels between patriarchal conditions in ancient Greece and today. The actual script used was an abridgment of the following translation. Cuts were made in the lines of the chorus, in long monologues of the principals, and in passages that sound moralistic or tediously tragic to a modern ear (although the cuts have been restored in what follows). The first half of the play was done as a comedy, as Euripides intended.

The set was a giant stylized painting of the face of Dionysos, and his gaping mouth was a stage-center entrance and exit. At first, the face seemed humorous, but as the play progressed it became more ominous, finally looking like the gaping maw of fate.

CAST OF CHARACTERS

DIONYSOS

The god of ecstasy, madness, and revelry; inventor of wine, master of the choral dance, and patron of transvestism; also known as Bakkhos, Iakkhos, and the Raving One.

Dionysos was born from the union of Zeus, the father of the gods, and Semele, a mortal woman. While Semele was pregnant with Dionysos, she was tricked by Hera, Zeus's jealous wife, into asking Zeus to manifest himself to her in his full glory as a god. Hera well knew that no mortal could withstand such a display of power.

When Semele persisted with this request, Zeus reluctantly agreed, and as a result she was burned to death, prematurely expelling her fetus, which Zeus took up and sewed in his thigh until it matured. In time, Dionysos was born from the body of Zeus, replete with the horns of a bull on his head and snakes in his hair.

In Euripides' play, Dionysos makes his first appearance in Greece, coming to the city of Thebes disguised as one of his priests, an effeminate young man with long hair. Seeking revenge for being rejected by the city's ruling clan, he inspires the women of Thebes to abandon their housework and worship him with wild rites in the mountains at night. Men are allowed to join the rites, but only if they wear the fawnskin hides that are viewed as a form of women's clothing.

In his quest to show that he is the Son of God, Dionysos first suffers and then prevails in a manner that later influenced similar Christian motifs. Euripides portrays him here with a wide range of qualities, alternately witty, noble, campy, and vindictive. In the first half of the play, when oppressed, Dionysos is at his most appealing; in the end, when triumphant, he is ruthless. Euripides, although a skeptic and a rationalist, nonetheless took more kindly to the god Dionysos than to many other Greek religious figures. In the end, however, even Dionysos falls before the judgment of Euripides' humanist values.

In this production, Dionysos wears a costume somewhat similar to that of San Francisco's Sisters of Perpetual Indulgence, an order of gay men who wear nunlike habits to enlighten people through satirical humor, but who also have developed a genuine sense of alternative religious ritual and public service. The man who played Dionysos in this production, Assunta Femia, was in fact an early precursor of the Sisters. At the end of the play, Dionysos appears in godlike glory, wearing a mask that displays horns, grape clusters, and snakes; dressed in golden balloon pants; and naked from the waist up, with his torso painted gold.

TEIRESIAS

An aged, blind seer living at Thebes. Although he is one of the few people to recognize the divinity of Dionysos, he is not taken very seriously by others, partly because of his penchant for pontificating bluster, which makes him seem tedious or ridiculous. Like many of those who specialize in cosmic truth, he is quite inept in dealing with people in practical situations. His appearance in this play is largely for comic interest. He wears gaudy drag and flashy sunglasses inset with rhinestones, and carries a large, floppy fennel stalk.

KADMOS

The founder of the city of Thebes and its ruling clan. Once, when much younger, he slew a dragon and planted its teeth in the soil, from which armed men sprang up and killed each other off until only five survived. One of them, Ekhion, married Kadmos' daughter, Agaue, who in turn gave birth to Pentheus, the king of Thebes at the time of this play.

Kadmos is portrayed here as a weak and vacillating character. He is corralled by Teiresias into putting on a woman's fawnskin drape in honor of Dionysos, but he would rather just stay at home out of sight. His appearance with Teiresias in the beginning of the play is largely for comic effect, but in the end, when he experiences a sudden resurgence of the power of his youth in the face of catastrophe, his role carries great pathos. In this production, Kadmos also appears in drag, which he feels most uncomfortable wearing.

PENTHEUS

The grandson of Kadmos, barely out of his adolescence, Pentheus has recently become the king of Thebes. Insecure in this new position, he feels a constant need to prove his masculinity both to himself and others. He has an arrogant attitude toward women and contempt for femininity in men. He is also alienated from his own sexual capacities, especially in regard to other men. The god Dionysos represents to him what he is most afraid of in himself. In this production, Pentheus has the manner of a young, bullying, up-and-coming executive and wears a natty three-piece business suit.

A HENCHMAN OF PENTHEUS

In this production, the henchman appears as a surly cop, somewhat rattled by the marvels he has seen of Dionysos but still loyal to the king.

A HERDSMAN

A young and innocent person of the fields, the herdsman is the first to give the king an eyewitness account of the amazing feats of the driven women of Thebes in the countryside. (As in the later gospel accounts this play influenced, those who keep watch over the flocks in the hills are the first to bear witness to the coming Son of God.) Pentheus is secretly fascinated with the physical beauty of the young herdsman but is horrified by his message. In this production, the herdsman is dressed like a Swiss shepherd.

A SLAVE

The king's personal attendant who has witnessed his death and immolation at the hands of the women of Thebes. In this production, the slave appears as the king's drunken chauffeur, dressed in black leather and with a Bronx accent, who has mixed feelings about the king's death. On one hand, the chauffeur resents the arrogant way the king has abused him and so is glad to see him fare ill, but on the other he is genuinely horrified by the ghastly spectacle he has seen. The slave's performance is the hinge of the play, since it is with his appearance that the action moves from comedy to nightmare.

AGAUE

The mother of King Pentheus. Her aristocratic values lead her to disdain the blurring of class and sex lines characteristic of the worship of Dionysos, whom she condescendingly dismisses. In retaliation, Dionysos drives her mad, and she leaves the city with her sisters Ino and Autonoe to join the wild mountain revels of the god.

Agaue goes through a radical transformation in the play, from raving Mad Woman to a very sober mother of sorrows. In her confrontation with the god at the end, she is completely overwhelmed by the superiority of divine power, yet maintains a kind of moral victory through her expression of humane values in the face of the nastiness of the triumphant Dionysos. She is really the central character in the play, and her depiction here is one of the most magnificent in Greek tragedy.

In this production Agaue wears a hunting outfit in the style of British aristocrats.

CHORUS OF BARBARIAN MAD WOMEN

The foreign-born attendants of Dionysos who have followed him to Thebes from Asia Minor in the East. They always remain loyal to Dionysos and to Kybele, the Great Mother. The leading matrons of Thebes treat them with great contempt since they are wild, unkempt foreigners. They get their vengeance by taunting the aristocratic Agaue in her madness.

The chorus should not be confused with the native women of Thebes. The latter have been driven out of the city by Dionysos and (with the exception of Agaue) never appear in the play, although their behavior is described by both the herdsman and the slave.

In ancient Greek productions, the lines of the chorus were originally sung in segments, and each segment was sung while, or after, the chorus danced from one side of the stage to the other ("turns" and "returns"). These choral movements are indicated in the text.

In this production, the chorus is dressed like a pack of psychedelic bag ladies. Their lines are never recited in unison, but divided up among individual members.

NATURE OF THE TRANSLATION

Throughout the play, I have aimed at translating the meaning and feeling of episodes rather than the literal denotation of individual words. In languages in general, and most particularly with ancient Greek, meaning is conveyed not only through words, but also by word order, inflection, idiomatic usage of moods and tenses, literary connotation, and historical allusion. Anyone who believes in a literal translation of Greek (including the Bible, by the way) is a believer in mirages, for Greek, when literally translated into English, is gibberish. For example, the opening lines of this play, when translated word for word, are as follows:

> Have arrived Zeus's son this of Thebans' land
> Dionysos, whom gives birth at length the Kadmos' daughter
> Semele, forced into labor by lightning-born fire.

This passage makes perfectly good sense in ancient Greek because of the conventions of meaning in that language, but it is totally useless in English, which has completely different conventions.

Euripides did not intend for his Greek script to be pored over by scholars in isolation but to be acted out on the stage before thousands. Hence I have aimed at creating an English translation that can be used for actual production of the play, and to that end have used words that are familiar and a syntax that is straightforward, in contrast to the archaic words and contrived sentence structure usually found in such translations.

Like all Greek playwrights, Euripides wrote his original text in metered verse. Although generations of scholars have argued over how to analyze Greek meter, the tragic poets themselves basically conceived of their lines as alternations of short and long syllables in a basic pattern of short-long, short-long, interspersed with a number of patterned exceptions (Raven, p. 27). To the ears of the Greek audience, the effect was that of a rhythm going da-DUM, da-DUM, the closest rhythm to that of natural speech, as Aristotle somewhere observes, but with numerous variations where the feeling or context of the action required a different beat, as in the songs of the chorus. To approximate in English the effect of the Greek sound patterns, I have used a style of meter I call iambic variameter—loosely structured successions of iambic feet with interludes of other meters where they feel appropriate.

Since some parts of the original text for this play have not survived intact, I have had to reconstruct them, based on existing fragments and indirect evidence. Such reconstructions are indicated by brackets.

CAST AND CREW OF THE ORIGINAL PRODUCTION

The following are the cast and crew for the original production of *The God of Ecstasy* as performed in the Valencia Rose Cabaret in San Francisco from December 4, 1984, through January 15, 1985:

CAST IN ORDER OF APPEARANCE:

Dionysos _____ Assunta Femia
Leader of the Chorus _____ Jackie Boykin

Chorus of Barbarian Mad Women _____	Chandria
	Diana
	Shessa
	Janet Tranbarger
Teiresias _____	Ben Gardiner
Kadmos _____	Jody Ellsworth
Henchman _____	Mark Borrowman
Pentheus _____	Earl Galvin
Herdsman _____	Mark Mardon
Slave _____	Jack Fertig
	(a.k.a. Sister Boom Boom)
Agaue _____	Michele Richards
Pallbearer _____	Ed Brophy

PRODUCTION CREW:

Director _____	Arthur Evans
Assistant Director _____	Jody Ellsworth
Staging Consultant _____	Carl Henry
Choreography _____	Randall Krivonic
Photography _____	Douglas Pickarts
	José-Luis Moscovich
Sound _____	Robert-John Florence
Lights _____	Nicholos Reigh
Set Design _____	David Larson
Set Construction _____	Michael Huckins
	Frederick
	Gary Rashman
	Steve Kocsis
	José-Luis Moscovich
Stage Manager _____	Ben Gardiner
Mask of Dionysos _____	John Soares
Costumes of Dionysos _____	Ray Graetz
Technical Assistance _____	Paul Stewart

THE
GOD
OF
ECSTASY

❂

ACT I

[Enter the god Dionysos, disguised as one of his priests, that is, as an effemi-
nate young man with long hair. In this production, he is dressed in a nunlike
costume. His opening style is alternately threatening, engaging, campy, and
ironic.]

Dion.   I am Dionysos—the Son of God!—
    And I have just arrived here in the land of Thebes.
    My mother was Semele, a mortal, Kadmos's daughter.
    While pregnant by Zeus
    She was hit by the fire of his lightning bolt
    And then gave birth . . . to me.

    I've changed my form from a god's to a man's,
    And here I stand by Thebes' two streams,
    The Ismenos and the River Dirke.
    Beyond, near houses and halls,
    I can see the tomb of my lightning-struck mother,

A ruin that smolders still
From the eternal flame of Zeus's fire—
A lasting offense by Zeus's wife,
Jealous goddess Hera.

Kadmos I commend,
For he made a sacred spot
Of the place where his daughter lies,
And I myself have covered it over
With the green of the grapevine's leaves.

From Lydia have I come and Phrygia,
The golden lands,
From sun-drenched plains in Persia,
From the walled cities of Baktria,
From the dreaded land of Media.

And I have passed through the whole of happy Arabia
And all of Asia Minor's coast
That lies along the salty sea,
Thronged with Greeks and barbarians thrown together
In beautifully towered towns.

This is the first Greek city I've come to
After bringing to others my chorus dance,
Establishing for them my rites,
Revealing myself a god.
Yes, in Thebes I first raised the women's cry
Of *olololo* in the land of Greece.
And I covered their bodies with a fawnskin dress
And put in their hands a weapon, the thyrsos,
My ivy wand.

But the sisters of my mother,
Those that I expected least,
Denied that I was born from Zeus.
They said some *man* had come and slept with Semele,
And she blamed the affair on Zeus.
They said her tale was a trick by her father, Kadmos,
And because she lied, they sneered,
Zeus had killed her.

And so from their homes I drove these sisters frenzied
To live beside themselves in hills,
Wearing the dress of my rites.
And I drove insane from their homes as well
All the women who reside in Thebes,
Each and every one.
Along with the daughters of Kadmos
They sit on rocks, beneath the boughs of silver firs,
Without a roof for their heads.

This city, a stranger now to my ecstatic rites,
Must learn its lesson well, although against its will:
I speak to defend my mother Semele
And reveal myself the god
That she conceived through God.

So then, Kadmos gave the throne of Thebes
To Pentheus, his daughter's son,
And Pentheus contends against the gods
By the way he mistreats me,
Excluding me from libations,
Forgetting me in prayers.
For that, I'll prove to him and all of Thebes
That I was born a god.

And when I set things right in Thebes,
I'll set my course for another land
And reveal myself a god.
And if the city of Thebes, in wrath, gets troops
And tries to take from the hills
The women who follow Bakkhos,
Generals will be routed by Mad Women.

So that's why I've changed and have a human face
And show the shape of man.

[*Turning to the Chorus, which is waiting concealed at the rear entrance of the theater:*]

Now you who left Mt. Tmolos,
Lydia's famous fortress,

My sacred band,
Women I've gathered from out of barbarian lands,
My comrades on the move, my aides,
Lift up, lift up your tambourines!—
The ones you brought from the land of Phrygia,
Devised by me and Mother Rhea.
Go to the royal palace there of Pentheus
And make them ring.
Let Thebes, the city of Kadmos, see!

I myself will go to the glens of Mt. Kithairon
And join the dance
With the women possessed by Bakkhos there.

*[Exit Dionysos. Enter the Chorus of barbarian Mad Women from the rear
entrance of the auditorium, howling, writhing, pulsating down the center aisle.
The lines of the Chorus are not recited in unison, but divided up among its
individual members.]*

[First Turn]

Chorus: From the land of Asia Minor
I left the holy mountain Tmolos.
I am flying with the Raving One—
What an easy chore! What a pleasant task!
I shout the cries of Bakkhos!

[First Return]

To all who are on the street,
To all who are in their homes,
Make way!
Let every tongue be hushed,
Made ready for the holy.
For now will I sing,
As always sung before,
The hymn of Dionysos.

[Second Turn]

Happy is she whose luck is to know
The rites of the gods,

Who makes her life into something holy,
Who joins her soul to the sacred band,
Who worships Bakkhos on mountains
With sacred rites of cleansing.
She observes the mysteries of Great Mother Kybele,
And shaking high her thyrsos,
Crowned with ivy,
Worships Dionysos.
Come, women of Bakkhos, women, come!
Raving Dionysos, a god's son, a god—
Bring Dionysos down from Phrygia's high peaks,
Yes, down, down to the very highways of Greece,
The Raving One!

[Second Return]

When his mother went into labor,
Forced by Zeus's bolt of fire,
Her womb expelled a fetus,
And she died from the lightning's strike.
The son of Kronos, Zeus,
Concealed the child at once
In a secret place for birth,
Enfolding him in his thigh,
And clamped it shut with a pin of gold,
Hidden from Hera.
And when the Fates matured him,
Zeus gave birth to a bull-horned god,
And crowned his son with a wreath of snakes.
And so the women possessed by Bakkhos catch wild
snakes
And weave them in their hair.

[Third Turn]

Oh Thebes, you who are the mother of Semele,
Put on a crown of ivy!
Blossom yourselves
With bright-green, red-berried milax vines,
And dance for Bakkhos with boughs of oak and fir.

Prepare a fringe of white-wool braids
To wear on spotted fawnskin clothes.
Prepare and bless the haughty fennel stalks.

The whole world now without delay
Will be a chorus line,
When he who raves conducts, from peak to peak,
His sacred band.
There the female sex, amassed, abides,
Driven by a god—Dionysos!—from shuttle and loom.

[Third Return]

Oh den of dancing warriors
And holy haunt in Crete where Zeus was born,
Where Kybele's thick-plumed priests
Devised in a cave this tight-skinned tambourine—
In the rites of Bakkhos they mingled its sound
With the clear, sweet air of Phrygian flutes,
And into the hands of a goddess, Mother Rhea,
They put the beat with shouts from Raving Women.
Frenzied satyrs then took the skin
From the Mother Goddess' hands
And mixed its sound
With the dance that's done on alternate years
In feasts that delight Dionysos.

[Finale]

What a delight he is in the hills
When he breaks from the speeding pack,
Down on all fours,
Clothed in a priestly fawnskin dress,
Stalking the blood of goats just killed—
Raw-flesh delight!—
Hurling himself from mountain to mountain
In Phrygia and Lydia,
Our priest and leader, possessed by Bakkhos—
Hai-ee!

211

[*Reconstructed lines:*]

> [And the women who surge and dance
> In the pine-thick peaks
> And toss their heads for the dancing god
> Suffer no lack,
> Though far removed from the granaries of men.]

[*Resumption of text:*]

> He makes the land to flow with milk, with wine,
> With the nectar of bees,
> [And so he makes them satisfied].
>
> The priest of Bakkhos,
> With pine-cone torch aflame
> And placed atop a fennel stalk,
> Its smoke like Syrian frankincense,
> Runs out,
> Inciting wanderers with dances,
> Shaking and shouting,
> Throwing his delicate locks to the air.
> With shouts of joy,
> He bellows as follows:
> "Oh come, women of Bakkhos, come!
> You are the glory of gold-filled Tmolos.
> Sing of Dionysos! Thump tambourines!
> Shout the praises of the shouting god
> With Phrygian screams and cries!
> And play on melodic and sacred pipes
> Your sacred and playful tunes
> In the journey from mountain to mountain."
>
> And so the women of Bakkhos, enthused by his call,
> Make quick, swift-footed leaps
> Like fillies with their grazing mother.

[*Exit the chorus. Enter Teiresias, dressed in drag and wearing a drape of fawnskin as well as flashy sunglasses inset with large rhinestones. Though blind, he feels his way along with determination, bellowing and shaking a large fennel stalk.*]

212

Teir. Is someone by the gate?
Then go and summon Kadmos from his house,
Agenor's son, who left Lebanon's city of Sidon
And founded the city of Thebes in Greece.
Go and say that I, Teiresias, a seer, but blind,
Am looking for him.
He himself knows why I've come—
What I, though old, agreed to do with one yet older—
Take up the thyrsos, put on a fawnskin hide,
Crown my head with ivy twines!

[Enter Kadmos, also in drag. He is apprehensive about how he looks but reluctant to offend the determined Teiresias, whom he tries to placate.]

Kad. Dear one, while in the house
I heard wise words
And one who was wise enough to speak them
And knew that it was you.
I've come prepared and wear *[clearing his throat]*
A god's attire.

Now since Dionysos is my daughter's son
And has appeared as a god to men,
We must, as best we can, exalt him.

But where shall we go to dance?
Where to kick our feet?
And where shall we shake our old gray heads?
Teiresias, be my leader, old man to old,
For you are wise.
I'll not tire by day or night
To pound my thyrsos up and down.
I'm glad to forget I'm old.

Teir. Yes, Kadmos, we feel the same indeed
I, as well, am in my prime
And want to try to dance.

Kad. *[Nervous about being seen]*
Shouldn't we drive our chariot, then,
Up to the mountain heights?

213

Teir. [Blustering and inadvertently hitting Kadmos when he flails
his arms around]
No! For the god would not have fitting honor.

Kad. [Grabbing his hand to protect himself]
Then I will take you by the hand,
Age ahead of age.

Teir. The god himself will lead us there with ease.

Kad. Are we the only men in Thebes
To dance with Bakkhos?

Teir. We alone received him.
All the rest did not.

Kad. Well then, let us go. Come, take my hand.

Teir. And here is mine, so there's a pair.

[They begin walking off, hand in hand]

Kad. I am but a mortal man. Who am I to slight the gods?

Teir. [With more bluster, loving to hear himself preach]
We cannot play the sophist with the gods.
The traditions handed down to us are old as time.
No logic will ever beat them,
Even with the sharpest minds.

They'll say I'm a disgrace in my old age
Wanting to dance with an ivy crown.
The god, in truth, does not divide
The young from old as to who must dance
But wants in common to be honored by all
And seeks no partial homage.

Kad. Since you, Teiresias, can't see this light,
I'll interpret and be your guide.

214

[He gazes to the rear of the theater and is startled]

> Why, here comes Pentheus hurrying home,
> Ekhion's son, to whom I gave the throne.
> How distraught he looks!
> I wonder what news he brings.

[Enter Pentheus from the rear of the auditorium, walking down the aisle, speaking to individual members of the audience. He is dressed in a three-piece business suit. He speaks with both anger and fascination about the rumors he has heard concerning Dionysos.]

Pen. While I by chance was away from this land,
   I heard bad things had reached the town—
   Our women here, spurred by phony fits of frenzy,
   Have left their homes
   To run about on dark-shaded mountain slopes,
   Holding dances in honor of Dionysos,
   Whoever he is, a newcomer god.

   I hear the bowls are full of wine amid their feasts
   And they sneak off to this or that deserted spot
   To service men in bed,
   Pretending to be some kind of raving priest,
   But serving, instead of Bakkhos,
   Love-goddess Aphrodite.

   So my men are guarding in the jail,
   Chained by their arms,
   All the women I've had arrested.
   And as for those who fled to the hills,
   I'll hunt them down:
   Agaue—my very mother!—
   As well as Autonoe and Ino,
   My mother's sisters.
   I'll tie them together with a net of steel
   And soon put an end to this evil frenzy.

   They say some stranger—a sorcerer, an enchanter—
   Has come to the city from the land of Lydia.
   He wears, they say, sweet-scented locks of auburn hair,

215

That his face is flushed,
That his eyes have the grace of a goddess, Aphrodite,
That by day and by night he stays with young women
And shows them ecstatic rites.

The day I get him in this building here,
I'll stop him from stamping his thyrsos,
From shaking his hair,
And from his body I'll sever his head.

He pretends Dionysos is a god
And once was sewed in Zeus's thigh—
He who was burned by the lightning's flash
And his mother, too,
Who lied about sleeping with God.
Whoever this stranger may be,
Such things are outrageous, I say,
And worthy of hanging's grim death.

[He sees Teiresias and Kadmos and is appalled]

What?! What a sight is this!
There's Teiresias, the blind seer,
Wearing a spotted fawnskin dress!
And there's my mother's father, Kadmos—a joke!—
Shaking a giant fennel stalk.

Father, you make me ashamed when I see
In old age how you've lost your mind.
Come now, throw that ivy crown away!
Oh father of my mother,
Toss that thyrsos out of your hand.

It was *you*, Teiresias, who brought him to this.
Ha, when you preach this new god to men
What you really want is pay
To interpret the flights of birds,
To expound the signs of sacrifice.
Were you not excused by the gray of your head,
You'd be sitting in jail with the women of Bakkhos
And teaching the mysteries of grief.

With women, when grapes appear at the feast,
The rites, I say, can never be good.

[A member of the Chorus, who has been sitting in the audience, rises and shouts out like a heckler at a political demonstration.]

Chorus. What disrespect you have for religion!
Stranger, don't you respect the gods
Or Kadmos, who planted the seeds
That grew from earth as men?
You, the son of Ekhion, shame your kin!

Teir. When the speaker is skilled and the cause good,
Speaking well is easy.
But with you, your tongue is slick, like someone smart,
But sense is not in your words.
A man who is bold, strong and able to speak,
But has no sense—
Ha! What a poor excuse for a citizen!

This new god, the one at whom you laugh,
I cannot say with words how great he'll be
Throughout the land of Greece.

[In pantomime, Pentheus pleads with Kadmos, who is greatly embarrassed and nervously points to Teiresias. The latter, in the meantime, is oblivious to their encounter and blusters away.]

The essential things for men are two, young man:
First the Goddess Demeter
(She is also Earth, call her what you will).
With dry-grain foods she rears the human race.
He who came in next, the son of Semele, Bakkhos,
Found the other half, the liquid food of grapes,
Which he gave to us to drink.
And when we enjoy to the full the grapevine's juice,
It stops the feeling of pain, brings sleep,
And makes us forget our daily ills.
For human woe, there is no better cure.
Being himself a god,
He is poured on our altars as an offering to gods,
And so through him do mortals have good things.

You laugh that he was sewn in Zeus' thigh.
I can show how that account is good.
Zeus snatched him from the lightning's fire
And took the infant god to Mt. Olympos,
But Hera, Zeus' wife, sought to throw him out.
So Zeus devised a plot against her
And one befitting a god.
He took a piece of the starry sphere
That surrounds the earth,
And *that's* the thing he gave as hostage to Hera,
Thus sparing that child himself from Hera's wrath.

Now since the god gave Hera a *hostage*
And *homeros* is the word for this in Greek,
Men in time said Bakkhos was nursed in Zeus' thigh,
Changing *homeros* to *ho meros*, meaning "thigh."

This god is a prophet,
For much of prophecy's power is found
Where ecstasy exists and madness.
When the god possesses their bodies in force,
He makes the Mad Ones tell what is to be.

And he has a role in Ares' sphere, the god of war.
When the enemy has come and arrayed itself to fight,
At times a sudden fear will come
And make them run in panic from the field
Before a spear is even thrown.
This madness, too, is a gift from Dionysos.

And one day yet
You'll see him on the cliffs of Delphi, too,
Where the god Apollo has his seat,
Bounding with torches on the twin-peaked plain,
Brandishing and shaking the branch
Of his ecstatic rites,
Renowned throughout the whole of Greece.

Oh heed me, Pentheus,
Don't boast that your rule extends over men
Or think that you yourself are very smart.

If you do, your mind is much deceived.
Receive the god into your land,
Make him an offering of wine,
Rejoice, and crown your head with ivy!

And Dionysos will *not* compel, in sex or love,
A woman to act with self-restraint.
No, for whether she is moderate or not
Is up to her own nature.
You must consider this:
Even in ecstatic rites,
She who is really moderate will not become corrupt.

Look, you yourself rejoice
When people stand by the gate
And the city extols the name of Pentheus.

And he as well, I think, enjoys himself when praised.
So Kadmos and I, at whom you laugh,
Will crown ourselves with ivy leaves and do the dance.
A gray-haired couple, true, yet dance we must.

I'll not heed your words and fight against the gods.
Grievous is your madness.
You'll not get a healthy mind
Even with the use of magic charms,
Though you would not be sick right now except for them.

[A member of the Chorus again speaks from the audience.]

Chorus. Old man, your words would please Apollo,
    Moderation's god,
    And when you praise the Raving One,
    You show how sane you are,
    Since's he's a god of greatness.

Kad. Son, Teiresias gave you good advice.
    Dwell with us and not outside the ancient way.
    You're troubled now; you don't make sense.
    And if, indeed, just as you say, he's not a god,

219

Still, why not claim he is? Tell a useful lie
So Semele will look like the mother of a god,
And praise will come to us and our whole clan.

You saw Aktaion's wretched fate, your cousin.
Flesh-eating dogs he trained for himself
Tore him apart in the open field
When he claimed to surpass at the hunt
The one who is its patron,
Goddess Artemis.
Let this not happen to you!
Come, crown your head with ivy.
Join us.
Show the god respect.

Pen.   Aawwgh! Don't beg me with your hands,
But go and dance with Bakkhos.
Your madness won't rub off on me!
This teacher of your folly here will get his due.

[Aside, to one of his thugs]

Have someone run with speed.
Go to the oracle's seat
Where the prophet Teiresias reads the signs.
Take clubs and overturn it, knock it upside down,
Scramble up his things.
In doing this, I'll get him good!

Let those who patrol the land of Thebes
Hunt till they find the effeminate foreigner
Who exposes our women to a strange obsession
And abuses the bed of marriage.
And when at last you catch him,
Bring him here in chains.
He'll soon see how Thebes has its own harsh rites
When he dies the death of stoning.

Teir.   How sad—you don't even know what you're saying.
Before you were losing control of yourself,
But now you're raving mad.

220

[Exit Pentheus in a huff.]

Kadmos, we'll go and intercede for him,
Although he's wild, and for the city, too,
So the god will do no harm.

Come, follow me, and bring the ivy wand.
Try to hold me up, and I'll help you.
What a disgrace for two old men to fall.
Well, so what. We have to serve the Son of God.

Kadmos, beware this grievous king
Does not bring grief upon your clan.
I say this not by prophecy's gift—
The events can speak for themselves.
A fool he is to speak such folly.

[Exit Teiresias and Kadmos, hobbling off hand in hand. Re-enter the Chorus.]

[First Turn]

Chorus.   Oh Heavenly Justice,
Queen of the Gods,
You who lower your golden wings to earth,
You see what Pentheus did.
You see it's against what's right,
This abuse against the Raving One,
Semele's son,
The god with his festivals and lovely crowns,
He who's happiest of all.

This is his role:
To revel in dance with his sacred band,
To laugh with the flute,
To scatter cares
Whenever the fruit of the vine
Is served at the feasts of the gods
Or when, at holidays decked with ivy,
A bowl of wine can clothe our cares in sleep.

[First Return]

The end is grief
For unchecked tongues
And thoughtless acts against what's right.
A quiet life of self-control
Remains intact and saves the home.

Though living far away and in the sky,
The gods can see the acts of men.

Smart is not the same as wise.
To act like we're above mankind,
That will make life short.
And if we chase what's great,
Perhaps we'll lose what's now at hand.
Such are the ways of those who are mad
And of men, I say, who are ill-advised.

[Second Turn]

I wish I were in Cyprus,
Aphrodite's land,
Where the Passions dwell
That enchant the hearts of men.
Or in that foreign land
Where no rain falls
Yet bursts in bloom from the River Nile
With its hundred feeding streams.
Or where Pieria is, fairest spot of all,
Olympos' holy slope,
The Muses' temple.
Oh Raving One, Ecstatic God,
Master of the Sacred Dance,
Take me, take me there!
That is where the Graces are
And young god Passion, too.
And there the ones possessed by Bakkhos
Are free to hold their rites.

[Second Return]

The god that is the Son of God
Delights in celebrations.

And he loves the goddess Peace,
The bearer of prosperity,
The nurturer of children.
To rich and poor alike
He gave the gift of wine that kills our pain.
He hates those men who aren't concerned
To live their days and treasured nights
In happiness and in joy.

It's wise to keep your heart and mind away
From those who are too smart.
The simple things
That common people love and use,
That's what I would take.

[Enter Henchman and Attendants, dressed like cops, with Dionysos as a captive. The Chorus flees. Pentheus enters on stage through the center-mouth.]

Henchman.   Pentheus!
Pentheus, my lord, your troops are here.
We caught the prey you sent us for.
We did not start out in vain.

This beast, though wild, was meek with us
And made no try to run away.
He surrendered of his own accord,
Not pale with fear, but with cheeks aglow.
With laughter he bid me bind and lead him on,
And then he waited, and made my job an easy one.
And I in shame addressed him thus:

"Not by my will do I take you, stranger,
But by decree of Pentheus, the King, who sent me."

Besides, those Raving Women you detained,
The ones you seized and bound in chains in jail,
They're gone, escaped, skipping off along the meadows
And calling on their raving god.
Their chains by themselves fell off their feet,
And the keys moved the door by a hand not human.

This man has come to us in Thebes with many wonders.
What happens next is up to you.

[In the following scene, Pentheus is both attracted to and repelled by Dionysos, several times approaching and fondling him and then suddenly pulling back. Dionysos, in turn, keeps enticing and teasing his captor.]

Pen. Release his hands. He's in my net.
He can't move fast enough to fly from me.

[Pentheus approaches Dionysos and starts fondling him
and then quickly pulls back his hand:]

So, stranger, your body's not bad . . .
At least as a woman would judge!
Which is why you came to Thebes.
[Feeling his hair]
And your hair's so long . . . no athlete you!—
[Feeling his cheek]
And falls below your cheeks . . . so full of lust!
[Feeling his hands]
And your skin is fair and pale . . .
Because of the life you lead!
Not in the rays of the sun, but in the dark,
You pursue with your beauty Aphrodite.
[Regaining his composure]
Well now, tell me what country you're from.

Dion. Nothing worth boasting, a small thing to say.
You've heard, I suppose, of Mt. Tmolos,
The range of mountains renowned for flowers?

Pen. Yes, it curves about the town of Sardis.

Dion. That's where I'm from. My home is Lydia.

Pen. Why have you brought these rites to Greece?

Dion. The Son of God, Dionysos, sent me.

Pen. Oh, is there some Zeus there who's fathering new gods?

Dion. No, but he who had sex with Semele *here.*

Pen. Did your god command you at night in sleep
Or openly during the day?

Dion. Eye to eye the rites were given.

Pen. What's the nature of these rites of yours?

Dion. It is forbidden to know the rites
For those outside the sacred band.

Pen. Do they bring the members some good?

Dion. You have no right to hear,
But they're certainly worth the knowing.

Pen. You've faked it so well, I want to hear.

Dion. The rites of this god
Detest a man who does not respect the gods.

Pen. So—you say you clearly saw this god.
What did he look like, then?

Dion. Just the way he wanted to. Do *I* determine that?

Pen. You evade this question, too,
By talking nonsense.

Dion. To the ignorant,
One who speaks with knowledge
Makes no sense.

Pen. Is this land the first to which you've brought the god?

Dion. All the barbarians dance these rites.

Pen. Of course, they have much less sense than *Greeks!*

Dion. In this case, more. Their customs are different.

Pen. These rites, do you do them at night or in the day?

Dion. Mostly at night. In darkness is holiness.

Pen. This is a treacherous way for women
And one not sound.

Dion. One can also find shame in the day.

Pen. You'll pay the price for your nasty tricks.

Dion. And you for stupidity
And your lack of respect for the god.

Pen. How bold this fan of Bakkhos is
And not untrained in words!

Dion. Well then, tell me how I'll suffer.
What awful things will you do?

Pen. First, I'll shave your dainty hair.

Dion. My hair is sacrosanct. I grow it as the god's.

Pen. Next, give me that thyrsos there!

Dion. No! You'll have to *take* it from me.
This staff I carry belongs to Dionysos.

Pen. I'll lock you up in prison.

Dion. The god himself will set me free
When I myself desire.

Pen. *If*, that is, you ever get to call on him
While out again with Raving Women.

Dion. He's close at hand right now
And sees what I am suffering.

Pen. Well, where is he, then?
He remains unseen to *me*.

226

Dion. He's right where I'm standing here.
        Your lack of reverence is your lack of sight.

Pen. Seize him! This man's in contempt of Thebes and me.

[Cops grab and rough up Dionysos.]

Dion. As sanity calling the sane,
        So I bid you not to bind me.

Pen. When it comes to the power to bind,
        My reach is greater than yours.

Dion. You don't know what you're saying,
        Or what you're doing,
        Or who you are.

Pen. I am Pentheus, the son of Agaue,
        And son of my father Ekhion.

Dion. Your name resembles *penthos*, Greek for "grief,"
        And fits you well for your misfortune.

Pen. Go! Lock him up nearby,
        Right in the horses' stable,
        So he'll gaze on the black of darkness.
        Dance *there!*
        And as for your cohorts in mischief,
        The women you brought here with you,
        I'll put them up for sale.
        Or else, when I stop their hands
        From pounding their tambourines,
        I'll keep them as slaves for the loom.

Dion. I'll go. But I'll never suffer what is not my fate.
        And I warn you this: the god Dionysos,
        The one you say does not exist,
        Will make you pay for these insults.
        In wronging me, you're leading *him* to jail.

227

[Exit all. Enter Chorus.]

[Turn]

Chorus. Oh River Dirke, Our Lady, happy maid,
        Daughter of Akheloios, who fathered all the streams,
        You once received in your waters the son of Zeus
        When the god retrieved him from the eternal flame
        To hide within his thigh.
        And Zeus then cried to his son:
        "Come, Dithyramb,
        Come enter this, my manly womb.
        Oh Bakkhos, by the name of *Dithyramb*
        I decree that Thebes shall call you."

        But now, oh happy Dirke, now you reject me
        While I stand before you with troops
        Who wear the ivy crown.

        Why, then, disown and spurn me? Why?
        By the clustered beauty of Dionysos' vine,
        I swear you will yet come to terms
        With the Raving God.

[Return]

        Pentheus lives up to his family's roots,
        To his father Ekhion,
        Who was born from the tooth of a dragon
        Planted in the earth by Kadmos.
        He's a wild-faced beast, no typical man,
        Bloody as a Giant who combats the gods,
        He'll soon have me, the follower of Bakkhos,
        Locked up in chains.
        Already he detains on the grounds of his palace
        My friend in the sacred band.

        Oh Son of God, Dionysos, god,
        Do you see how those who reveal your will
        Have to contend with force?

Come, descend, Oh Lord, from the heights of Olympos!
Come and shake your golden wand!
Suppress the crime of a violent man!

[Finale]

Dionysos, where on Mt. Nysa, then,
That haunt of ferocious beasts,
Do you summon with thyrsos your sacred band?
Or where on the peaks of Parnassos?
Perhaps in the thick-wooded glens of Olympos,
There where Orpheus, playing his lyre,
Once called the trees through song,
Once called the beasts of prey.

Oh happy Pieria,
The God of Ecstasy reveres you
And will come with revelry and with dance.
He will cross the swift-flowing stream of Axios
And will lead his Mad Women whirling.
And he will cross as well the Lydias River,
The father of rivers, the source of blessings to men.
It enriches, I hear, with the loveliest of streams
A land renowned for its steeds.

[Dionysos calls to the Chorus from off-stage in the voice of a god, answering their prayer for help.]

Dion.   Oh, listen, listen, listen to me!
           Oh, women of Bakkhos, women, oh!

Chorus.   What?! Who's that?
           The voice of Ecstasy?
           Where is it calling me from?

Dion.   Oh, oh, again I cry,
           The son of Semele, the Son of God.

Chorus.   Oh Lord, my lord,
           Come and join our sacred band,
           You who rave, who rave—

Dion.   Let Goddess Earthquake shake the land!

[*An Earthquake strikes with great rumblings and flashes of light. The members of the Chorus stagger about, each delivering a subset of the following lines:*]

Chorus. Ahhhhhhhh!
Soon the palace of Pentheus will be shaken down!
Dionysos—look, he moves upon the palace!
May he be praised!

Yes, praise the god!

Look, the stone caps there on the columns,
They're starting to move!

Within the walls, within the walls,
A Raving God is screaming.

[*Dionysos again calls from offstage*]

Dion. Strike, fiery flashes of lightning, strike!
Burn the royal house of Pentheus down!

[*Crash of cymbals*]

Chorus. Look, look,
Can't you see, right there,
Fire around the tomb of Semele?
It's the very flame of Zeus' bolt
That remained behind when she was hit.

Oh Raving Women of Bakkhos,
Throw yourselves to the ground and shake,
For he is upon the palace
Now to tumble it down,
Our Lord, the Son of God!

[*The Chorus throws itself to the floor, pounding feet and fists on the stage and screaming. Dionysos, still in the same disguise, enters from the side. The noise suddenly stops, the Chorus looks up, and he begins quietly and rather coyly . . .*]

Dion. Barbarian women,
So struck with fear

230

You've thrown yoursleves to the ground?
No doubt you saw how Bakkhos
Shook down the house of Pentheus.
Come, stand up, take heart,
Don't shake.

[The Chorus rises and huddles around him.]

Chorus.   It's you,
The leading light in our ecstatic rites.
How glad I am to see you.
Before I felt so lonely.

Dion.   Did you despair when I was taken in,
In fear I would succumb
While in the dark of Pentheus' jail?

Chorus.   I did. For who would then protect me
If you should meet misfortune?
But how did you get free
After falling in with that unholy man?

Dion.   Why, with ease I saved myself without a strain.

Chorus.   But didn't he bind your hands with chains?

[The Chorus recedes, as Dionysos steps forward to tell his story, in which the Chorus takes delight with audible laughter.]

Dion.   This is how I made a *fool* of him:
I made him think he jailed me
When in fact he neither touched nor bound me
But fed on expectations.

By the stable there where he had led and held me
He found a bull
And tied a rope around its knees and hooves.
And all the while he dripped with sweat,
Seethed with hate,
And bit his lips.
Nearby I sat at peace and watched.

While this was taking place,
Bakkhos came and downed the palace,
And then his mother's tomb burst into flames.
When Pentheus saw the tomb,
He thought his house on fire.
He ran about in circles, back and forth,
And told his slaves to fetch some water.
And every slave went at the task,
But that was pointless.

And then he thought that I'd escaped,
And so gave up this task
And seized a sword of iron
And rushed into his house.

And then the Raving One—
Or so it seems to me, it's just my guess—
Put a phantom image in the yard.
Pentheus jumped, then ran and jabbed the empty air,
As though he were slaying *me*.

And Bakkhos did this to him besides:
He smashed his house all to the ground,
Now a ruin in a thousand pieces,
So Pentheus would know how harsh my chains.

And when the fight had worn him out,
He dropped the sword.
For though a man, he dared do battle with a god.
And so I left the house, heedless of Pentheus,
And came to you.

Wait,
I think I hear his footsteps now within the house.
He'll soon be at the door.
In view of all that's happened,
What can he possibly say?

Well, I'll put up with his rantings,
Even if he comes in a huff.
A wise man out to practice being even-tempered.

[The Chorus flees. Pentheus enters nearly delirious.]

Pen.   A terrible thing has happened to me!
The stranger has escaped,
The one just put in chains.

Say, say—here he is! What's going on?
How'd you get out to stand before my house?

Dion.   Hold it! In anger, take an easy step.

Pen.   How'd you escape from your chains and get out here?

Dion.   But didn't I say, or didn't you hear,
That one would come and free ̄me?

Pen.   Who? Your words are always weird.

Dion.   He who makes the grapevine grow for men.

Pen.   *[Reconstructed line:]*
[Yes, and makes them act besides themselves.]

Dion.   You'd *blame* Dionysos for a thing so fine?

Pen.   *[Aside, to one of his thugs]*
I command that all the gates around be locked.

Dion.   What, you think the gods can't scale the walls?

Pen.   Oh, you're smart, real smart,
Except for where it counts.

Dion.   I *am* smart, you're right,
And exactly where it counts.

But stop now and listen to this herder's story.
He's come from the heights with news for you.
I'll wait.
I'll still be here.

233

[A young Herdsman rushes down the aisle from the rear of the theater, breathless and highly agitated.]

Herd. Pentheus, Lord of the land of Thebes,
I come from Mt. Kithairon,
Where the snow's bright, white glare
Has never failed.

Pen. What heavy news have *you* come to tell?

Herd. I have seen the screaming Mad Women
Who ran barefoot and frenzied from this land.
If I may, I've come to tell the city
And you, my lord,
They do strange things, beyond belief.
I want to know if I may freely speak to you
Of these events or else hold back the tale.
For I fear the edge of your moods, my lord,
Your temper, and the caprice of royal power.

[The Herdsman is young, innocent, and cute, and Pentheus is much taken with him. As the herdsman proceeds with his tale, Pentheus becomes increasingly agitated, and Dionysos pleased.]

Pen. Speak, you'll go scot-free of me, whatever said.
To be angry with the just is wrong!
The worse you say of those who follow Bakkhos,
The more I'll punish this man here,
Who conveys these arts to women.

Herd. I was taking a herd of cattle up the summit slope
Just as the morning sun sent forth its rays
To warm the land.
And I saw three troops of women dancers:
The first was led by Autonoe,
The second by your mother, Agaue,
The third by Ino.
All were resting, their bodies relaxed.
Some leaned back on boughs of firs,
Some lay casually about with heads on oak-leaf mounds.
All were sober, despite what you say,

234

Not drunk from bowls of wine and the sound of flutes,
Not lost in the woods
In pursuit of the goddess of love.

Agaue, your mother,
When she heard the horned cows moan,
Stood up amid the women of Bakkhos
And gave the cry of *olololo*
To rouse their bodies from sleep.
And they threw the weight of night from their eyes
And stood erect,
Their ordered response a wonder to see,
Both young and old and maidens who still were single.
And at first
They shook their hair to their shoulders,
And those whose bands came loose
Re-set the tops of their fawnskin drapes
And attached their spotted hides
With snakes that licked their cheeks.

Others were cuddling fawns and wild wolf cubs
And nursed them with their milk,
All the city's new mothers, with breasts still full,
Who had left their babes at home.

Then they donned their crowns of ivy
And oak leaves and flowery milax.
And one took her thyrsos and hit a rock,
From which sprang forth a stream of water,
Fresh as dew.
Another took and sank her staff to earth,
Through which the god sent forth a spring of wine.
And whoever thirsted for the pure white drink,
By scratching earth with finger tips,
Found streams of milk.
And from an ivied thyrsos top
There dripped sweet honey drops.

So had you come and seen these things,
You would have neared with prayer
The god you now condemn.

We herders and shepherds assembled ourselves together
And argued each to each,
Since strange are the things they do, amazing.

And a certain traveler came from the town,
One skilled in words, and said to all:

"You who live in the majestic mountain peaks,
Come, let's flush out Agaue, Pentheus' mother,
Out from the rites of Bakkhos,
To do the King a favor."

He seemed to us to put it well,
So we hid in ambush beneath a shrubbery cover.
And when the appointed time had come,
Each woman took and shook her wand in dance
And called with common voice to Iakkhos,
The Son of God, the one who raves.
And all the mountain joined and danced along,
Wild beasts, too. Nothing escaped the rush.

Now Agaue happened to leap right by,
So I jumped and tried to grab her,
Up from the thicket where I had hid myself.
She cried:

"My hunting hounds,
We're being chased by these *men* here.
Come and follow me!
Take thyrsos in hand and charge!"

Then *we* were the ones to run,
Not to be torn apart by Raving Women.

They attached with naked arms
Cattle that grazed on the grass nearby.
Then you'd have seen your mother,
With her own two hands,
Tear a bellowing, fat-uddered cow in two,
While others ripped the cattle to shreds.

Ribs and hooves could be seen all around,
While pieces of flesh hung from the trees,
Spattered and dripping with blood.
Belligerent bulls in the front stampeded,
Tripping themselves to the ground,
Pulled by myriad hands of maidens.
And sooner did they strip the victims' skins
Than you could blink your royal eye.

And then, like birds in flight,
They swooped to the plains below,
There by the streams of Asopos River
Where the fruitful harvest of Thebes is grown.

Then onward to Hysiai and Erythrai, too,
Which lie below the cliffs of Mt. Kithairon.
Like a troop of invaders,
They descended and ravaged all.
Children they seized from their homes,
And whatever they took and put on their shoulders,
There without a strap it would stay,
And nothing would fall to dark-black earth,
Neither iron nor bronze.
And upon their heads they carried fire,
But their hair remained unburned.

Now the men grew angry at the women's pillage
And so took arms against them.
But the sight, my lord, was awful to see:
Their sharpened spears could draw no blood,
While *they*, the women, hurling the thyrsos
From out of their hands,
Wounded and routed the men.
So a god, no doubt, was with them.

And then they returned to their original haunts,
To the place where the god had made their springs,
And they washed the stains of blood from themselves,
While snakes, with flicking tongues,
Licked clean the spots from their cheeks.

Master, this god, whoever he is,
Welcome him now to Thebes.
His greatness is seen from these many things
And in this form, too: He gives, I hear,
The pain-killing vine to men.
Now if wine is removed,
Then so is Kypris, the goddess of love,
And all other joys beside for men.

[Exit Herdsman.]

Chorus.   [Again, a Chorus member in the audience]

Before the King I fear to speak free words,
Yet nonetheless it must be said:
Among the gods,
Dionysos is second to none.

Pen.   [Highly agitated]
By now the Raving Women's outrage burns nearby,
A grave reproach to Greeks.
And I must not hold back!
Go to Elektra's Gate,
Assemble all the troops
That fight on foot with heavy shields,
And all the knights
Astride their swiftly running steeds
And all the archers who brandish smaller shields
And twang the strings of bows.
We march against the Bakkhic women!
For this, indeed, is just too much—
Am I to continue to suffer so at *women's* hands?

Dion.   Pentheus, you've heard my words,
But not been moved at all.
Though you abuse me, yet I advise:
You must not bear arms against a god,
But instead keep still.
The Raving One will not abide
The women of Bakkhos to be driven by you
Away from ecstasy's hills.

238

Pen. What—*you* teach *me!*
      Don't forget you just escaped from jail
      Or you'll soon be punished again.

Dion. Better to offer him sacrifice
      Than get enraged and kick against the goads,
      A man against a god.

Pen. I'll give him sacrifice enough—
      Many women's bodies, as they deserve,
      When I rout them there in Mt. Kithairon's glens.

Dion. You'll all be put to flight,
      And this will be your shame:
      To turn and run with shields of brass
      Before the wands of Raving Women.

Pen. Damn, what a hold this alien wrestler has me in.
      And whether on top or on the bottom,
      He won't shut up!

Dion. But sir, you still can make things turn out right.

Pen. How is that? Am I to play the slave to women?

Dion. I can bring them here, and without the use of arms.

Pen. Ha! You're up to something once again.

Dion. How so, if I want to save you by my arts?

Pen. You've made a pact with them in this,
      So you can keep your rites alive.

Dion. Oh, I made a pact, for sure,
      But with the god.

Pen. Bring out my arms! You—shut up.

Dion. Well,
      But wouldn't you like to *spy* on them there,
      All gathered in the mountains?

Pen. Why, yes . . .
I'd give a pile of gold!

Dion. Why does that arouse you so?

Pen. I want to watch them when they're stinking drunk.

Dion. What!
You want to watch what galls you?

Pen. Yes, but hidden among the pines.

Dion. But even if you came unseen,
They'd track you down.

Pen. Hmm. Well, in the open then. You're right.

Dion. Want me to show you how to reach that place?
Do you really want to take this trip?

Pen. Get on with it then.
I resent the time I have to spend with you.

Dion. Okay, first put on a linen dress.

Pen. What's that!?
Am I, a man, to be reduced to a woman?

Dion. But if they see you're a man, they'll kill you!

Pen. Hmm, you're right again.
You've been a smart one all along.

Dion. My school was Dionysos.

Pen. Tell me how you want to carry out
This clever plan of yours.

Dion. Why, I'll go inside with you and dress you up.

Pen. How? Like a woman? But I'm ashamed!

Dion. But don't you want to watch the Raving Women?

Pen. Well . . .
What *kind* of a dress will you put me in?

Dion. First I'll cover your head with a long-haired wig.

Pen. And then what's next?

Dion. A full-length dress,
Then some ribbon for your hair.

Pen. Is that it then?
Is there anything else besides?

Dion. Why yes, a thyrsos for your hand,
And a hide of spotted fawnskin.

Pen. I can't put on a woman's dress!

Dion. But if you charge the women of Bakkhos in battle,
Yours will be the blood that flows.

Pen. You're right. First I have to go and spy.

Dion. Well, it's a smarter thing, for sure,
Than to set yourself up for harm.

Pen. But how will I get through Kadmos' town
And not be seen?

Dion. We'll take a path no one else would take.
I'll lead the way.

Pen. To be the laughingstock of Raving Women
Would be the worst of all.
I'll go inside and see what plan is best.

Dion. Suit yourself. Whatever plan you choose,
I'm prepared.

Pen. Either marching with arms
      Or following your plan,
      I'll go!

[Exit Pentheus into the center mouth-exit of the set.]

Dion. Oh women of Bakkhos, he stands before the trap.
       He'll come to you and through his death
       Will pay his debt.

       Dionysos, here's your chance,
       For you are not far off. Let's punish him!
       First, drive him from his mind
       And then inflict a giddy madness.
       He'll never wear a woman's dress when sane,
       But driven from his mind he will.

       I'll have him as the laughingstock of Thebes
       When led through streets in woman's form,
       And this, because his previous threats
       Had made him such a dread.

       I go to put on Pentheus
       The dress he'll wear to Hades
       When his mother's hands destroy him.
       And this he'll come to know:
       The Son of God, Dionysos,
       Although to mortals he's most gentle,
       By nature is a god of dreadful power.

[Dionysos exists stage center through the mouth and reappears with Pentheus, who follows him to the center of the mouth with a dazed look, like a bull being led to slaughter. He is, in fact, quite mad at this point. While the Chorus enters and delivers the following lines, Dionysos takes off all of Pentheus' clothes and dresses him as a woman.]

[Turn]

Chorus. When will I lift my naked feet
         In the night-long dance of Bakkhic frenzy
         And toss my head to the dewy sky?—

Like a fawn
Who frolicks in the pasture's verdant pleasure
When she escapes, out of watcher's sight,
The dreaded hunt,
And leaps above the fine-knit hunting nets.
The hunter incites his snarling hounds.
She strains, she makes fast swerves and runs,
She bounds across the river plain
And finds delight in a wild land free of men,
Safe in the thick of the forest's shade.

[With sarcasm]

What's as smart or a better gift
From gods to men
Than to have the upper hand on foes?
"A good thing always pleases."

[Return]

The power of the gods—it hardly moves—
But yet is something sure.
It corrects those men who laud their own excess
When moved by a clouded mind,
But fail to respect the gods' concerns.

The gods are crafty and lie in wait for a length of time
To jump the man who lacks respect.
What we know and what we plan
Cannot surpass their ancient ways.
The cost is slight to understand
That these two things prevail:
First, of course, whatever the gods themselves ordain
And then whatever through length of time
Has ever been the rule.

What's as smart or a better gift
From gods to men
Than to˙have the upper hand on foes?
"A good thing always pleases."

[Finale]

Blessed is he who flees from the storm at sea
And comes to find his port.
And blessed is he who masters his toil.
Here and there this one competes with that
For money and might.
Thousands of men and thousands of hopes,
Some of which will end in wealth,
And others, dashed.
But whoever is happy in the life of day-to-day,
That one, I say, is blessed.

[Exit Chorus. Dionysos goes downstage, turns and addresses Pentheus, now standing in the center of the mouth, dressed as a woman. In the Valencia Rose production, he appeared in the likeness of San Francisco's prudish mayor, Dianne Feinstein.]

Dion.   You there,
You who are eager to see the forbidden
And search for what should be shunned,
Pentheus, come out in front of your house.

Let me see you wearing a woman's dress,
The dress of a woman who raves,
The dress of a woman of Bakkhos,
You who would spy on your mother
And on her band.
You look just like a daughter of Kadmos!

[Pentheus comes forward, giddy and campy, with falsetto voice.]

Pen.   Oh, I think I see two suns in the sky
And two of seven-gated Thebes.
And you look like a bull to me,
Leading me on in front,
And your head has grown two horns.
Say, have you ever been a beast?
Why, you really are a bull!

Dion. The god, though hostile once,
Is with us now in peace.
You see as you should.

Pen. Well then, how do I look?
Do you think I could pass for Ino?
Or for Agaue, my very mother?

Dion. In seeing you, I seem to see them too.
But look, this strand of hair is sticking out,
As if beside itself,
Which is not the way I put your headband on.

Pen. I knocked it loose
When I shook and jerked my head about inside,
Rapt with Bakkhic frenzy.

Dion. Well, it's up to me to see you're taken care of,
So let me put it back.
Here, hold still, don't move your head.

Pen. All right, then, you can fix it.
See—I offer you my head.

Dion. Oh, but now your belt is loose,
And your hem is all uneven.

Pen. Hmm, it does seem so,
At least for the leg on the right,
But it looks okay on the left to me.

Dion. Now let me tell you this:
You'll think me the best of your friends
When you get to see,
Despite what some may say,
How terribly sober the women of Bakkhos are.

Pen. Which looks most like a woman of Bakkhos—
To hold the thyrsos on the right,
Or on the left, like this?

245

Dion. It goes on the right,
To be raised with the beat your right foot keeps.
I commend your change of heart!

Pen. Will I be able to bear on my back
The glens of Mt. Kithairon
And all the women of Bakkhos, too?

Dion. You can if you want.
The mind was unsound you had before,
But now it is as should be.

Pen. Do I need to bring a crowbar?
Or should I put my arms and shoulders
At the bottom of the peaks
And tear them up by hand?

Dion. No,
You mustn't destroy the Nymphs' sacred places
Or shrines where the sounds of Pan are heard.

Pen. You're right.
The women must not be taken by force.
I'll hide myself in boughs of fir.

Dion. You'll hide yourself in the hiding you must
When you sneak to spy on those who rave.

Pen. I do believe they keep themselves
In sweetest snares of marriage beds
Just like birds in nests.

Dion. For that, then, be on guard.
And perhaps you'll even catch them there—
Unless they catch you first.

Pen. Lead me on,
And right through the middle of Thebes!
I alone am *man* enough to dare these things!

[Dionysos leads Pentheus off the stage, into the audience, and toward the side entrance of the theater.]

Dion. Yes, what you alone will do will save this city,
You alone.
And the struggle awaits you there that had to be.
Now follow me.
I will be your guide and keep you safe till there.
But someone else will bring you back.

Pen. Yes, she who gave me birth!

Dion. And your fame will be known to all.

Pen. That's why I go—

Dion. And you'll be carried when you return—

Pen. In splendid luxury, yes—

Dion. And in your very mother's hands.

Pen. You'll have me spoiled!

Dion. Spoiled, indeed.

Pen. Just as I deserve!

[Dionysos shoves Pentheus out the side door, then turns to address the audience with determination and fury.]

Dion. Such a rugged, rugged man you are,
And so rugged will be the suffering you find there
That you'll see your name raised up to heaven.
Stretch for your hands, Agaue!
And you,
Daughters descended in common from Kadmos!
To a rugged struggle I send this youthful man.
And I shall win and be revealed the Raving One,
And that shall prove all else.

[Exit Dionysos. Enter the Chorus, furiously surging in.]

[Turn]

247

Chorus. Go, go, speeding hounds of the Goddess Fury!
Go to the heights where the daughters of Kadmos
Keep their sacred band!
Goad them into a frenzy,
Goad them onto him who wears a woman's dress,
The frantic one who spies on Raving Women.

As he stalks from smooth-round rock or tree,
His mother will see him first
And call to Raving Women:

"Who is that who's come from peak to peak
To track the hill-traveling daughters of Kadmos,
Oh women of Bakkhos?
Who could have given him birth?
He couldn't be born from a woman's blood—
No, this one was born from a lion
Or the race of Libyan Gorgons."

Let Justice come forth in the flesh!
Let her come with sword in hand
And slit the throat
Of the godless, lawless, unjust one,
The monster son of Ekhion.

[Return]

He started out, Lord Bakkhos,
With a mind opposed to what is right,
An anger opposed to law,
A raging heart, a delerious intent,
All aimed against your rites
And those of your mother, too,
In order to defeat by force
The one who cannot lose.

A life that's free from grief—
For men, that means to have a balanced will
And truly respect the affairs of the gods,
As befits a mortal soul.

248

Not compelled, but our of choice,
I delight in what is wise.
And here's another thing
That leads a life to what is good:
To prove you're pious,
Live an open life, both day and night,
And to prove that you esteem the gods,
Turn away from things unjust.

Let Justice come forth in the flesh!
Let her come with sword in hand
And slit the throat
Of the godless, lawless, unjust one,
The monster son of Ekhion.

[Finale]

Come, and be revealed a bull, my Raging One!
Be a many-headed dragon!
Be a lion, spurting flames!
Come, and with a smiling face
Throw a deadly loop of rope
On him who seeks to hunt and seize
A herd of Raving Women!

[The Chorus gives a blood-curdling scream, and the lights go out. End of Act I in the Valencia Rose production.]

ACT II

[Act II begins with the entrance of the Slave from a side door of the theater. In this production, he is the King's chauffeur, dressed in a black leather jacket and dark pants and having a bald head. He is drunk, and takes a good swig from his bottle before beginning to speak. The Chorus is already on the stage.]

Slave. Oh Thebes,
You who prospered once throughout the land of Greece,
You, the home of Kadmos, Sidon's ancient man
Who planted a crop of dragon's teeth
To spring from earth as men,
For you I grieve, though I myself am but a slave.

Chorus.	What's this?
	Do you have some news of the women of Bakkhos?

Slave.	Pentheus,
	The son of his father Ekhion,
	Pentheus is dead.

Chorus.	What?!
	My Lord, the Raving One,
	How great a god you are revealed!

Slave.	Well, what is that supposed to mean?
	So, women,
	Does it make you glad to see my master not do well?

Chorus.	Hai-ee! Hai-ee!
	Though I'm a stranger here,
	I'll sing my homeland's songs.
	Your jails don't scare me now!

Slave.	Do you think that Thebes is so devoid of men
[Reconstructed line:]	
	[That none can manage foreign women?]

Chorus.	Ha! Thebes is not my lord,
	Dionysos is.

Slave.	Women, perhaps this might be pardoned you,
	But it's wrong to rejoice at someone's evil fortune.

Chorus.	Come, tell me, say it, say it—
	What kind of death did that man of injustice die?
	And what injustice was he up to then?

Slave.	When we left the dwellings of the land of Thebes
	And crossed beyond the Asopos River,
	We entered the ridge of Mt. Kithairon,
	Both Pentheus and I (for I followed behind my lord)
	And also the stranger, our journey's guide.

Then first of all
We seated ourselves on a grassy field,
Preserving the silence from sounds of foot and tongue,
So we could see but not be seen.

Nearby was a grove, with cliffs all around,
Well watered with streams, shaded by pines.
And there the Mad Women sat,
Their hands devoted to pleasant pursuits.
Some decked out anew their tired wands
With curls of ivy,
While others slipped off their dappled robes,
Like fillies their yokes,
And answered each other in raptured song.

The luckless Pentheus,
Who couldn't quite see the female crowd,
Said this:

"Stranger, from where we stand,
I can't make out those phony Raving Women.
If I could only climb a hill or lofty fir,
I'm sure I'd see their obscene acts much better."

At once, I saw the stranger do a wonder—
He took a fir by the top of a branch
That reached the sky
And pulled it down and down and down,
Right to the earth itself.

It curved like a bow,
Or the way a line, when drawn with compass,
Assumes the shape of an arc.
Thus the stranger held the mountain branch in hand
And shaped it down to earth,
And did a feat not human.

And he took and seated Pentheus on the topmost
branch,
Then smoothly released the trunk,
Sliding it up through his hands,
Careful it wouldn't throw him.

It rose straight up, open to the open sky,
And there, seated on the top, my master,
Seen more by Raving Women than seeing them.

And hardly was he seated, plain to see, above,
And the stranger now no longer seen,
When someone's voice came from the sky,
Dionysos, as it seems to me, and cried:

"Oh maidens,
I bring and offer up to you
The one who laughs at you,
At me,
And at my secret rites.
Avenge yourselves on him!"

No sooner had he spoken thus
Than in the sight of earth and heaven
He flashed a bolt of fire,
Sublime and dreadful.

The air fell silent.
Leaves in the forest glen stood still.
You couldn't hear a living sound.

And all the women there,
Because they didn't quite make out the voice,
Shot up
And rolled their eyes.

He called to them again.

And when the daughters of Kadmos
Clearly made out the cry of Bakkhos,
They surged ahead with the speed of birds in flight,
Straining, propelled, with rapid-beating feet,
Both Mother Agaue and her native sisters
And all the women of Bakkhos.

Along the valley's verdant river bed
And over crags they bounded,
Frenzied by whispers that came from a god.

And when they saw that Pentheus
Was seated on top a tree,
First they climbed a rocky mound
To have a launching site,
And then from there with rage threw stones at him
And tossed a fir tree's limbs,
While others hurled through air their staffs
And made a scary shooting scene.

But they couldn't reach their mark.
The height at which the poor man sat,
Bewildered and confused,
Surpassed the women's zeal.

At last they approached with branches of oak
As though with thunder bolts
And tried to pry the fir tree's roots
With bars not made of iron.

And when they failed to gain their efforts' goal,
Agaue said:

"Mad Women, come, from a circle around this tree.
Grab a branch so we can catch this beast of prey
That waits to spring on us,
Or he'll expose the secret bands of Bakkhos."

And so they laid a hundred hands upon the tree
And tried to pull it up from earth.
Shaken from his seat above,
Pentheus with a host of screams slid down to earth,
Aware a dreadful thing was near.

His mother, priestess,
First to start the sacrifice,
Attacked.
He threw the wig and ribbons from his hair,
So wretched Agaue would know him,
Not kill him,
And touched her cheek and said:

"Mother, look, I'm Pentheus, your son.
You gave me birth in Ekhion's house.
Have pity, Mother, on me,
And don't, for the wrong that I have done,
Slay your son."

But she,
With foam already drooling from her mouth,
With contorted face and rolling eyes,
Was far beyond herself,
Possessed by Bakkhos.

And he could not persuade her.

And then she grabbed his hand on the left,
Planted her foot against the doomed man's chest,
And ripped his shoulder out,
Not by her own arm's might,
But the god gave power to her hands.

And Ino, also tearing at his flesh,
Finished off the other side.
Autonoe attacked, and then the Bakkhic pack entire.
And one great cry at once arose,
The groaning man,
When and if he had a chance to breathe,
And the women ever howling
Like men who charge in war.

One tore off an arm, one a foot complete with shoe.
His ribs were stripped by tearing.
Back and forth with blood-stained hands
All batted parts of Pentheus' flesh.

His body was diversely laid,
One part under jagged rocks,
One deep away in forest brush,
None an easy task to find.

The doom-struck head,
Which had come by chance to his mother's hands,

She impaled on top her thyrsos
And carried like a mountain lion's mane
Around the midst of Mt. Kithairon,
And left behind her sisters there
In packs of Raving Women.

Exulting in her ill-starred prey,
She moves within this city's very walls,
And summons Bakkhos by the names
"Fellow Leader of the Pack"
And "Glorious Partner in the Hunt,"
A hunt from which she brings as trophy tears.

I myself, therefore, will leave
To get beyond the pale of this disastrous scene
Before Agaue comes to reach her house.

[With an audible belch]

Live a balanced life,
Respect the affairs of the gods—
That's the noblest thing.
And that's the smartest thing, as well, I think
For mortal men to do.

[Exit Slave, staggering off.]

Chorus.   *[With great venom]*

Let's dance for Bakkhos!
Let's sing for the doom of Pentheus,
The dragon's son!

He took for himself a woman's dress
And a sharpened fennel stalk
(What a worthy thyrsos for Hades!)
And followed a bull to guide his doom.

Oh women of Bakkhos,
Daughters of Kadmos,
You've turned his famous victory song
Into a dirge of tears!

And what a noble struggle it is
When the hand that drips with blood
Takes hold upon her child!

[A high-pitched olol” *scream is heard from the rear of the theater.]*

But look,
I see the mother of Pentheus, Agaue—
Her face contorted, with rolling eyes.
She's rushing home.

Welcome to the God of Ecstasy's merry crowd!

[Agaue comes rushing down the center aisle from the rear of the theater, carrying a leather bag which contains the head of her son, Pentheus. (In ancient productions, she carried the head impaled on a thyrsos.) She is raving mad, thinking she carries the head of a mountain lion, and completely oblivious to the acid sarcasm with which the chorus now taunts their aristocratic enemy. Agaue's movements are spastic and jerky here, her voice alternatively breaking with shrill laughter and deep sobbing.]

Agaue. Oh women from Asia Minor—

Chorus. What would you have me do?

Agaue. From the peaks of the mountains down to my home,
I bear a blessed beast of prey,
A stalk just cut.

Chorus. Oh sister in our fun, I see and welcome you.

Agaue. Look at what I caught and without a trap—
A mountain lion's young offspring,
As you can plainly see.

Chorus. What desolate place did you bring it from?

Agaue. Mt. Kithairon.

Chorus. Mt. Kithairon? And just what happened there?

256

Agaue.   That's where it was slaughtered.

Chorus.   Who was she who attacked him first?

Agaue.   The prize is mine!

Chorus.   Oh *lucky* Agaue—

Agaue.   That's what they call me in the sacred band.

Chorus.   But what of the others?

Agaue.   Well, those of Kadmos—

Chorus.   Kadmos? Kadmos what?

Agaue.   Daughters of his came after me,
Yes, *after* me,
And took the beast in hand.
Oh what a lucky catch!
Come, let's eat it!

Chorus.   Eat what, pathetic one?

Agaue.   [*Sticking her hand in the bag and feeling Pentheus' face*]
The beast is young
And under furry head
Has grown not not long ago
A downy jaw.

Chorus.   [*Laughing*]
How like a beast of prey to be distinguished
By its mane!

Agaue.   Sharp hunter Bakkhos goaded Raving Women sharp
To hunt this prey.

Chorus.   Our Lord, the Hunter!

Agaue.   Do you approve?

Chorus. You couldn't know how much I do.

Agaue. And soon the sons of Kadmos—

Chorus. And your son Pentheus, too—

Agaue. Will praise his very mother
Who caught this raging mountain lion.

Chorus. So—
Your pride is great in this great catch?

Agaue. I'm glad that through this hunt
I've done a thing that's great,
Great and clear to all.

Chorus. Then why not show the people now,
Oh ill-starred one,
Your victory-token,
The one you caught and brought here with you?

Agaue. [Stepping forward triumphantly]
Oh you who live in the land of Thebes,
In the town with lovely towers,
Come forth and see the prey
That we, the daughters of Kadmos, caught
And not by use of Thessaly's hunting spears,
And not by traps,
But by the strength
Of pale white arms and hands.

And we have this boast:
We didn't need the weapon-maker's wares.
Why, we ourselves with our own bare hands
Seized upon this beast
And tore him limb from limb.

Where's my father, old and wise?
Let him come to me.
And Pentheus, my son, where is he?
Have him get a ladder

And set it up against the house
So he can nail against the wall
The lion's head I caught to give him.

[Kadmos enters from the rear entrance of the theater. Two attendants follow him, carrying a large trunk filled with the bloody remains of Pentheus. Kadmos is still in drag, but he is spattered with blood. The Chorus flees except for the leader, who remains watching off to the side.]

Kad.   Servants, come and follow me
And bring the pitiful mass of Pentheus
Before the house.
From endless, tedious searches
I bring the body here.
I found it scattered in Mt. Kithairon's glens,
And not in one same site,
But strewn about the tangled forest floor.

I heard about my daughters' violent acts
As I walked along the town within the walls,
Just back with old Teiresias
From the Raving Women's rites.
So back to the mountains I returned
To retrieve a son just slain by mad ones.

And there I saw Autonoe,
The wife of Aristaios and mother of Aktaion,
And Ino also,
Wandering still amid the underbrush,
Woe-begone and frenzied.

Agaue, I was told,
Returned by driven feet to here.
And what I heard was true,
For I see her coming now,
And not a happy sight.

Agaue.   Father, a great thing you have to boast of:
To be the father of the very best of daughters.
I mean us all, but especially me.

259

I left the shuttle and the loom
And have come to something better,
To be a hunter of beasts with my own two hands.

I bear in my arms, as you can see,
The trophy of victory that I have won,
So you can nail it on your house's wall.

Father, come and take it here.
Be proud of what I've caught
And call your friends to feast.

How blessed you are, how blessed,
By the things that I have done.

Kad. Ohhhh such grief!
Grief that can't be told!
Grief too much to see!
Oh slaughter done by those cursed hands!

First you go and slay this one,
Though a victim that is royal,
As an offering to the gods.
Do you then ask Thebes and me to feast?!

Alas for your misfortune first, then mine.
How the god, the Raving One, Our Lord,
Justly indeed, but oh too much,
Has vanquished us,
Though once our friend and kin.

Agaue. How peevish has men's old age become
And glum of face. I hope my son takes on
His mother's ways to be a lucky hunter
When he seeks with Thebes' young men
To catch his prey. But all he now can do
Is fight the gods. The task is yours
To warn him, Father. Who will call him here
Within my sight so he can see how blessed I am?

Kad. Ohhh— Ohhh—
      The day you know what kind of thing you've done,
      You'll feel an awful grief.
      But if you keep to the end of your days
      The state of mind that now you have,
      Although not blessed, at least you won't seem cursed.

Agaue. Why is this so bad? Why a cause of grief to you?

*[Agaue becomes apprehensive and hostile, sensing that something is about to be
revealed she does not want to hear. Kadmos, angered and emboldened, begins
to approach her. She feels menaced and swings out at him. With a sudden
burst of determination and energy, Kadmos lunges at her. She screams wildly
like a cornered cat and fights back. Kadmos overcomes her, wrestles her to the
floor, and holds her. Sobbing, she begins to return to a sober mind.]*

Kad. Now, lift up your eyes to see the sky.

Agaue. I see. But why look there?

Kad. Is it still the same? Or can you see some change?

Agaue. *[Slowly coming around.]*
        Why . . .
        It's getting clearer . . .
        It's more focused than before . . .

Kad. Is your mind, then, still distraught?

Agaue. *Distraught?*
        I don't know what you mean.
        Yet . . .
        Yet I think . . .
        I think I'm coming 'round.
        I'm . . .
        I'm returning to myself.

[Kadmos helps Agaue rise.]

Kad. Can you understand my words?
      Can you make a clear reply?

261

Agaue. Why, I've completely forgotten, Father,
        The things I just was saying!

  Kad. When you were given in marriage,
        Whose household did you join?

Agaue. You gave me to Ekhion, the dragon's son, they say.

  Kad. And who was the son you gave to Ekhion there?

Agaue. Pentheus, from my union with his father.

  Kad. Now—
        What head is in your hands?

Agaue. A lion's—
        Or so they say who caught it.

  Kad. Well, why don't you take a look.
        That should be an easy task.

[Agaue opens the leather bag, gazes in, and collapses in horror.]

Agaue. No! No!
        What's this I see!
        What's this thing my hands have brought on me!

  Kad. Yes, take a good, long look.
        Learn it well.

Agaue. I see the weight of grief.
        I'm crushed!

  Kad. Not much like a lion, is it?

Agaue. No, I hold the head of Pentheus
        And despair.

  Kad. It caused despair
        Before you just now learned it.

262

Agaue.   Father, who has taken this man's life?
         And why am I the one to hold his head?

Kad.   Oh awful truth,
         When will time be right for you?

Agaue.   Speak! My heart withholds its coming beat.

Kad.   *You* killed him, you and your sisters.

Agaue.   *[Reconstructed line:]*
         [What?! No! It cannot be! But how?]
         [Continuation of text:]
         And where? At home? Or somewhere else?

Kad.   Where dogs before tore off Aktaion's flesh.

Agaue.   What made this man of grief go to Mt. Kithairon?

Kad.   To sneer at you and at your reveling sisters.

Agaue.   But why did we ourselves fly off to there?

Kad.   You all were raving mad.
         Thebes went wild for Bakkhos.

Agaue.   Ahhh—now I see—
         It was *Dionysos!*
         He's the one who doomed us.

Kad.   He suffered from your insolence,
         For you did not accept him as a god.

Agaue.   Father, where is the precious body of my son?

Kad.   I scarcely was able to search it out
         And have it . . . here.

Agaue.   And have you put it back together right . . .
         With all the parts?

Kad.   *[Reconstructed lines:]*
[The most important one I could not find.
But you have brought it here.]

Agaue.   What role did Pentheus have in all my madness?

Kad.   He was just like you. He would not respect the god.
And so we three were joined in one sad fate,
Pentheus, you and me.
And the god cut off the family line.

Now I've become without a son for heir
And had to see, oh woman of sorrows,
The fruit of your womb, my son,
Shamefully, horribly killed.

His family revered him.
Yes, my son, born of my daughter,
You kept us all together.
You awed the city of Thebes.

And no one dared insult your aging father,
When they turned their eyes toward you.
You always took a worthy vengeance.

But now, disgraced,
I'll have to be an exile from my land—
I, Kadmos, Kadmos the Great,
I who sowed the seeds of Thebes
And reaped the noblest harvest.

Dearest of men, though you no longer live,
Still I count you, child, among those most dear.
Your hand no longer will touch this cheek.
No longer, child, will you embrace and call
Your mother's father, saying:

"Who has wronged you, old one?
Who shown disrespect?
Who has hurt your heart or been a source of pain?

Speak, Father,
And I will punish the one who wronged you."

But now I'm lost, and you, a thing to pity.
Your mother is a sight for sorrow;
Her sisters, a misery.

[Possibly an interpolation:]
If anyone exists who slights the gods,
Let him see this death and then believe.

[The leader of the Chorus, who has been watching from the side, speaks all the
remaining lines of the Chorus in this scene.]

Chorus.   I grieve for your suffering, Kadmos.
Your son has paid the price that was just for him,
But what a grief for you.

Agaue.   Oh Father, you see how all my world has changed.
[Except for a few fragments, the remainder of Agaue's lamentation here has
been lost. The following is a reconstruction. In ancient productions of the play,
Pentheus' dismembered body parts were probably exposed to view during this
scene (Whitehorne, p. 65).]

[To think that I was like a queen,
The noble daughter
Of one who raised a race from dragon's teeth,
The honored mother
Of one who ruled in lovely-towered Thebes.
But now I'll have no peace in Thebes
Or anywhere in Greece,
For I have stained myself,
And the city, too,
With murder.

To you, old one,
I've now become a source of bloody grief.
And as for Pentheus here,
He's dead, dismembered,
A victim of his mother's hand.

Oh face most dear, the very cheek of youth,
Pentheus, son,
I held you as a babe
That day you first caught sight of heaven's light
And watched you grow
Like bursting barley stalks
When favored by a warming wind
And cleansing rain
And glorious light of sun.
And I and Thebes rejoiced to see you King,
Protector of your people and the law.

Yet such a thorough-tearing death you died
That I cannot embrace your form as when you lived.
For how am I, your grieving mother,
To hold you to my breasts?
And how am I to mourn my son
And not embrace his flesh?
Ahhh, Ahhh—
My heart is ruptured in its grief
As was your body when you died.

Oh, I wish we had received the god in Thebes
When first he came with wine and joy.
But I could not accept his claim
That such a one could be the Son of God,
And you went out among the rocks
To spy on Raving Women,
And so brought down a tearing doom

Yes, they ripped off every limb,
And so I kiss and mourn in piecemeal parts
The flesh that once, as whole,
I raised and nursed.
And it would today still live as whole
If I had not, by my own hands,
Seized my special doom.

Come, old one,
Let's take the head of this sad one
And put it where it used to be.

And let's connect, as best we can,
What once was known as Pentheus.

I cover your head
And all your blood-stained limbs
With one pale shroud entire—
And with my tears.]

Chorus.   [Reconstructed lines:]

[How deep is a mother's grief
When the son she loved has died.
And greater still the pain
When she comes to know she helped, albeit unawares,
To take his precious life.
I weep for Agaue and for Thebes.]

[A bell rings in the rear of the theater. A light comes on, illuminating the god
Dionysos standing on an elevated platform in the rear. He is nude from the
waist up, with his body painted gold. He wears a striking mask that displays
horns, ivy leaves, clusters of grapes, and snakes. The eyes of Agaue, Kadmos,
and the leader of the Chorus are lifted to behold the sight.]

Kad.   [Reconstructed lines:]

[He who came to Thebes a man of joy
And was rejected,
Festive Dionysos,
Approaches now in victory as a god
To render searing judgment.
Behold the Son of God.]

Dion.   [Most of the first part of Dionysos' speech here has been lost.
Accordingly, the section in brackets is a reconstruction. In
this scene, Dionysos is nasty and implacable.]

[When I came with dance and song and wine,
The Happy One,
This city cast me out and said I was no god,
Though it might have acted otherwise.
But now I come to punish and to pain,
And the city has no choice.

267

Harsh was the doom of Pentheus,
Harsh but just.
I advised, but he would not listen.
I warned, but he only grew more insolent.
Thinking his power reached to the heavens,
He tried to bind a god.
Had I not possessed the strength
Of one who was born divine,
The Son of Zeus,
He surely would have slain me.
And then he schemed to enslave or kill
All my Raving Women.
And so he was murdered by those
Who least of all ought slay him,
And justly did he suffer.

And you, Agaue, and your sisters, too,
Refused to acknowledge the Son of Zeus
And abused my mother, Semele.
For that, you've stained your hands
With the blood of your son
And yourself with the crime of murder.
And hence you cannot stay,
Nor your sisters either,
And pollute the land of Thebes,
But shall wander from place to place till death,
No more to see your native land.

And Kadmos, too,
You had your share in this disaster.
Too weak, too weak you were to rule a son
Who fought against the gods,
And more concerned with the fame of your house
Than slanders against your daughter Semele.
And here's how you will suffer:]

[Resumption of text:]

You shall undergo a change and be a snake,
And your wife, Harmonia, Ares' daughter,

Whom you wed while still a man,
Shall be shaped anew, a beast,
And assume a serpent's form.
And as the words of Zeus foretold,
You shall have dominion among barbarians
And with your wife shall drive a cart of beasts
And with a countless host
Shall plunder many states.

And when they've sacked Apollo's seat,
They'll make a wretched journey back.
Then Ares will rescue Harmonia and you
And extend your lives forever
[With irony]
To live in the Isles of the Blessed.

And I, Dionysos, declare to all,
I who am no mortal father's son,
The Son of God:
Had you learned to balance your lives
At the time you did not wish,
You would have lived a happy life,
Having Zeus' son as friend.

Agaue. We've wronged you, Dionysos, and we beseech—

Dion. Too late, too late you've come to know me.
When you should have, you did not.

Agaue. [Becoming more defiant]
I know. But in your vengeance, you're too harsh.

Dion. [Shouting]
But didn't you abuse me, though I was born a god?

Agaue. [Quietly but with determination]
It ill befits the gods
To mold their wrath on men's.

Dion. This fate was long ago decreed by Father Zeus.

Agaue. Ai-ee!
       It's all been settled, then, old man—
       Exile, misery!

Dion. [With a snotty tone]
      Then why, indeed, delay what fate has said must be?

[The light on Dionysos goes out, and the god is suddenly gone.]

Kad. What an awful end, my child,
     We all have come to—
     You, your sisters doomed,
     And I, pathetic, to live among barbarians,
     An aging alien.
     And then my fate to lead against the Greeks
     A barbarian horde of troops!
     And Harmonia, Ares' child, my wife,
     Possessed by a snake's wild form,
     Led by her serpent husband, in command with spears,
     Against the tombs and altars of Greece.

     And I, most sad of all,
     Shall never see the end of grief
     Nor sail the stream that descends to the dead
     And so arrive at peace.

Agaue. Oh Father, I'm deprived of you and banished—

Kad. Would you enfold me with your arms, poor child,
     Like a snowy swan its feeble father?

Agaue. But where can I go without a home?

Kad. I don't know where, my child.
     Little help your father now.

Agaue. My home, goodbye.
       And goodbye, my city, my country.
       I leave you behind to go and seek misfortune,
       An exile from my house and bed.

Kad. Well, travel first to the house of Aristaios,
      Autonoe's husband . . .

Agaue. Father, you make me cry . . .

Kad. And you, my child, me.
      And I weep for your sisters, too.

Agaue. [With defiance again]
        Lord Dionysos is the one
        Who brought this doom upon your house.

Kad. [Nervously looking back to where Dionysos had been]
      Yes, but look what he suffered because of you,
      And his name found no respect in Thebes.

Agaue. [Exiting]
        Father, farewell.

Kad. [Slumping down to the floor, in front of the large mouth of
      the stage set]
      Farewell, my grieving daughter.
      I know you won't be coming back this way.

Agaue. Lead on, attendants, to where I can find
        My suffering and exiled sisters.
        And let me go
        Where blood-stained Mt. Kithairon
        Will never catch its sight of me again,
        Where my eyes will never see Kithairon,
        Where the memory of the thyrsos
        Will never again be raised—
        That I leave to other Bakkhic women.

        [Exit Agaue.]

        [The leader of the Chorus steps forward.]

Chorus. How varied are the gods' displays of power:
         What we often don't expect,
         That they bring to pass.

271

And what we look for most,
That goes unfulfilled.
And for the least expected things,
A god will find a way.
And thus did these events transpire.

[Lights out]

Mask of Dionysos (by John Soares). *Photo by Rink © 1984*

The coming of Dionysos is proclaimed by the Chorus of Mad Women (left to right: Shessa, Chandria, Jackie Boykin, Diana, Janet Tranbarger). *Photo by José-Luis Moscovich*

The leader of the Chorus (Jackie Boykin) extols the joys of the rites of Dionysos. *Photo by José-Luis Moscovich*

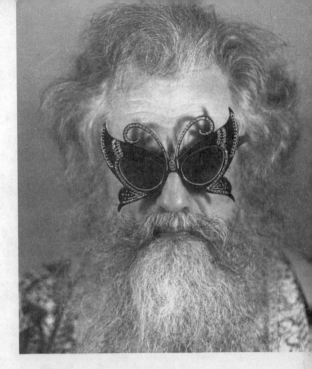

The blind seer Teiresias (Ben Gardiner) summons the city to worship Dionysos. *Photo by Douglas Pickarts*

The captive Dionysos (Assunta Femia) is about to be interrogated ·
Photo by José-Luis Moscovich

King Pentheus (Earl Galvin, right) fondles the captive Dionysos (Assunta Femia). *Photo by José-Luis Moscovich*

King Pentheus (Earl Galvin), driven insane because of his rejection of Dionysos, dresses up as a woman. *Photo by José-Luis Moscovich*

The slave (Jack Fertig, a.k.a. Sister Boom Boom) describes how women possessed by Dionysos tore King Pentheus apart with their bare hands. *Photo by José-Luis Moscovich*

The aristocratic Agaue (Michele Richards, center) is surrounded by the barbarian followers of Dionysos (clockwise from lower left: Diana, Janet Tranbarger, Assunta Femia, Chandria, Jackie Boykin, Shessa). *Photo by Douglas Pickarts*

The insane Agaue (Michele Richards, center) is taunted by two followers of Dionysos (Shessa, left, and Chandria). *Photo by José-Luis Moscovich*

Dionysos (Assunta Femia) reveals himself as a god. *Photo by Rink © 1984*

SELECT BIBLIOGRAPHY

❂

GREEK AND LATIN SOURCES

AISKHINES, *Against Timarkhos*
AISKHYLOS, *Endonians* (Fragments)
ARISTOTLE, *Poetics*
Politics
CICERO, MARCUS TULLIUS, *On Law*
CLEMENT, *Exhortation*
DEMOSTHENES, *On the Crown*
DIODOROS, *Historical Library*
EURIPIDES, *Bakkhai*
Hippolytos
GREGORY OF NAZIANZOS, *The Passion of Christ*
HERODOTOS, *History*
HOMER, *Iliad*
Odyssey
HOMER (PSEUDO), *Hymns*
LIVY [TITUS LIVIUS], *From the Foundation of the City*
NONNOS, *The Epic of Dionysos*
PAUSANIAS, *Geographical Description*
PHILOSTRATOS, *Paintings*
PLATO, *Defense of Socrates*
Gorgias
Kratylos
Laws
Republic
PLUTARCH, *Lives*
Moralia
STRABO, *Geography*

SECONDARY SOURCES

ALAND, KURT, "The Problem of Anonymity and Pseudonymity in Christian Literature of the First Two Centuries" in *The Authorship and Integrity of the New Testament*, The Talbot Press (SPCK), London, 1965.

ALDERINK, LARRY J., *Creation and Salvation in Ancient Orphism*, The American Philological Association, American Classical Studies no. 8, Scholars Press, Chico, California, 1981.

AUGER, DANIÈLE, "Le jeu de Dionysos: déguisements et métamorphoses dans les Bacchantes d'Euripide" in *Dionysos, le même et l'autre*, ed. by Michel Bourlet, Nouvelle Revue d'Ethnopsychiatrie, no. 1, La Pensée Sauvage, 1983, pp. 57–80.

BACHOFEN, JOHANN J., *Das Mutterrecht*, 2 vols., 1861; reprinted by Benno Schwabe & Co., Basel, 1948.

BERGER, PAMELA, *The Goddess Obscured. Transformation of The Grain Protectress from Goddess to Saint*, Beacon Press, Boston, 1985.

BETHE, E., "Die Dorische Knabenliebe," in *Rheinisches Museum für Philologie*, v. 62, 1907, 438–475.

BIANCHI, UGO, "Prolegomena. The Religio-Historical Question of the Mysteries of Mithra" in *Mysteria Mithrae*, ed. by Ugo Bianchi, E. J. Brill, Leiden, 1979.

BILLIGMEIER, JON-CHRISTIAN, AND JUDY A. TURNER, "The Socio-Economic Roles of Women in Mycenaean Greece: A Brief Survey from Evidence of the Linear B Tablets" in *Reflections of Women in Antiquity*, ed. Helene P. Foley, Gordon and Breach Science Publishers, New York, 1981, 1–18.

BOBER, PHYLLIS, "Cernunnos: Origin and Transformation of a Celtic Divinity," *American Journal of Archaeology*, v. 55, 1951, 13–51.

BOMATI, YVES, "Les légendes dionysiaques en Étrurie," *Revue des Études Latines*, v. 61, 1983, 87–107.

———, "Phersu et le monde dionysiaque," *Latomus*, v. 45, 1986, 21–32.

BOURLET, MICHEL, "L'orgie sur la montagne" in *Dionysos, le même et l'autre*, ed. by Michel Bourlet, Nouvelle Revue d'Ethnopsychiatrie, no. 1, La Pensée Sauvage, 1983, pp. 57–80.

BRAMBS, J. G., ED., *Christus Patiens [The Passion of Christ]*, Greek text of *Khristos Paskhon* with German Commentary, B. G. Teubner, Leipzig, 1885.

BREMMER, JAN, "An Enigmatic Indo-European Rite: Pederasty," *Arethusa*, v. 13, 1980, 279–298.

———, "Greek Maenadism Reconsidered," *Zeitschrift für Papyrologie und Epigraphik*, v. 55, 1984, 267–286.

BRIFFAULT, ROBERT, *The Mothers*, v. I, Johns Reprint Corporation, New York, 1969.

BURKERT, WALTER, "Craft Versus Sect: The Problem of Orphics and Pythagoreans" in *Jewish and Christian Self-Definition*, v. 3, ed. Ben F. Meyer and E. P. Sanders, Fortress Press, Philadelphia, 1982, 1–22.

————, ED., *Orphism and Bacchic Mysteries*, The Center for Hermeneutical Studies, Protocol of the 28th Colloquy, Berkeley, California, 1977.

BUTTERWORTH, E.A.S., *Some Traces of the Pre-Olympian World*, Walter de Gruyter and Co., Berlin, 1966.

CALAME, CLAUDE, *Les choeurs de jeunes filles en Grèce archaïque*, v. 1, Dissertation, Edizioni dell'Ateneo & Bizzarri, Rome, 1977.

CARRIÈRE, JEAN, "Quelques mots encore sur les Bacchantes d'Euripide," *Mélanges Edouard Delebecque*, Université de Provence, Aix-en-Provence, 1983, 89–99.

CARTLEDGE, PAUL, "Spartan Wives: Liberation or Licence?", *Classical Quarterly*, v. 31, 1981, 84–105.

CHILDS, BREVARD, *The New Testament as Canon*, Fortress Press, Philadelphia, 1984.

COWARD, ROSALIND, *Patriarchal Precedents. Sexuality and Social Relations*, Routledge and Kegan Paul, London, 1983.

DANIÉLOU, ALAIN, *Shiva and Dionysos*, trans. K. F. Hurry, East-West Publications, London, 1982.

DAVIS, GLADYS M. N., *The Asiatic Dionysus*, G. Bell and Sons, Ltd., London, 1914.

DAWSON, CHRISTOPHER, *The Age of the Gods*, Howard Fertig, New York, 1970.

DE SMEDT, CAROLUS, ET AL., "Passio antiquior SS. Sergii et Bachii, graece nunc primum edita," *Analecta Bollandiana*, v. 14, 1895, 373–395.

DETIENNE, MARCEL, *Dionysos à ciel ouvert*, Hachette, 1986.

————, *Dionysos Slain*, trans. Mireille Muellner and Leonard Muellner, Johns Hopkins University Press, Baltimore, 1979.

DEVEREUX, G., "Greek Pseudo-Homosexuality," *Symbolae Osloenses*, v. 42, 1968, 69–92.

DODDS, E. R., ED., *Euripides' Bacchae*, Greek text and commentary, 2nd edition, The Clarendon Press, Oxford, 1960.

DONLON, WALTER, *The Aristocratic Ideal in Ancient Greece. Attitudes of Superiority from Homer to the End of the Fifth Century B.C.*, Coronado Press, Lawrence, Kansas, 1980.

DOVER, K. J., *Greek Homosexuality*, Vintage Books, New York, 1980; reprint of 1978 edition.

ENGELS, FRIEDRICH, *The Origin of the Family, Private Property, and the State*, 1884; reprinted by International Publishers, New York, 1972.

EVANS, ARTHUR, *Witchcraft and the Gay Counterculture*, Fag Rag Books, Boston, 1978.

FERGUSON, JOHN P., "The Great Goddess Today in Burma and Thailand: An Exploration of Her Symbolic Relevance to Monastic and Female Roles" in *Mother Worship. Theme and Variations*, ed. James J. Preston, University of North Carolina Press, Chapel Hill, 1982, 283–302.

FORD, CLELLAN, AND FRANK BEACH, *Patterns of Sexual Behavior*, Harper, New York, 1951.

GALLINI, CLARA, "Il Travestismo Rituale di Penteo," in *Studi e Materiali di Storia delle Religione*, v. 34, 1963, 211–228.

GESELL, GERALDINE C., "The Place of the Goddess in Minoan Society" in *Minoan Society. Proceedings of the Cambridge Colloquium*, ed. Olga Krzyszkowka and Lucia Nixon, Bristol Classical Press, 1983, 93–99.

GIMBUTAS, MARIJA, *The Goddesses and Gods of Old Europe, 6500–3500 BC. Myths and Cult Images*, 2nd Edition, University of California Press, Berkeley, 1982.

GOLDEN, MARK, "Slavery and Homosexuality at Athens," *Phoenix*, v. 38, 1984, 308–323.

GOULD, HARRY E., AND J. L. WHITELY, EDS., *Titus Livius*, Book I, Latin text, MacMillan, London, 1952; reprinted 1973.

GOULD, JOHN, "Law, Custom and Myth: Aspects of the Social Position of Women in Classical Athens," *The Journal of Hellenic Studies*, v. 100, 1980, 38–59.

GRAHN, JUDY, *Another Mother Tongue*, Beacon Press, Boston, 1984.

HAMMOND, N.G.L., *A History of Greece*, The Clarendon Press, Oxford, 1967.

HAWKES, JACQUETTA, *Dawn of the Gods*, Chatto and Windus, London, 1968.

———, "Prehistory" in *History of Mankind*, v. 1, by Jacquetta Hawkes and Leonard Woolley, Harper & Row, New York, 1963.

HENRICHS, ALBERT, "Changing Dionysiac Identities" in *Jewish and Christian Self-Definition*, ed. Ben F. Meyer and E. P. Sanders, v. 3, Fortress Press, Philadelphia, 1982, 137–160.

———, "Greek Maenadism from Olympias to Messalina," *Harvard Studies in Classical Philology*, v. 82, 1978, 121–160.

———, "Loss of Self, Suffering, Violence: The Modern View of Dionysus from Nietzsche to Girard," *Harvard Studies in Classical Philology*, v. 88, 1984, 205–240.

———, "Response" in *Orphism and Bacchic Mysteries: New Evidence and Old Problems of Interpretation*, The Center for Hermeneutical Studies, Protocol of 28th Colloquy, Berkeley, CA, 1977.

HUMBERT, JEAN, ED., *Homère, Hymnes*, L'Association Guillaume Budé, Paris, 1951.

JEANMAIRE, H., *Dionysos. Histoire du culte de Bacchus*, Payot, Paris, 1978.

KALKE, CHRISTINE, "The Making of a Thyrsos: The Transformation of Pentheus in Euripides' Bacchae," *American Journal of Philology*, v. 106, 1985, 409–426.

KERÉNYI, C., *Dionysos: Archetypal Image of Indestructible Life*, trans. Ralph Manheim, Routledge and Kegan Paul, London, 1976.

KEULS, EVA, *The Reign of Phallus. Sexual Politics in Ancient Athens*, Harper & Row, New York, 1985.

KRAEMER, ROSS, "Esctasy and Possession: The Attraction of Women to the Cult of Dionysus," *Harvard Theological Review*, v. 72, 1979, 55–80.

LA RUE, JENE A., "Prurience Uncovered. The Psychology of Euripides' Pentheus," *The Classical Journal*, v. 63, 1967, 209–214.

LAWLER, LILLIAN B., *The Dance in Ancient Greece*, Adam and Charles Black, London, 1964.

LERNER, GERDA, *The Creation of Patriarchy*, Oxford University Press, New York, 1986.

LEWIS, CHARLTON T., AND CHARLES SHORT, *A Latin Dictionary*, The Clarendon Press, Oxford, 1966.

LIDDELL, HENRY G., AND ROBERT SCOTT, *A Greek-English Lexicon*, revised by Henry S. Jones, 9th edition, The Clarendon Press, Oxford, 1966.

LÜDEMANN, GERD, "The Successors of Pre-70 Jerusalem Christianity: A Critical Evaluation of the Pella-Tradition," in *Jewish and Christian Self-Definition*, v. 1, ed. by E. P. Sanders, Fortress Press, Philadelphia, 1982, 161–173.

MARKALE, JEAN, *Women of the Celts*, Gordon Cremonesi, London, 1975.

MARTIN, VICTOR, AND GUY DE BUDÉ, EDS., *Eschine. Discours, Tom I, Contre Timarque*, Société d'Édition "Les Belles Lettres," Collection des Universités de France, Paris, 1927.

MASON, PETER, *The City of Men. Ideology, Sexual Politics and the Social Formation*, Edition Herodot, Göttingen, 1984.

McCALL, DANIEL F., "Mother Earth: The Great Goddess of West Africa" in *Mother Worship. Theme and Variations*, ed. James J. Preston, University of North Carolina, Chapel Hill, 1982, 304–323.

McNALLY, SHEILA, "The Maenad in Early Greek Art," *Arethusa*, v. 11, 1978, 101–135.

MEIER, M.H.E., *Histoire de l'amour grec*, Stendhal, Paris, 1930.

MORGAN, LEWIS H., *Ancient Society*, Charles H. Kerr & Co., Chicago, 1877.

MOSS, LEONARD W., AND STEPHEN C. CAPPANNARI, "In Quest of the Black Virgin: She Is Black Because She Is Black" in *Mother Worship. Theme and Variations*, ed. James J. Preston, University of North Carolina, Chapel Hill, 1982, 53–74.

MUELLER, C. O., *The History and Antiquities of the Doric Race*, John Murray, London, 1839.

MURRAY, MARGARET, *The Witch-Cult in Western Europe*, Oxford University Press, London, 1921.

NANCY, CLAIRE, "Euripide et le parti des femmes" in *La femme dans les sociétés antiques*, ed. by Edmond Lévy, Actes des colloques de Strasbourg, May 1980 and March 1981, Strasbourg, 1983, 73–92.

NETTLESHIP, HENRY, AND J. E. SANDYS, EDS., *Dictionary of Classical Antiquities*, Originally by Oskar Seyffert, Meridian Books, New York, 1966 Reprint.

NEW AMERICAN BIBLE, trans. the Catholic Biblical Association of America, P. J. Kennedy and Sons, New York, 1970.

NIETZSCHE, FRIEDRICH, *The Birth of Tragedy*, trans. William A. Haussmann, Russell and Russell, New York, 1964.

NILSSON, MARTIN P., *The Dionysiac Mysteries of the Hellenistic and Roman Age*, reprint of 1957 edition, Arno Press, New York, 1975.

———, *The Minoan-Mycenaean Religion and Its Survival in Greek Religion*, 2nd

Revised Edition, C.W.K. Gleerup, Lund, 1950.

O'BRIEN, JOAN, "Nammu, Mami, Eve and Pandora: 'What's in a Name?'" *The Classical Journal*, v. 79, 1983, 35–45.

PARKE, H. W., *Festivals of the Athenians*, Cornell University Press, Ithaca, New York, 1977.

PICARD, CHARLES, "Sabazios, dieu thraco-phrygien: expansion et aspects nouveaux de son culte," *Revue Archéologique*, v. 2, 1961, 129–176.

PICKARD-CAMBRIDGE, *Dithyramb, Tragedy and Comedy*, revised by T.B.L. Webster, The Clarendon Press, Oxford, 1962.

POMEROY, SARAH B., *Goddesses, Whores, Wives and Slaves*, Shocken Books, New York, 1975.

PUTNAM, HILARY, "After Empiricism" in *Post-Analytic Philosophy*, ed. John Rajchman and Cornel West, Columbia University Press, New York, 1985, 20–30.

RANDALL, JOHN HERMAN, JR., *Hellenistic Ways of Deliverance and the Making of the Christian Synthesis*, Columbia University Press, New York, 1970.

RATTRAY, R. S., *Ashanti*, The Clarendon Press, Oxford, 1932.

RAVEN, D. S., *Greek Metre. An Introduction*, Faber and Faber, London, 1962.

RAWSON, PHILIP, "Early History of Sexual Art," in *Primitive Erotic Art*, ed. Philip Rawson, G.P. Putnam's Sons, New York, 1973.

RING, GEORGE C., "Christ's Resurrection and the Dying and Rising Gods," *The Catholic Biblical Quarterly*, v. 6, 1944, 216–229.

RORTY, RICHARD, "Solidarity or Objectivity?" in *Post-Analytic Philosophy*, ed. John Rajchman and Cornel West, Columbia University Press, New York, 1985, 3–19.

SANDYS, JOHN E., ED., *The Bacchae of Euripides*, Greek text and commentary, revised edition, Cambridge University Press, London, 1885.

SCHOFF, WILFRED, "Tammuz, Pan and Christ," *The Open Court*, v. 39, 1912, 513–532.

SCHUTTE, OFELIA, *Beyond Nihilism: Nietzsche Without Masks*, University of Chicago Press, 1984.

SEGAL, CHARLES, *Dionysiac Poetics and Euripides' Bacchae*, Princeton University Press, 1982.

———, "The Menace of Dionysos: Sex Roles and Reversals in Euripides' Bacchae," *Arethusa*, v. 11, 1978, 185–202.

SERGENT, BERNARD, *L'homosexualité dans la mythologie grecque*, Payot, Paris, 1984.

SLATER, W. J., "Artemon and Anacreon: No Text Without Context," *Phoenix*, v. 32, 1978, 185–194.

SPUNBERG, BERNARD, "Androgyny Prevails." Review of *The God of Ecstasy* in *Bay Area Reporter*, v. 14, no. 50, December 13, 1984, p. 27.

STARHAWK, *The Spiral Dance*, Harper & Row, San Francisco, 1979.

STERN, J. P., *A Study of Nietzsche*, Cambridge University Press, Cambridge, 1979.

SYMONDS, JOHN, *A Problem in Greek Ethics*, Areopagitica Society, London, 1908.

TUILIER, ANDRÉ, ED., *La Passion du Christ*, Les Éditions du Cerf, Paris, 1969.

TUMASONIS, DONALD, "Some Aspects of Minoan Society: A View From Social Anthropology" in *Minoan Society. Proceedings of the Cambridge Colloquium 1981*, ed. O. Krzyszkowska and L. Nixon, Bristol Classical Press, 1983, 303–310.

TURCAN, ROBERT, "Les Religions de l'Asie dans le Vallée du Rhone" in *Études Préliminaires aux Religions Orientales dans l'Empire Romain*, v. 30, E.J. Brill, Leyden, 1972.

TYSON, JOSEPH B., *The New Testament and Early Christianity*, The MacMillam Co., New York, 1984.

VAN GENNEP, ARNOLD, *The Rites of Passage*, University of Chicago Press, Chicago, 1960.

VERNANT, JEAN-PIERRE, "Le Dionysos masqué des Bacchantes d'Euripide," *L'Homme*, v. 25 (no. 93), 1985, 31–58.

————, *Myth and Society in Ancient Greece*, trans. from the French by Janet Lloyd, Humanities Press, Atlantic Highlands, New Jersey, 1980.

WALKER, MITCH, ET AL., *Visionary Love*, Treeroots Press, San Francsico, 1980.

WALTON, J. MICHAEL, *Greek Theater Practice*, Contributions in Drama and Theater Studies, no. 3, Greenwood Press, Westport, Connecticut, 1980.

WARREN, LARISSA B., "The Women of Etruria" in *Women in the Ancient World: the Arethusa Papers*, ed. John Peradotto and J. P. Sullivan, State University of New York, Albany, 1984, 229–239.

WEST, CORNEL, "Afterword: The Politics of American Neo-Pragmatism" in *Post-Analytic Philosophy*, ed. John Rajchman and Cornel West, Columbia University Press, New York, 1985.

WHITEHORNE, JOHN, "The Dead as Spectacle in Euripides' 'Bacchae' and 'Supplices,'" *Hermes*, v. 114, 1986, 59–72.

WILLETTS, R. F., *Cretan Cults and Festivals*, Greenwood Press, Westport, Connecticut, 1980 reprint.

WINNINGTON-INGRAM, R. P., *Euripides and Dionysus. An Interpretation of the Bacchae*, Cambridge University Press, Cambridge, 1948.

INDEX

281

Orphism, 160; and Rome, 116, 118–19, 126–27
Honey, 60
Horatia, 123
Horatius, 123
Horned god, 130, 139, 140, 141, 142–43, 161, 172, 187, 188
Hulla, 142
Human: /animal/divine cleavages, 49–50, 54, 140; consciousness, modes of, 192–93; nature, 191–92; sacrifices, 46–47, 134
Humbert, Jean, 63
Hurry, K. F., 130
Hymn to Dionysos (Pseudo-Homer), 23, 137
Hyrcanos, King, 162

I-it vs. I-you relationship, 181–82
Iliad (Homer), 23, 39, 49, 55, 97–98, 100
India, 60, 127, 130, 131–36
Indo-Europeans, 100, 130–31, 141
Intoxicants, 60, 131, 184–85, 188–91
Inuus, 120, 140
Isis, 138, 140

James (Jacob), 164–65
Jeanmaire, H., 24, 148
Jerusalem, 165, 170
Jesus of Nazareth, 119, 144, 145, 148–49, 161, 162–67, 168–70, 193
Jews, 150, 162, 165, 170
John, 151
Jones, Henry S., 21, 33, 156
Judas Maccabeus, 162
Judea, 161, 162
Jupiter, 124
Justin, 120

Kadmos, 8, 26, 28, 48, 49, 69, 145, 159
Kalke, 8
Kerényi, C., 21, 33, 37, 41, 42, 46, 48, 49, 57, 59, 65, 67–68, 78, 79, 80, 149, 160
Keuls, 19, 51, 109
Kinsey, 177
Korybantes or *Kouretes*, 65, 132
Kouros, 131
Kraemer, Ross, 25
Kratylos (Plato), 156
Kronos, 65, 136
Kumara, 131
Kwaternik, 143
Kybele, 63, 64, 65, 66

Labyris, 44, 47–48
Latini, 131
Lavihia, 124
Laws (Plato), 24–25, 77, 103
Lenaia, 19
Lerner, Gerda, 67, 78, 84, 86
Lesbianism, 73–74, 75, 79, 85, 108, 171, 183, 185
Lesbos, 73
Lewis, Charleton T., 74, 120
Liber, 80, 140
Liddell, Henry G., 21, 33, 156
Likhnon, 160
Linear A, 40, 44
Linear B, 41, 59
Linga Purana, 131
Literary evidence, 12
Lives (Plutarch), 46, 157
Livy, 112–25
Logical positivism, 195–96
"Logos," 161–62, 165–66, 170
Lucian, 19
Lüdermann, Gerd, 165
Lupercalia, 120
Lupercus, 120
Luther, Martin, 165
Lybians, 136

McCall, Daniel F., 174
Macedon, 55–56, 90
McNally, Sheila, 24
Mad Women, 5, 8–10, 11–16, 18, 70, 82, 134, 136, 148, 151; and dancing, 55–58; and males, 24–28; and sex, 71–73, 75, 79
Maenadism, 11–14, 17–18, 19, 24, 27–28, 197
Magnesia, 12
Male bias, 66–67
Malinowski, Bronislaw, 88
Mark, 163, 170
Markale, 139
Mars, 119
Martello, Leo, 185
Martin, Victor, 95
Masculinity, 176–78
Mason, Peter, 77, 99–100
Matriarchy, 88–90
Matronae or *Matres*, 139
Meier, M.H.E., 126
Menelaus, 41
Messiah, 162, 163–64, 170
Metaphysics, 195–96
Milesia, 13, 15